Keep Your Courage

Keep Your Courage

A Radical Christian Feminist Speaks

Carter Heyward

scm press

Published in 2010 by SCM Press
Editorial office
13–17 Long Lane, London, EC1A 9PN, UK

SCM Press is an imprint of Hymns Ancient and Modern Ltd (a registered charity)
13A Hellesdon Park Road, Norwich NR6 5DR, UK
www.scm-canterburypress.co.uk

British Library Cataloguing in Publication data

A catalogue record for this book is available from the British Library

978-0-334-04378-2

Typeset by the *Church Times*

Printed and bound by
CPI Antony Rowe, Chippenham SN14 6LH

Contents

v

I dedicate this book with love to the young ones:
Rob   Isabel   Kate   Ramsey   Candice
Will   Marissa   Nicole
Kristen   Maria
and Katie S. B.

As long as you're afraid of this horse, she'll scare you.

Linda Levy, my riding teacher

In every generation wisdom passes into holy souls and makes them friends of God, and prophets; for God loves nothing so much as the person who lives with wisdom. She is more beautiful than the sun, and excels every constellation of the stars. Compared with the light she is found to be superior, for it is succeeded by the night, but against wisdom evil does not prevail.

Wisdom of Solomon 7.27b–30

Acknowledgements

Over the past decade, many people have searched with me for words with which to speak and, often by their courage, have inspired me to try to keep mine. Without them, the pieces in this book might well not have taken shape at all and certainly would not have taken the shape they did: I can't begin to name them all, but I've dug into my date books and memory to name as many as I can, some with whom I have vigorously disagreed politically, theologically, professionally, or personally. Yet, without these folks – friends, colleagues, family, and in a few cases people I don't see any more – I wouldn't have been able to speak theologically with any confidence during the dubious and disastrous Presidency of George W. Bush or today, more hopefully, as Barack Obama tries to help salvage our sinking ship – as a nation, as global communities, as planet earth.

First, heartfelt thanks to the five who helped bring this book to life: to Darlene O'Dell, herself a brilliant writer and teacher, for a sharp editorial eye and sweet sisterly wisdom in working through each piece in this book with me; to Janine Lehane, remarkable poet, artist, and clown, for joining Darlene in witty and wonderfully perceptive read-throughs of twice this much material from me; to Kody Kinsley, multitalented community organizer and public servant, who just might be President of the United States in about twenty-five years. In the meantime, Kody's computer skills have given this project its shape; to Bev Harrison, beautiful friend and life-companion for many years, whose reading and suggestions were, as usual, incisive and clarifying – and whose personal courage in the face of mounting age and infirmity never ceases to amaze and encourage me; and to Natalie Watson, insightful and good humoured Senior Commissioning Editor of the SCM–Canterbury Press in London, for inviting me to publish this collection and for shepherding our little team along. In the beginning, and the end, Natalie's word was reliable, gentle, and definitive.

In addition to these five are others who must be named: Sue Sasser, my other cherished life-companion, who has encouraged me to speak and write, regardless, and has been there for me. Sue and I laugh, cook, hike, trail ride, travel, run a farm together, scatter fertilizer and seeds, do road work, listen to each other's tales of the day, read Harry Potter (we're just now finishing a second reading of the whole series!), usually agree but sometimes argue about politics, and stay amazed and often delighted in the world around us. Sue inspires me to meet each day and be glad in it.

'Redbud Springs', our residential community outside Brevard, North Carolina, has been a mainstay of encouragement and deepening friendships over the years. In addition to Sue and Bev, our evolving community has included Gerrie Kiley, Jennifer Rouse, Nancy Richards, Peg Hall, Gerry Azzata, Gretchen Grimshaw, former interns Debra Sue Chenault and Lisa Nafziger and, until her death, Sr Angela, CC. Other friends who live near us and join in many Redbud activities include Deb and Preston Pruitt, Ann Franklin and Elly Andujar, Joyce Rouse, Darlene O'Dell and Janine Lehane, and Norene Carter, a trustworthy friend and companion in theological and political work for decades.

Along with the members of Redbud Springs, there are others who, in special and particular ways, have helped me claim my theological voice and speak out during the last decade: I am thinking especially of three beloved friends: Jan Surrey, partner in exploring mutual relation as a vibrant spiritual, psychological, and political basis of whatever is good; Alison Cheek, sister priest in the struggle for a more fully mutual world and church, and B. K. Hipsher, who has accompanied me up and down the East Coast, across the nation, and to Europe and back in our shared effort to

ACKNOWLEDGEMENTS

teach and preach a radical gospel of justice love. I cherish these three.

Then, there are quite a few other sister and brother theologians, bishops, priests and pastors, writers, teachers, poets, artists, musicians, healers, community organizers, and friends who have inspired me during this past decade. Steve Bergman, Marvin Ellison and Frank Brooks, Jim Willems and Christina Fernandez, Esu Lackey, Webb Brown, Muffie Moroney, Angela Moloney, Demaris Wehr, Reinhild Traitler, Thalia Meehan, Kwok Pui-lan, Christopher Duraisingh, Joan Martin, Gale Yee, Joanna Dewey and Fairbairn Powers, Bill Rankin, Steven Charleston, Ed Rodman, Rick McCall, Lucretia Yaghjian, Ian Douglas, Bill Kondrath, Chris Medeiros, Karen Montagno, Ben Matlock, Alcurtis Davis, Nancy Davidge, Elisa Lucozzi, Rosanne Hebert, Sheryl Kujawa Holbrook, Fredrica Harris Thompsett, Angela Bauer, Larry Wills.

I'm also grateful to Beverly Hall, Tom Shaw, Gene Robinson, Barbara Nielsen, Barbara and Fred Plimpton, David Conolly, Anne Gilson and Judith Davis, Robin Gorsline, Robert Griffin, Mari Castellanos and D.D. Gomez de Molina, Patricia and Rob Brennan, Bonnie Engelhardt and Susan Graesser, Anne Carroll Fowler, Bill Blaine-Wallace, Frank Clarkson, Emily Hewitt, Lee McGee, Merrill Bittner, Alla Bozarth, Louie Crew, Betty Lane, Andrea Shirley, Janie Van Zandt and Alan Knight, Mary Anne Osborn, Ann Wetherwilt and Peg Huff, Shirley Krogstad, Megan Crouse and Chris Morton.

Others who've contributed greatly to my life and work during this past decade include Kathy Meacham, Jeannie Matthews Sommers, Sandra Smith, Philippa Hackett, Roger Riggers, Hilary Dirlam, Mary Gordon, Melissa Saxton, Marion Stott, Mary Page Sims, Mel Bringle and Shirley Arnold, Kathy Hart, Carol Dodson, Shelly Webb, Sandra Kremer, Rob Field, Nathan and Summer Griffin, John and Charlotte Cato, James Harrison, Hal Wildung, Mary Glasspool, Irene Monroe, Virginia Ramey Mollenkott, Kelly Brown Douglas, Catherine Keller, Rosemary Ruether, Delores Williams, Lisa Isherwood, Larry Rasmussen, Nyla Rasmussen,

Pam Gilchrist, Katja Linke, Peggy Cleveland, Ann Elliot, Steve Shoemaker, Murdock Smith, Doug and Edna Lou Aldridge, Maner Ware, Debbie Parrish, Holly Hardgrove, Jane Wildung Lamphere, Mary Jane Evans, Fay Walker, Tom Brackett, Catherine Tupper, Janet Benway, Jim and Annette Cullipher, Michael Collins, Maureen Copelof, Sara Schade, Jan Swenson and MeiMe Vandenburg.

Other friends and colleagues who have inspired me include Liz Bounds, Toddie Peters, Randy Styers, Marilyn Legge, Traci West, Pam Brubaker, Jane Hicks, Mel and Beth Kaiser, Jean Hammond, Selisse Berry and Cynthia Martin, Dawn Rouse, Sheila Baker, Steve Jennings, Denise Jones, Mary Margaret Camalo, Liw Bringleson and Gloria Nafziger, Beverly Ellison, Ryan McKisson and Mary Chaney, Jim McKinley, Christina Nance, Ruth Nicholson, Susan Shackelford, Susan Petersen and Tom Mahan, Chris Blackburn and Dar Nicgorski.

And the list goes on. Thanks to Desmond Tutu, David Siegenthaler, Robert Kramer and Jean Hiatt Kramer, Jean Austin and Libby Kennedy, Laurie Auffant, Alice O'Donovan, Mykel Johnson, Rose Eddington, Sissi Loftin and Janet Brocklehurst, Laine Calloway, Bob Johnson, Drew Hanlon, Matthew Cadwell, Dan Spencer, Michael Clark, Dorlee Dilschneider, Ulrike Guthrie, Karen Meridith, Nancy Harbison Dotson, Elizabeth Kaeton, Jan Sheperd, Brigitte Lowe, Pam Blevins and Karen Shaffer, Peggy Culbertson, Sue and Jim Null, Barbara and Leah Howell, and Nancy Wilson.

My siblings Robbie Heyward and Ann Heyward live with hearts open to the world. Their lives are grounded in a passion for justice as well as strong senses of compassion and great senses of humour, which help keep us all relatively sane. I adore them and celebrate them, and I imagine they'll find this book, much of it, to their liking.

Earlier in the decade, Linda Levy helped me learn to trust my own horse Red, and myself with Red. Linda, an exceptional equestrian, taught me much about horses, humans, and (to her surprise and, I believe, delight) the divine Spirit moving between us. Today, my chief 'horse buddy' Liz Galloway rides with me twice a week and has become one of my best friends in the world. She not only teaches me about horses. Her connection with these large creatures never fails to offer spiritual insight. Along with Linda and my incredible sister-horsewoman-sister priest and soul-mate Gretchen Grimshaw, Liz has become a powerful spiritual mentor.

As I was just beginning my life with horses, a fine horseback riding teacher Sandi Thompson taught me so much about horses, and I'll be forever grateful. She and her veterinarian husband Mark Thompson continue to be wonderful mentors as well as true friends. Other 'horse people' who've worked or played with the horses and me, and with whom conversation about many things has been rich, include LaVonda Blackwell, Keith Galloway, Jason McCall, Jennifer Grey, Hollan Schwartz, Barbara Jean Sorenson, Eleanor Boatright, Betsy Boatright, Kathy Morrow, Carolyn Bane, Anne Westall, Marilyn Thompson, Charlotte Page, Anna Ripley Faulkner, Julie Kerr, Kristen McCauley, Maria Fisher, Elise Ellinghausen, Peggy McGoldrick, Veheda Fuller, Juanita Dixon, Nancy Searles, Julie Robins, Chuck and Libby Cordray, Lillie Ware, Jane Williams, Kay Hunter, Reed Patton, Gail and Billy Hagler, Jill Wildung Schmidt, Wendy Wildung, Lisa Wildung, Matthew Wildung, Priscilla Donham, equine massage therapist Dave Jacobi, farriers James Gash and Bernard Pellatier, and equine veterinarians Kris Woodaman, John Freeland, Mickey Coleman, Michael Lowder and the staffs of Tryon Equine Hospital and Appalachian Equine Hospital in western North Carolina.

One more horse-person must be mentioned: Robie White is a talented and gentle trainer in Shelby, North Carolina. Over a three year period, he worked with my young horse Feather, who has a chapter in this book, helping her become a stunning and reliable companion, a horse I hope to grow old with.

The Mountain Community of Saint Clare has been an important spiritual resource for those of us who founded it in

2002. Its members, past and present, have been spiritual teachers to me and one another for most of the past decade: Its current members are among my most engaging theological colleagues: Jennifer and Ray Henley, Eleanor and Peter Mockridge, Billy and Gail Hagler, Bev Harrison, Darlene O'Dell and Janine Lehane, Kathleen Moore, Norene Carter, Lucy Teeter and Sue Null. Shelly Mae Simmons is off at seminary; and Charles and Marion Huston are in a retirement community down the mountain from us; but each has played a major role in my theological thinking in recent years.

Others with whom I've spent a lot of time during the last decade and who have often touched me with their courage and integrity include the community of the Episcopal Divinity School in Cambridge, Massachusetts, from which I retired after 30 years in 2005; the staff, board, volunteers, students, and of course horses of Free Rein Center for Therapeutic Riding in Brevard, North Carolina; participants in our See Off Homesteaders group on the top of the mountain, where we live in North Carolina; my band-mates in our women's oldtime string band, 'The Bold Gray Mares'; the residents of the Cedar Mountain House in Cedar Mountain, North Carolina, a retirement community at which our Mares play every month; and participants in our local Democratic Party in western North Carolina, who helped put Obama in the White House. To name all the folks in these groups who've made such a difference to my life would take many more pages and, even so, I'd leave out many. You know who you are, and I thank you.

For the last decade and a half, a women's 'consciousness raising group' I belonged to at Union Theological Seminary in the early 1970s has met bi-annually to catch up. The seven of us inspire and challenge each other every time we meet. Love and thanks to these special sisters: Barbara Gerlach, Emily Jean Gilbert, Maurine Doggett, Susan Savell, Sarah Bentley and Linda Clark.

Along with their partners, spouses, families, and animal companions, members of CLOUT – Christian Lesbians OUT – have been sources of friendship and lasting inspiration over the years. Thanks to Janie Spahr, Jan Griesinger, Melanie Morrison, Diana Vezmar-Bailey, Chris Page, Roberta Robles, Irene Monroe, Mari Castellanos, Virginia Mollenkott, and the many other brave, brazen, and wonderfully witty CLOUT women who continue to carry it on. You are The Best.

My family of origin continues to be a strong support network for me and for each of us, and I want to thank them for this: Along with my siblings Robbie and Ann, and their spouses Betsy Alexander and Robert Dulin, I want to thank Luther Carter, Marsha Carter, Amy Perry Carter, Marsha Carter Davis, Bill Davis, Rob Drinkwater, Isabel Drinkwater, Ramsey Dulin, Candice Dulin, Albert Dulin, Celeste Dulin, Bruce Drinkwater, and my mother's beautiful care giver Ofa Tonga. The younger ones too give me great hope: especially Robbie and Betsy's sparkling little daughter, Kate Alexander Heyward, and Marsha and Bill Davis' talented teenagers, Will and Marissa Davis, and Bruce and Colene Drinkwater's bright and lively daughter, Nicole Drinkwater. I wonder also about my many Heyward cousins and their kin, scattered here and there. I wish I could see more of them, because they matter to me, I think of them. In special memory of my good, kind and intelligent dad, Bob Heyward, I wish them blessings of love, justice, and joy.

The Wildungs and the Sassers (Bev's and Sue's families of origin) have also played wonderful roles in my life during this past decade. Members of these families have been great conversation partners and, more importantly, great spirits during good times and sad times as all of us have lost loved ones along the way.

I cannot imagine being in this world without animal friends. My companions and I have a farm in western North Carolina, where we have been fortunate to have quite a gathering of creatures over the last ten years, some given to us, some rescued, some chosen, some who have died, some still with us, all cherished. I am grateful for each and every one: the horses – the eldest now departed Sugar, my young Feather and her mom Red (both prominent in the pages of this book), our senior horse

Macho, our shyest Patience, our round and whimsical Pumpkin, our sweet and gorgeous Fanny, and all the others; dogs Brennan, who died in 2003, Buddy, the senior lab with us now, Shelly Pom Pom, the little one who arrived as a rescue last spring, Jennifer Rouse's beautiful black Bear (whom I sometimes call 'Sirius Black', as he streaks through the woods) and the other great dogs in our community; and of course the cats – Rubyfruit, who died at age 23 in 2005, Tigger and Panther, who disappeared into the woods, Piglet and Pooh, who still rule the roost in Bev's house, and the others.

In special ways, I give thanks for those human loved ones who have 'jumped the twig' in the past decade. I think especially of Robert McAfee Brown, Angela Solling, Mary Spotswood 'Spots' Pou, Dorothee Soelle, Sue Hiatt, Robert L. DeWitt, Ryan Jones, Katrina Martha Welles Swanson, Bennett Sims, Eben Alexander, Chris Hart, Jason Palmer, Al Surrey, Travis Cox, Doris H. Sasser, Abb Allen Jeffcoat, Cindy Acuff, Caroline Elliot, Audrey Wildung, Dick Wildung, John Mack, Leon Howell, Dale Weil, Mary Ann Heyward, Mary Daly, Carroll Teeter, and Milly Morrison. Readers may notice some of these spirits interweaving through the pages of this book, more I suspect than we know!

Finally, my thanks to Linda Crosby for her good-humoured, collegial help in proofing the text of this book, Mary Matthews, Editorial Manager at SCM Press, and others who have worked to bring this book out.

Introduction

Sparking courage in a fear-based situation

In the United States today, there are lots of frightened people who call Barack Obama a 'socialist'. By extension I suppose that means that many millions of other justice-loving people are also 'socialist' – simply because we believe in universal health care and other basic human rights for all people, not just for those privileged men and women who can afford the luxuries of good education, medical treatment, a place to live, and food on the table. For Obama and others of us to be labelled 'socialist', because we are trying to love our neighbours as ourselves, reflects a stunning historical ignorance. It also conveys terrible fear of change and, as is often the case in relation to Barack Obama, a strong resistance to having a black man as President of the United States.

I have never been economically savvy enough to be a serious 'socialist', though, like many justice-loving sisters and brothers, I do indeed aspire to many of the ideals of the nineteenth-century Christian Socialist movement with its origins in England. Looking back, I think I became a 'liberal' when I was seven years old and took the part of Adlai Stevenson, the 1952 Democratic Presidential candidate, in a second grade debate. I remember liking Mr Stevenson, because he was said to be an advocate of the 'common man'. I don't recall hearing that Stevenson was called a 'socialist', but he was probably called that, and much more. This was, after all, in the era of McCarthyism, so I imagine Adlai Stevenson was, in some conservative quarters, suspected of having 'communist' leanings. In any case, by the time I was in my mid-teens, I had become supportive in every way I could of those politicians and religious leaders who struggled for civil rights and economic fairness. Now fifty years later, while not as naïve and utopian in my politics, I am still enthusiastically committed, as a Christian, to struggles dedicated to building a world in which every person is entitled, by law, to basic human rights. I have come to realize, as I move along into my mid-sixties, that what justice-loving people most need in these times, and in all times, is courage to speak and act on behalf of this world.

My desire in this book is to spark such courage and stir imagination. I am inviting readers to think outside the boxes most of us have grown up in. I want to draw folks toward the roots of our shared humanity and creature-being. Though I write as a Christian, these pieces, in their deepest meanings, transcend the boundaries of any one religious or spiritual tradition. For example, to affirm God as the source of compassion, and compassion as a basis of a holy life, is both a Christian affirmation and a thread, which runs through many spiritual traditions. Christians have no monopoly on spiritual or ethical truths, and neither does any other religion.

I offer these pieces at this time in response to the stranglehold that fear has on people in the United States and elsewhere. Social and religious historians remind us that this is not the first time in the history of the United States, nor in Western history, that a fear of change and of the 'alien' or 'other' has taken such a prominent position in the daily news. Fear, alienation, and scapegoating, especially of persons and cultures, which seem 'foreign' to us, are recurrent themes, which surge from time to time through our societies and religious traditions, especially in times of economic or military stress, both so pervasive in the United States and Europe as we enter the second decade of the twenty-first century.

I speak here as a citizen of the United States, a national culture distinct in many ways from that of the United Kingdom. And yet the United States is systemically and historically connected to

Europe in general and to the British Isles in special ways, given the origins of the United States as a modern nation and the overlap of many Anglo cultural assumptions on either side of the Atlantic pond. Some of these assumptions are splendid, such as our shared commitment to participatory democracy and common investments in economic, educational, artistic, scientific, and other creative social endeavours. Some of our shared assumptions, however, are disturbing: our legacies of white racism come immediately to mind. Similarly, we share strong traditions of heterosexist and patriarchal privilege as well as structures of capitalist exploitation. These structures of oppression shaped the empire built by the United Kingdom over several centuries and were carried on by the United States, beginning early in our efforts to obliterate Native American tribal peoples and cultures. There is little doubt that the fear which permeates the United States today has corollaries in the United Kingdom and other parts of Europe and the world. There is also little doubt that the fears we experience – of change, of difference and otherness – have moorings in some of the more confounding and morally reprehensible structures and dynamics which we in the United States, and in the United Kingdom, and in other parts of the so-called 'developed' world have set in motion historically.

Today, in the United States of America, fear has taken a heavy hand as large numbers of white people, men and women, stand ready to angrily denounce the nation's first black president, regardless of what he does or does not do; and large numbers of people of all colours march against Spanish-speaking immigrants from Mexico and further South. Media pundits in the United States, right-wing bloggers, and the leadership of the Republican party are purposely stirring fear and alienation among those ready to believe any lie about Barack Obama, as long as it serves to negatively reinforce 'American traditions' of strong fear-based alienations – traditions that set white against black and brown; rich against poor; conservative against liberal; Christian against 'others' (especially since 9/11, the people of Islam); 'traditional'

Christians and 'patriotic' Americans against those advocating significant social change in areas such as gay marriage, full acceptance of openly gay and lesbian soldiers, health care as a universal human right, and sane immigration policies grounded in compassion and common sense.

The so-called 'Tea Party' has struck a chord among these white Christian traditionalist men and women who are pushing the already very-conservative Republican Party even further to the right. It would take some chutzpah – courage – from Republican leaders to push back against the Tea Party by struggling to transform their 'Grand Old Party' (GOP) into the more moderate, socially and economically centrist party which lives on in the fading memories of my generation and that of my parents.

This book, however, is not primarily about electoral politics in the United States. It is about the courage needed to cut through the fear in which anger and violence threaten to undo our life together. Without the spiritual gift of courage – which we generate only by embodying it ourselves – we are doomed to live in the grip of fear. Living in fear of change, of difference, of otherness, invariably leads us to hatred and violence and to apathy, resignation, and depression. We may say, oh no, we will never resort to violence, but let us not lie to ourselves: we commit violence all the time. Regardless of our politics or religion, we perpetuate violence every day either actively or, more often, passively as onlookers, bystanders, or as people who choose not to notice. We stand by and watch, or we close our eyes and ears, as wars get concocted and hate rhetoric soars because we are afraid to act, frightened of speaking up, reluctant to become involved in the struggles for justice and peace, healing and liberation.

As a feminist liberation theologian who wrestles with these fears myself, I am presenting God in these pages as the wellspring of our courage to speak up, the sacred source of justice-love and of our capacity to keep our courage, take heart, get involved. These essays, speeches, and sermons span most of the first decade of the new century, a period marked dramatically in the

United States, United Kingdom, and elsewhere in the world by a fear of Islamic 'terrorism'. In these pieces, each written in this fear-based historical and social context, God takes many shapes and names, among which Courage is probably the most urgent for our life together.

Yes we are afraid, and in the midst of our fear, if we let her, God's Wisdom – 'Sophia' in the Greek – finds ways to touch and comfort our hearts, minds, and bodies. Paul describes Jesus as the Sophia/wisdom of God (1 Cor. 1.23–5; 2.6–8). Feminist biblical scholarship shows that the Logos (Word) which the Fourth Gospel equates with God was originally assumed to be the Sophia (Wisdom) of God (John 1). Sophia/Wisdom is the spiritual energy at the heart of God. She gives birth to courage, and courage becomes our passage through fear. Our fear is not negated by courage; it does not disappear. We are not suddenly unafraid. Our fear is passed through and, in a sense, tamed. It becomes a familiar, intimate feeling, and its debilitating power over us is diminished. Wisdom literally en-courages us. She en-lightens our hearts to experience that which we had feared – the changes, the other, the scary enemy – in ways we had not dreamt of before. With Wisdom as our guide, we find ourselves imagining and experiencing the other, the different one, as a possible friend, perhaps even a partner in our efforts to take care of ourselves and one another. Even the perceived enemy, while unlikely to be our friend or partner, may become more human to us, someone whose way of being in the world evokes our interest and compassion rather than our terror.

'Keep your courage'

In 1974 in the city of Philadelphia, Episcopal Bishop Robert L. De-Witt and three other bishops ordained eleven women deacons to the priesthood prior to the Episcopal Church's authorization of the ordination of women. Even before this 'irregular' ordination, Bishop DeWitt had become a 'spiritual dad' to me (see Chapter

34) and, from the time of the ordination until his death in 2003, he usually signed his letters to me and the others he had ordained, 'Keep your courage'. This was Bishop DeWitt's pastoral charge to us in the context of a church he knew would be hostile to women priests. He knew that, if it got the upper hand, our fear – of being scorned, being unable to find work, being physically harmed – would deplete us mentally, physically, and spiritually. Bishop DeWitt's apt words made me think of Paul Tillich's *The Courage to Be*, in which Tillich lifted up courage as a spiritual path to God, the Ground of Being itself. I believe Bob DeWitt would be pleased to 'sign off' in the title and pages of this book.

The subtitle identifies me as a 'Radical Christian Feminist'. What do I mean? Let me say a little about *liberals* and *radicals*. I often identify myself as a *liberal* Democrat in the United States, someone devoted to principles of universal human rights and to society's primary responsibility to care for all of its people, especially its poor. Sometimes I seem to be more liberal than our President, with whom I disagree on a number of issues, such as gay marriage (he is opposed) and a single payer or 'nationalized' healthcare system (he is opposed), but then I am not the President of the United States, and I do not have to squeeze my principles into strategies. While *liberals* are advocates for inclusivity and broad principles of fairness and equality, *radicals* dig deep to locate the rot at the base of our institutions and systems. Radicals can be liberal or conservative. I *aspire* to be radical as well as liberal in my politics. I *am* radical and liberal in my faith, but I am more inclined to identify myself a 'radical Christian' than a 'liberal Christian', because the liberal church is still a fundamentally patriarchal institution that does not take many women as seriously as it takes most privileged men.

In this context, to identify myself a 'radical Christian' is to affirm that I am committed to digging near the foundation of Christian theology to help root out sexism, racism, Antisemitism, and other structures of oppression which the church has cultivated over the years. I have spent several decades helping clear away the weeds which are choking the life out of Christian faith and practice. With other radical Christian feminist theologians, I want Christians to be able to enjoy and celebrate the more creative, liberating foundations of Christian faith.

As a 'radical Christian', I acknowledge both my continuity with the Jesus-tradition, which is the root of my faith, and the extent to which I aspire to live and breathe as close as I can to its foundation – the Christic Spirit of Jesus. I have already identified this Christian Spirit as Sophia/Wisdom, the same spiritual energy that Christians have called 'Christ'. As a radical theologian, I have worked at the margins of the institutional church. Still, I am a Christian and also a priest. The priesthood is an order of ministry in the Catholic tradition which functions as a window through which people can look and see themselves, other people and all creatures as sharing in the Christic/Sophia Spirit of Jesus. All human beings are invited by the radically inclusive Spirit to embody, through our lives as lovers of justice, compassion, and peace, the humanity and divinity of the brother from Nazareth.

As for 'feminist', well, it's the spiritual and political air I breathe. Without feminist interpretations of biblical and other texts, and without the camaraderie of other feminists in the church, I would not have remained Christian. I agree with the bumper sticker which reads, 'I'll be a post-feminist in a post-patriarchy.' And what is a feminist? A feminist is a woman or man who is thoroughly committed to women's well-being and to the inclusion of women's voices, not just white privileged women, but women of all colours and cultures and classes, all ages and conditions. Feminists, in my judgment, always have a moral and political mandate to help make connections between and among the various structures of injustice and oppression – to ask, for example, how race, gender, and class interact in the oppression of many black and brown women in the United States today. We feminist theologians who strive to make connections among the many varied structures of oppression usually identify ourselves as 'feminist liberation theologians'.

The three parts of this book

The three parts of this book reflect the primary foci of my life and work as a feminist liberation theologian over the past decade: Part 1, 'Messages to the Empire', includes pieces which give voice most emphatically to the ongoing struggles for justice. In Part 2, 'Remembering Who We Are', I speak of who we are created to be, sisters and brothers, connected at the root of our humanity and our creatureliness, joined with other species as well as creatures 'like us'. Part 3, 'Celebrating our Friends', bears witness to the power of relation in our lives and work. It testifies to how beautifully, joyfully, and ultimately sadly, we are bound up in each other's love and work, life and death.

The reader might wonder why Part 2 doesn't come first since it focuses on our spiritual identity not merely as Christians, but more basically as *human* sisters and brothers. Doesn't our 'being' precede our 'doing'? Don't our senses of who we are in the world root and ground the more explicitly political and activist shape of our lives, which provide the basis of Part 1? Yes and no. Certainly, a strong theological case could be made for wrestling first with the matter of our spiritual identity as people of God and then allowing our ethics, how we live in the world, to follow. On the basis of this logic, I probably would have reversed the order of Parts 1 and 2 myself, so strongly do I believe that our activities are seasoned and sharpened by the clarity of our senses of identity as people connected at the root of our common humanity. At the same time, it is equally true that what we do shapes, even creates, who we are; our values and actions generate our identities because, as long as we live,we are changing and growing, and we are always more or less becoming who we are.

Today, I am a citizen of a nation whose foundations are being shaken by economic injustice and volatile fears of 'otherness' and change. In this theological and political climate, I am responding in Part 1 to a moral urgency we share, we in the United States and people throughout the world: to participate in the struggles for racial, economic, gender, sexual, and environmental justice. In deciding which pieces to publish, and in what order, I came to see that, if I had been asked to choose twelve pieces to publish in a book one third the length of this one, many of the pieces in Part 1 would have had to be included. That's how urgent their messages seem to me.

Part 2, which may, on the whole, read as less 'heavy' than Part 1 is, I submit, by no means less morally serious or spiritually significant. Without compassionate pastoral sensibilities and the humility and gratitude in which our psychological well-being is seasoned, our activism and politics are doomed to drive us, and others, nuts. Without a strong sense of spiritual or moral identity as people who belong, people who are basically good, people whose souls are well, all the Christian feminism in the world will fail to liberate women, personally or politically, and all the liberation and postcolonial movements in the world will come to naught. We do not have to be religious, but we do have to be moral and, I would say, we need some sensibility of being connected to one another's lives socially, economically, politically – a sensibility which I call 'spirituality' – in order to have the staying power to keep on keeping on in the struggles for a better world.

Part 3, in which nine individuals are celebrated and re-membered, could have been placed anywhere in the book; or its chapters could have been interwoven throughout these pages. I chose to place it last, because it is a fine coda to a book on courage – nine lives which have embodied it in ways bold and brilliant.

Repetition

Anyone reading this whole book will meet some of the same characters again and again and will encounter some of the same materials from chapter to chapter. Over a decade, many events, people, stories, controversies, and themes impacted my spiritual journey so significantly that they appeared repeatedly in my public work. In putting this book together, I decided to leave each piece intact, with several exceptions. This means that repetition plays a role in this volume. My hope is that it will underscore the creative, liberating power – in my life, and in the world around us – of such characters as Sister Angela of the Clare Community in New South Wales, one of my most cherished friends and spiritual mentors; and Sue Hiatt, the great pioneer in the movement for the ordination of women. Other people, too, and stories and creatures, appear and reappear from time to time in these pages, weaving their ways through what I trust will be read as our collective call to courage.

God images

Anyone familiar with my theological work would be shocked, and maybe disappointed, if my theological language were not unorthodox. I don't often use gendered references to God, either masculine or feminine; when I do, I often use the feminine – She, Her, Mother, Sister. This is because as a woman and, earlier as a girl, I have always appreciated those Christian and other theologians who have dared to image God as Woman. In the context of our overwhelmingly patriarchal religious traditions, it's the least we can do. And perhaps even more importantly, the Sacred is truly neither and both – male and female, gendered, transgendered, and omnigendered. She and He are It and They. The God images in this book are many and varied. On the whole, they are non-theistic and impersonal, yet able to be experienced as deeply personal and imaged in ways which bring us to life.

Death and grief

The last five pieces in this book are talks or sermons I gave at the memorial services of five of my most beloved friends, including my mother. Gathering these pieces together for this book heightened my awareness of the major role which death has played in my life during this decade. Most of the people in my life have not died tragically, and none has been victim of the awful violence which comes daily, routinely, to countless brothers and sisters around the world. My personal experiences of death, to date, have been gentler. But the loss of friends, parents, and mentors has tossed me about from time to time in waves of loneliness and fear, leaving me tired in my bones, often more than I have realized until later. Yet here I am today, a vibrant and, as far as I can tell, healthy woman in my mid 60s, who is buoyed by communities of friends and companions, and who has much work, play, love, and life yet to come. I have every reason to be grateful for all that has been, and I am. I stand to give thanks, my body and spirit bending and swaying in the present, my heart opening toward a future which I cannot imagine.

Carter Heyward
Brevard, NC
1 May 2010

Part 1: Messages to the Empire

Introduction

The eleven chapters in Part 1 were selected because each wrestles with moral and theological problems of oppression and injustice and our sacred power to participate in the struggles for liberation. Chapter 1, 'Messages to the Empire', my commencement address in 2004 at the Episcopal Divinity School in Cambridge, Massachusetts, sets the tone and themes for Part 1. Subsequent chapters in this part are arranged chronologically to reflect the development of my interests and commitments as the decade progressed.

Chapters 2, 4 and 10 are brief 'op ed' (opinion editorials) written for local newspapers in the United States South (only one was actually published). Chapter 2, 'Beyond Shameful Theology', was published in *The Charlotte Observer* (Charlotte, North Carolina) several days after the 11 September 2001, terrorist attacks in New York City and Washington DC. This piece was a response to the Reverend Jerry Falwell's charge that the attacks were God's response to 'pagans, feminists, gays and lesbians', and others trying 'to secularize America'. Chapter 4, 'The Passion of Mel Gibson', discusses director–actor Mel Gibson's powerful and, in my judgment, theologically mistaken and misleading 2004 film, *The Passion of the Christ*. In Chapter 10, 'The Wisdom to Lead', I discuss my enthusiastic support of Barack Obama's Presidential bid in 2008 and my hope, at the time, that an Obama Presidency would open the door for Americans of different races to begin to come together across lines which historically have divided us. As

I write this Introduction, almost two years later, my optimism in this piece seems unfounded, or, we can hope, premature, so great is the fear holding us in its grip.

Chapter 3 is a brief sermon, or homily: 'Queer Christ', which I preached at the Episcopal Divinity School in 2004. In it, the term 'queer' first appears in these pieces as a theologically descriptive term for the holy and serendipitous spirit which surprises us, bursting our expectations and keeping us honest. In my work, 'queer' never refers only to lesbians, gay, bisexual, and transgender people, nor simply to the phenomenon of gender-bending. To be 'queer' is to be allied with efforts toward sexual and gender justice and, perhaps, to be lesbian, gay, bisexual, or transgender oneself. But it is more than this. To be 'queer' is to burst out of boxes and cross boundaries constructed to diminish and mute us. In Chapter 3 I link the term 'queer' with both the free spirit of nineteenth-century English theologian Frederick Denison Maurice and my eighty-eight-year-old happily heterosexual mother, and I suggest that a 'dynamic dimension of queerness – and Christ – is the holding together of qualities which only appear to be contradictions', qualities like anger and hope. Like Christ, queerness has a paradoxical dimension: what is fully human can be also fully divine; what is deeply spiritual can be also sharply political; what is strongly 'feminine' can be also sweetly 'masculine'.

In Chapters 5 and 6 I wrestle with questions of gay, lesbian, bisexual and transgender justice, especially in the context of the Episcopal Church and Anglican Communion. Chapter 5 is excerpted from a letter I wrote my friend, Tom Shaw, Episcopal Bishop of Massachusetts, in 2004, explaining my reasons for refusing to follow his directive that priests in Massachusetts not officiate at same-sex weddings. Chapter 6, 'Make Us Prophets and Pastors', is an 'Open Letter to Gay and Lesbian Leaders in the Anglican Communion'. This essay was first published in 2005 in response to Anglican leaders' decision not to ordain gay and lesbian people nor bless our relationships.

Chapter 7, 'Some Violent Connections', examines dynamics of violence and raises questions about connections between the economy, war, religion, fear, and women. This chapter is a reconstruction, on the basis of my notes, of a keynote address I gave in 2006 at a workshop on violence sponsored by various groups at the University of Indiana and the Episcopal Diocese of Indianapolis. This piece is a critique of global capitalism and explores its connections to the Iraq War, religious fundamentalisms at home and elsewhere, and the fear of women in which such religions are steeped.

Chapters 8 and 9 are addresses I gave at Martin Luther King celebrations in Brevard, a small town in the mountains of western North Carolina, where I live. The Human Relations Council of Brevard invited me to give the first of these speeches (Chapter 8: 'Strong Faith') at a Prayer Breakfast for religious leaders and justice advocates in 2006. Because the response to this presentation was positive, the Council asked me to address a larger, more general audience the following year on the theme 'The Dream Continues'. I did so in January 2007, and my talk appears here as Chapter 9. Unlike my address the previous year, this presentation provoked outrage from some in the audience, who accused me of being hostile to the good white citizens of our town and of trying to link Dr King to 'unrelated issues', like gay, lesbian, bisexual, and transgender justice.

Following the op ed piece on Obama (Chapter 10, 2008), I conclude Part 1 with some reflections on 'Feminism and Love', a speech at the closing ceremony of Holy Ground, a feminist spiritual centre in Asheville, North Carolina, which was shutting its doors after fifteen years. I include this piece in this book, because it addresses the apparent waning of feminism as a strong, vibrant social force among religious women in the United States at this time.

1

Messages to the Empire

Every year the graduating class at the Episcopal Divinity School in Cambridge, Massachusetts, invites a member of the faculty to preach at its Commencement Eucharist. I preached this sermon on 19 May 2004. The word 'Empire' refers here not, primarily, to the United States of America but rather to the structures of global capitalism and militarism which generate economic and social injustice in the United States and throughout the world.

Sister Angela (see also Chapter 31), a contemplative Anglican nun, mystical priest, and beloved friend of many of ours here at the Episcopal Divinity School told a story about a three-year-old Australian boy named Bobby whose parents overheard him one night leaning over the crib of his newly arrived sister: 'Baby! Baby! Wake up and tell me about God, because I've begun to forget what God is like!' This is the kind of story we cherish because it makes us happy, even perhaps ecstatic, to imagine such a God and such a child as little Bobby. I love this story! I believe this story, and I wanted to share it with you, because it is a beautiful introduction – and counterpoint – to a Commencement service about loving such a God in the age of Empire.

Be clear that the God whom young Bobby is trying to remember is the same God about whom we have been hearing in today's lessons, appointed by the Prayer Book as lessons for 'Ministry'.[1] They are lessons which need to be heard as lessons about ministry in the Empire: a ministry of speaking truth to power, of speaking up in the context of a deafening silence. It is a ministry we share with our christic brother from Nazareth – a ministry of solidarity

---

1 Exodus 19.3–8; 1 Peter 4.7–11; Matthew 16.24–7; Psalm 15.

4

with those left standing outside the centres of power; a ministry today of helping save the people, like Bobby, his sister, and all creatures great and small from the devastation we will surely endure if our nation continues to pursue its policies of arrogant and reckless disregard, of waging war for the sake of profit and making profit for the sake of the rich.

If Mel Gibson's slasher film *The Passion of the Christ* has any theological merit, it is in its portrayal of how Empires treat those who, like Jesus and his disciples, are experienced as troublemakers. Rome was Jesus' imperial context and that of the early church. Ours today is the United States of America and a world being shaped by it. Our context as Christians is also the Church. So let's try to hear this afternoon, in this double context of world and Church, what Bobby's God is saying to the Church.

In the reading from Exodus, we hear God exhorting the people of Israel, through Moses their leader, to obey God's voice and keep God's commandments. And why should they do this? Because they, the people of Israel, are a chosen people. It is a tradition Christians share with Jews – to think of ourselves as chosen by God. It is a tradition fraught with danger, especially the danger of mistakenly lifting ourselves above others as a people set apart by God to be his *only* chosen, an exclusive people, a 'designer people'. It is a dreadful mistake shared too often by Christianity, Judaism, and Islam to the exclusion of one another and of all other 'heretics' and 'infidels' within and beyond the 'chosen' tradition.

But listen to what Psalm 15 has to say about being God's chosen people: 'O Lord, who may abide in your tent? Who may dwell on your holy hill? Those who walk blamelessly and do what is right. Those who speak truth from the heart.' God isn't saying that only Israelis may abide in the tent or that only Palestinians may dwell on the holy hill or that only Christians will inherit eternal life. God is not talking about who we are, dear friends, or what religion we may profess. God is interested in how we act, what we do, whether we love our neighbours as ourselves, whether we forgive our enemies as we wish to be forgiven. In our advanced capitalist global order, as graduate Brad Brockmann reminds us, God is choosing us to lift the burden – literally, the debt – from off the back of the poor, so that the poor can live and thrive with us, our sisters and brothers, in God's world.

To live as people chosen by God is thus to extend our wings as far as we can and – with the Holy Spirit as the wind beneath our wings – to soar toward inclusivity, seeking out those who have been marginalized by us or others, those cast out by the dominant social order and, too often, by the deafening silence of the liberal church. Indeed, our critique of the world must always include a critique of the Church, because our religious organizations are shaped by the same social forces, fear and greed, which are distorting the shape of the world around us.

So one message we are called to bring to the Empire is that, whatever our identity, whatever our social location, *we are never, ever, chosen by God to be an exclusive people.*

As you graduates can attest, the EDS curriculum includes a required course called 'Foundations', hardly anyone's favourite course, because it calls us all to a vocation of self-criticism, of studying critically our power relations as people of different races, cultures, classes, genders, sexualities, religious traditions, and other varieties of social location. Learning how to be self-critical, to notice how we are shaped by, and often benefit from, power relations, helps prepare us *spiritually* to speak truth to power.

So then, to be chosen by God is to learn about power, to make justice roll down like waters, to love mercy, to walk humbly with our God, understanding ourselves as rooted and grounded in the same God as every other creature, human and other, on earth and throughout and beyond the cosmos.

To be chosen by God in this cosmos is also to dare to dream big spiritual dreams – to envision an earth upon which no one is an alien, a world in which there is no terrorism because there is no poverty, no oppression, no Guantanamos. Can we imagine a world in which there would be no suicide bombers because all horrific systemic oppressions which sap the human spirit would have been dismantled and laid to rest? Can we dream such a world in which there would be no Departments of Homeland Security, because religious fanaticism would have given way to respect for spiritual and cultural differences?

Can we stretch our minds and hearts to imagine our own involvement in the un-doing of the major evil of the postmodern world – the greed of unfettered global capitalism? Dare we dream that our own small lives can make a big difference as we struggle toward that utopian realm – Jesus called it the 'kingdom of God' – when the lust for profit has finally succumbed to the 'constant love for one another' of which 1 Peter speaks?

Can we bear to imagine ourselves sharing the christic willingness to lose our life – our security as religions and as nations – in order to find our life as a people chosen and blessed by God?

Bear in mind that one of the ways the Empire keeps us in bondage is by trivializing our dreams. The Empire badly wants us to dream small dreams about computers and clothes and chocolate. The Empire uses fear as a tool, wanting us to be overly preoccupied with staying safe. We are well-trained by the Empire to be good consumers and good citizens, cultivated to ignore our big spiritual dreams. After all, fear shrinks us spiritually – and the Empire, like its capitalist foundation, is cemented in a collective fear crafted to make us believe that the less things change, the better.

So, another message we are to bring to the Empire and to our churches is the stuff of big spiritual dreams – *a message of God's universal love, of his dances of universal peace, of her dreams of a 'common language',* in the words of the remarkable Jewish lesbian feminist poet Adrienne Rich.

Still another message we should send to Empire and to the Church today is that *we will not let ourselves be silenced*, as church people or as citizens, by the predictable plea for patience with injustice and oppression. Jesus asks us to consider what it will profit us – as a nation – to gain the whole world, what it will profit us – as a church – to contain all the people, and especially the ones with money, if we lose our rootedness in the Spirit of justice-making, reconciliation, and compassion, especially for those most marginalized?

Martin Luther King wrote in 1963 from a jail cell in Birmingham, Alabama, that the white moderate who envisioned peace as a absence of conflict rather than as the 'presence of justice' had deeply disappointed him and had proved to be a more problematic 'stumbling block' to freedom than those members of the White Citizen's Council or of the Ku Klux Klan.

Let us beware of the constant temptation we face as clergy and lay leaders in the world and Church – to mistake appeasement with love and efforts to minimize tension with peace. This is the mistake of the liberal church's current response to the jubilant 'gay marriages' blossoming in the Spirit all around us here in Massachusetts today. Thanks be to God!

This leads me to suggest that we should be clear to the Church in these times that *we, the people of God, are called to help lead the way* through these confounding times.

Those who believe that God's spirit arcs toward justice,[2] those who believe that love is concrete, economic, and nonviolent, those who have faith that God's love is for all persons and creatures, those persons, you, I, and many, many others are called to help lead the way in both world and Church today, not to follow along once it seems safe. What a feckless vocation that would be!

Our former colleague and pioneer for the ordination of women, Sue Hiatt (see Chapter 32), often made the point that whenever in the journey for justice church leaders slow down for fear of going too fast and getting too far ahead of the people, the Church winds up getting rear-ended – and is shown, yet again, to be the caboose rather than the engine in God's movement for a better world.

A final message the people of God should send to the Empire is that life in the Spirit, *life in the struggle, is a blessing and often a joy*

---

2 Martin Luther King, Jr, often used variations of this phrase in his sermons and speeches. The original quotation, by abolitionist Theodore Parker, dates from the mid-nineteenth century: 'The arc of the moral universe is long, but it bends toward justice.'

experienced with gratitude and humility. It's not only dangerous to live in the Spirit, although it is that, but it's also a pleasure. It's not about long faces and over-serious attitudes. To live willingly and gratefully in God's Spirit is to be good-humoured and enthusiastic, not because it's an easy way to live, but because it's such a wondrous opportunity to learn and grow and teach together, to pray and play and march together, to protest and rest and love and work together!

Of course, living together in this Spirit of mutuality and joy means that our spiritual engine must keep chugging along on tracks which run counter to, and often cross, those of the dominant capitalist spirituality and its politics in a postmodern world. There will be many collisions and more than a few casualties. So one of our tasks as God's people is to help one another learn how to weather conflict and how to survive, if possible, our crashes with the Empire within and beyond the Church.

The founders of Alcoholics Anonymous figured it out: It is only as a team, only together – understanding our survival, our sanity, and our spiritualities as utterly bound up in one another's – that we have even a chance of surviving the violence and insanity, which threatens to suck us collectively, as well as individually, into the abyss.

And so, my friends, here we are at this commencement, a time of new beginnings, of going our separate ways. May we never forget that we go together in God. May the Holy One of Mary and Jesus, the Liberating Spirit of Church and world, give us the serenity, courage, and wisdom to live faithfully in Her Spirit, wherever on this planet we may find ourselves. May we keep learning, forever learning, how better to share the earth, how better to love one another, how ever more gracefully to let ourselves be borne on eagle's wings, soaring in the Spirit which arcs toward justice, the same God that little Bobby asked his sister about, the One who is our first and final home. God bless us one and all!

2

Beyond Shameful Theology

This piece was published in The Charlotte [NC] Observer *on 24 September 2001. I wrote it in response to the Reverend Jerry Falwell's contention that the terrorist attacks of September 11 were God's punishment of the United States because of the presence of lesbians, feminists, abortionists, and liberals. Falwell was interviewed by the Reverend Pat Robertson on Robertson's television show* The 700 Club, *where Falwell said:*

I really believe that the pagans and the abortionists and the feminists and the gays and lesbians who are actively trying to make that an alternative lifestyle, the ACLU, People for the American Way, all of them who have tried to secularize America, I point the finger in their face and say 'you have helped this happen'.

Christians everywhere must emphatically reject the theology of the Reverends Jerry Falwell, Pat Robertson, and other narrow-minded Christians who are inclined to interpret the terrible events of September 11 as God's judgement upon this nation or upon any group of people in it. As Episcopal Bishop Jane Holmes Dixon of Washington DC has stated in the strongest possible terms, this theology is 'beyond shameful'. It has nothing to do with the love of God or Jesus of Nazareth. It also has nothing to do with Christian morality, which is about the deeply human struggles for right relation, not self-righteous judgements upon everybody except oneself and one's own.

We who are Christians, as well as people of other spiritual traditions such as Islam, Judaism, Buddhism, and Wiccan need to be clear and public in our shared affirmation of the power of love in history. This Sacred Power, which most Christians call 'God', heals the wounds which divide us. This God is a Spirit which 'arcs toward justice', as Martin Luther King, Jr., said. In no way is this God ever involved in terrorist activities, except as God is deeply present with the victims and their loved ones.

The notion of a deity, who violently wipes out his enemies, is a terrible misinterpretation of Christian scripture with historic roots in our deep fear of 'enemies' and in our very human inclination to make 'God' in the image of this fear. The best that can be said about the Falwell–Robertson charge that – due to the presence among us of feminists, lesbians, gay men, abortionists, and other liberals – God chose not to 'protect' the United States from terrorism is that this spiritually ignorant view reflects its proponents' own fears and moral confusion. It would be simply a pathetic view if its proponents had not become so politically influential over the last several decades.

As it is, the fear-based theology of Falwell–Robertson has become a political instrument of division and destruction being wielded against those whom they believe to be the enemies of God. This weapon is being used not only in the name of a judgmental and violent God but also, increasingly, in the name of the United States of America. This theology of fear and hate needs to be named for what it is: shameful and blasphemous in relation to the God of love, justice, and compassion, the One whom Jesus loved, and the One whom Moses and Mohammed also loved.

Especially chilling at this moment is the realization that the Falwell–Robertson version of Christianity is a very close cousin to the theology of those who bombed the World Trade Center and Pentagon with hijacked commercial airliners last week. What we witnessed in horror as the planes hit their targets, taking with them thousands of our brothers and sisters, was the dramatization of a theology of fear, hatred, and narrow-minded absolutism in which its proponents assumed that they, and they alone, could speak for God and indeed represent God in the wiping out of his enemies. Whether a perversion of Islam (as it seems to have been in this case) or, in other instances, a perversion of Judaism or

Christianity, this wretched theology of judgement and violence is a primary source of evil among us. In the name of God, we must reject it.

What, then, can be a loving and just response to Jerry Falwell and other peddlers of this shameful stuff? This is an important, ongoing question for Christians and others as well. Its answers are neither clear nor simple, and we must pray for the wisdom and courage to know how best to respond. But I am sure that the most genuinely inspired responses have to do with learning how to love our enemies, rather than simply attacking them, even as they attack us.

Real love is justice-making with compassion. It poses a mighty spiritual challenge in these times to imagine what such enemy-love actually might require. But I also am sure that the justice–love of God is so vast, so broad, so high that it forever threatens to transform us – you and me, Jerry and Pat, even perhaps the terrorists who struck such a mighty blow to the heart of our nation last week.

3

Queer Christ:
Transforming Anger into Hope

I preached this homily at the Episcopal Divinity School's weekly Eucharist on 19 February 2004. We were celebrating the life and work of Anglican theologian Frederick Denison Maurice, much appreciated among progressive Anglicans for the breadth and depth of his theological interests as well as for the prophetic temper of his theological voice in mid-nineteenth century England.

Most folks, gay and straight, are uncomfortable with the word 'queer' and most of us also prefer, whenever we can, to disown anger as a real, embodied feeling. I have been musing over a couple of emails the seminary has received this week from someone self-described as a 'gay Episcopalian', who is angry about our use of the term 'queer Christ' in the announcements we made about this service. This person asked me to let you know that there is at least one gay Episcopalian who wishes to be disassociated from this service and its blasphemous linking of queerness with Jesus Christ. We are not surprised because both queerness and anger evoke strong responses. Why? Because each signifies something we fear way deep inside ourselves, does it not? Yet we have come here this morning to celebrate the affirming presence of an angry and queer Christ.

The term 'queer', as I am using it, let me be clear, is not simply a code-word for gay, lesbian, bisexual, transgender, and other ways of being at odds with dominant gender culture. 'Queer' is not simply a reversal of a negative epithet so often hurled against GLBT folks in homophobic culture. Nor is 'queer' simply a synonym for being 'odd', 'unusual', or 'out-there'.

Queerness is bigger than GLBT lives.
Queerness is more than a linguistic reversal.
And queerness is way deeper than merely 'odd'.

Queerness is public solidarity in the struggle for sexual and gender justice, of irrepressibly making connections to other struggles for justice, compassion, and reconciliation. By this definition, the Episcopal Divinity School is, by the grace of God, a queer seminary.

Some of you have heard me say that my eighty-eight-year-old happily heterosexual mother is the queerest member of my family! Yes, she has a dyke for a daughter, whom she loves, and many other lesbians and gay and bisexual and transgender folks in her life, whom she loves and respects. And yes, she is an odd character in this nation at this time. Even now from her room in an extended care facility, she is feisty in her righteous contempt for the current occupant of the White House, who she does not believe would be there had the 2000 election been fair and honest. And yes, my mother – like the gay Episcopalian who has emailed us – is not especially comfortable with the term 'queer', because she is after all a Southern Christian lady who likes to steer clear of unseemly and offensive language.

Yet queer she is to me and to many. What makes my mother so queer is not simply that she is supportive of her lesbian daughter and my friends and communities; and not simply that she is at strong odds with the prevailing political culture in both the world and Church in which she has grown old. What makes my mother queer is her irrepressible interest in making connections among justice struggles and making these connections public. She refuses to hide her convictions under a barrel, to remain silent when everyone around her would be more comfortable if she were sometimes a little less in their face about Bush, the war, and gay marriage. At the same time, you will never meet a gentler, kinder, more compassionate soul than my mother Mary Ann Carter Heyward (see Chapter 35).

Is she in your face about injustice? Yes.
Is she open to you and eager to know what really makes you tick? Yes.
Is she angry about the injustices we join in and perpetuate? Yes.
Is she compassionate and forgiving toward everyone she has met who has hurt her or done her wrong? Yes.

The queerest thing of all about my mother is that she is such a bundle of *apparent* contradictions. She is confrontational and compassionate, angry and gentle, representing for me One through whom we meet God face to face. There are many people, including many right here in this chapel, who embody Christ for me in stunning ways. But there is no one through whom I catch stronger intimations and glimpses of the Wisdom of God, Christ herself, than my own queer mother.

This is because the most dynamic dimension of Queerness – and Christ – is the holding together of qualities which only appear to be contradictions, qualities which are not in fact contradictory or oppositional, qualities which taken together are, well, simply 'queer'. Each brings out something in the other, revealing it more fully for what it is: humanity and divinity, anger and compassion, the struggle for life and the letting go of it, a capacity to wrestle fiercely against the enemies of justice and to love them concretely, which means trying to do them no harm, trying not to humiliate them, respecting them as brothers and sisters, whether or not they recognize us. Like the humanity and divinity we meet in Jesus and – through him as our spiritual lens – in one another, we also can experience anger and compassion, anger and gentleness, anger and forgiveness, anger and hope not as contradictory feelings but rather as mutually interactive dynamics of human being and divine being which work together in us and make us whole.

Frederick Denison Maurice, whose day this is in our church calendar, would be, I believe, pleased to be recognized as the queer man he was in mid-nineteenth century England, when he was frequently at odds with the ecclesial and academic context in which he worked as priest, professor, and theologian. One of the founders of Christian Socialism in England, a founder of one of the first colleges for women, the proponent of ecumenical dialogue and a universalist in his Trinitarian faith, Maurice lost his job as a theology professor at Kings College in London, because he wrote an essay in which he rejected the notion of a God who would condemn anyone to eternal hellfire.[1] His superiors fired him, because, they said, this theology would undermine morality. (Without the threat of hell, where would we be?) F. D. Maurice and his Christ were too queer for Kings College. If Episcopal Divinity School has patron saints, Maurice is surely among them. He's even been memorialized in a stained glass window there in the rear of this chapel's nave.

Beverly Wildung Harrison, Professor Emeritus of Christian Ethics at Union Theological Seminary in New York City, a renowned feminist social ethicist in this and other lands, and one of my life-companions in North Carolina, wrote an essay in 1980, which has been published in various languages around the world. Among her many remarkable pieces of ethical analysis, 'The Power of Anger in the Work of Love' is probably Bev Harrison's most widely read and admired essay. Her central insight is that, far from being a bad emotion, anger is an essential resource for living vibrant, responsible, liberating lives in an unjust world. Without anger, Professor Harrison writes, we cannot live moral lives. Without anger, we cannot be good Christians.

So, yes, we do remember the murders of our brothers and sisters, people like Matthew Shepherd, and we are angry! We listen ad nauseam to the fear-based voices of legislators, governors, candidates, president, bishops, popes, and they make us angry! We

---

1 F. D. Maurice, 1953, *Theological Essays*, Cambridge: Macmillan, pp. 377–407.

are beaten up by absurdities dressed in Christian rhetoric and by hate disguised as Christian love. Of course we are angry! And if we are not angry, dear ones, we are dead or we are dying.

But deeply embedded in our queerness is an ability to hold and celebrate our anger as a gift and a blessing. Like all blessings from God, anger is a resource of transformation. Anger carries us beyond a sense of powerlessness toward a realization of our strength in the Spirit. It lifts us above the perpetration of violence against one another and ourselves toward recommitting ourselves every day, recommitting ourselves every hour, recommitting ourselves as sisters and brothers in the ongoing journey toward justice, compassion, and reconciliation. That is what we are here to do.

4

The Passion of Mel Gibson

In 2004, Mel Gibson's blockbuster film The Passion of the Christ *hit the big screen to critical acclaim. I went to see it immediately and participated in several public forums about it. I wrote this review, but have made no effort to have it published until now.*

I had expected to hate *The Passion of the Christ* – what I'd heard about its over-the-top violence; its anti-Semitic inferences, if not explicit portrayals, of cruel and evil 'Jews'; and its overall theological message reflecting the ultra-traditionalist Catholic views of Mel Gibson. I emerged tired and troubled from Mr Gibson's *Passion*, but I can't say that I hated the movie or even that it was, for me, the horrible experience I'd been dreading. I found it interesting and provocative. You might wonder why, with such low expectations, I'd gone in the first place. It's because, as an Episcopal priest and teacher of theology, I felt some professional obligation to see the film.

At a very personal level, my tiredness was, I am sure, simply an effect of a psychosomatic disconnection from the film's violence, as I gazed numbly at the seemingly endless scenes of scourging and crucifixion. It was how I made it through the film. As I exited the theatre, I felt like I'd been on a psycho-spiritual treadmill for two hours rather than sitting in the comfort of a Harvard Square theatre. At another level, my exhaustion was a more complex visceral response to Mel Gibson's particular spin on the Christian story. His movie illuminates a medieval (not biblical) interpretation that the blood of Christ saves humankind. Not Jesus' life, not his healings or his wisdom, not his teachings or his compassion, not his passion for justice, but rather his death on the cross is what

18

saves humankind. Moreover, his death on the cross is willed by his Father God who requires him to suffer this excruciating death as payment for the sins of the world. This view of the Passion, as a blood sacrifice to God, is still shared by most traditionalist Catholics and evangelical Protestants. Mr Gibson has been clear, not only in the film but in interviews, that this particular understanding of Christianity is what saved him. And who am I to doubt a brother's salvation story?

What troubles me is not Mel Gibson's personal story but rather his, and his church's, certainty that this salvation story is *the* Salvation Story for everyone and that unless we worship this suffering Christ – the rest of Christ's life is almost entirely absent from the film – we are lost as Mr Gibson declares himself to have been. It's the spiritual arrogance that troubles me, and not just Mr Gibson's but that of other Christians like him who assume that they, and those who agree with them, know The Way, The Truth, and The Life that is 'The Christ'. One of the problems, historically and still today, with this sort of absolutist understanding of 'The Christ' as the only way to God is that it is, by definition, hostile not only to Jews but to adherents of all other religious or spiritual traditions as well as to dissenting Christians.

To me, a dissenting Christian woman, the medievalist understanding of Christ's blood sacrifice as salvific is the antithesis of my experience of the love and healing power of God, who has never required the unjust death of a human son or daughter or, for that matter, a goat or a dove. I am bone tired and fed up with this theology, which promotes violence in the image of a sadistic Father, who requires suffering and a masochistic Son, who willingly goes along with such a scheme. There is no divine love in this drama, but only the narcissistic projections of men who seem to imagine themselves in the image of a harsh and punitive Father and/or a mild and obedient Son.

As for the charge that the film is antisemitic: it is anti-Jewish in the same way much Christian theology is. Christian Antisemitism is a problem *anyone* making a film about Jesus has to face, because, unless read and interpreted through serious critical lenses, parts of the New Testament, and especially the Fourth Gospel, are anti-Jewish.[2] In this movie, Mel Gibson has handled the problem of Antisemitism no worse than most Christian storytellers, and actually better than some. Still, because he portrays the Jewish throngs and Caiphas, their ruthless High Priest, as bloodthirsty in contrast to the rather more likeable Roman leader, Pontius Pilate, the movie is likely to stir anti-Jewish sentiment wherever it is waiting to be stirred. Gibson says he was trying to be true to the biblical portraits of these people. But other Christians, myself included, see these characters very differently in scripture. More importantly, because Christian scripture *is so often, and so easily*, read as anti-Jewish, should not Christians say something critical about this in our public presentations?

Are we not morally obligated to critique our own tradition, including the Christian Bible, especially when it has been used historically as a weapon against particular groups of people? Most well-educated and faithful biblical teachers candidly point out problems, such as anti-Judaism and sexism, which are present in the Christian Bible. Such leaders encourage Christians to be aware of these problems and to strive to overcome them, living by the spirit and not the letter of the Bible.

Theology is never simply a private opinion, nor is it a politically neutral resource. Theology impacts, and should impact, how we vote, what we stand for, the kind of society and world we want to help build. The theology of Mel Gibson, as I understand it from both his film and various public interviews, is very close to the theology of George W. Bush and the dominant forces within the Republican Party. It is a theology which reflects an arrogant and faulty assumption that all right-thinking people share the same values, which in turn shape our understanding of

---

1 See Rosemary Radford Ruether, 1974, *Faith and Fratricide: The Theological Roots of Anti-Semitism*, Boston: Seabury Press; Joel Carmichael, 1992, *The Satanizing of the Jews: Origins and Development of a Mystical Anti-Semitism*, New York: Fromm; William Nicholls, 1993, *Christian Antisemitism: A History of Hate*, New York: Aronson.

marriage, sexuality, patriotism, war, capitalism, and other matters of consequence. There is precious little space for moral complexity or political differences in the world of Mel Gibson or his Christ.

5

Why I Decided to Solemnize Marriages between Persons of the Same Sex

In November 2003, the Commonwealth of Massachusetts became the first state in the United States to legalize 'gay marriage'. Subsequently, the Episcopal Bishop of Massachusetts ruled that Episcopal ministers in Massachusetts could not officiate at such marriages, because the Episcopal Church in the United States and the worldwide Anglican Communion of which it is a member had not yet affirmed marriage between persons of the same sex. As an Episcopal priest canonically resident in the Diocese of Massachusetts, I wrote Bishop Tom Shaw a letter detailing my reasons for having decided to disobey his ruling. What follows below is a portion of my letter to Bishop Shaw, dated 6 June 2004. Several years later, following the national Episcopal Church's lifting of the ban against its ministers blessing same sex unions, Bishop Shaw lifted his 2004 ruling.

This was not the decision I expected to make, nor could I have imagined making it, several months ago. I am among those who believe that the Church should get out of the marriage business altogether. However, the current controversy about marriage, in Massachusetts and throughout the United States, reflects a muddle of confusion between civil rights and patriarchal religion, in which most Christian churches are attempting to put the brakes on the *civil* movement for gender and sexual justice. In this context, I find myself 'marrying folks' because, against the tradition of Christian marriage which is patriarchal to its core, marriage between persons of the same sex has become a momentous justice issue in relation to which Christian churches which profess a love for Jesus as Liberator, Healer, and Reconciler should be leading the way.

In April, during a community meeting at the Episcopal Divinity School, which came on the heels of Bishop Shaw's telling diocesan clergy that we would not be allowed to solemnize gay marriages, I heard person after person pour out grief and anger about how betrayed they felt by the diocese. 'Betrayed' is the word I have heard in this context more than any other. It is as if a whole group of people – Episcopal gay men and lesbians in this instance – experience themselves (I should say 'ourselves') as having been literally 'left at the altar' by the Church. Sitting in that community meeting, I knew – as a priest, a lesbian priest – that some of us needed to act on behalf of our lesbian sisters and gay brothers rather than on behalf of the cohesiveness of the institutional Church, a unity being held together on the bodies of gays and lesbians. The biblical image which came to mind that day, and stays with me, was that of people 'harassed and helpless, like sheep without a shepherd' (Matt. 9.35–8). That night, I phoned the two lesbian couples whose weddings I had declined to solemnize, and I told them that I had changed my mind, and why. Here were, and are, my reasons:

1 *Pastoral responsibility as a priest.* Quite simply, it became clear to me that, as a priest, I have a pastoral responsibility to the whole people of God, especially in this context and at this moment to those who are Episcopalians. This includes more than a few LGBT sisters and brothers who have been faithful Episcopal Christians for decades.

2 *Strategy for social change.* Our situation today is analogous to the Episcopal Church's predicament 30 years ago in relation to women's ordination. Then and now, I believe (as do many others) that, *for the Church to change, the Church must act its way into new ways of thinking.* The Episcopal Church will not be able to think its way successfully toward an inclusive gay-affirming reimaging of Christian marriage until there are many

gay and lesbian Episcopalians who are married. People act –
only then do the laws change. The canons and liturgies catch
up with people's lives over time. That's how laws get changed
inside and outside the Church.

3 *Canons and prayer book do not forbid marriage between persons
of same sex.* Nowhere in the Constitution and Canons – the laws
– of the Episcopal Church or its Book of Common Prayer is 'gay
marriage' rejected or forbidden. It is simply never mentioned
because it was never anticipated. Therefore, to read these
documents as expressly excluding marriage between persons
of the same sex is *an* interpretation but it is by no means the
only possible one. To interpret 'holy matrimony' as an unambiguously heterosexual institution is to strengthen its
unambiguously patriarchal moorings. Is this what the Bishop of
Massachusetts, or the Presiding Bishop, or the Archbishop
of Canterbury intend? Surely not. Why not render a more
inclusive interpretation of the canons and the prayer book? Why
not do it now – and allow the General Convention of the whole
Episcopal Church in 2006 to consider supporting what the
Diocese of Massachusetts has done on behalf of sexual and
gender justice?

4 *Political situation in the Commonwealth of Massachusetts.* The
Massachusetts Supreme Judicial Court said in their November
2003 ruling that anything other than marriage constitutes
discrimination and injustice. The Episcopal Church's official
'ban' against its clergy solemnizing gay marriages, along with
similar rulings in other churches, will be used politically by the
opponents of gay marriage to support their efforts to secure
a constitutional amendment to ban same sex marriage in
Massachusetts. The Episcopal Church's pastoral, sacramental,
and liturgical leaders need to be standing *against* this unjust
amendment-movement with our bodies, liturgies, and
vocations. More than anywhere else in the United States, the
two dioceses in the Commonwealth of Massachusetts have a
unique opportunity in this important historical moment to

help forge a path to new theologies, ethics, and liturgies of marriage which in turn will help secure civil rights for LGBT people everywhere.

5 *Unity of the Church.* When Episcopalians talk about 'unity', they should be asked – '*Unity with whom?*' With the Bishops of Nigeria and South Carolina or with the suicidal gay teen in South Carolina and the Nigerian lesbian beaten and raped, because someone discovered she's lesbian? The 'unity of the Church' argument has been used against every justice movement which has ever threatened to change the Church. Our unity isn't worth much if it's not rooted and grounded in justice, healing, and reconciliation which take time – but which do not ever require us to perpetuate injustice. Our unity – as Episcopalians and, globally, as Anglicans – will be woven historically, over time, generations, and continents, as efforts for racial, sexual, gender, class, tribal, religious and other forms of justice move along, interfacing, colliding, reconciling, being stirred and sparked by the Spirit of God.

6 *Different roles to play in the Church at this time?* Our bishops may believe that their primary role in such a situation is to protect the 'unity of the Church' and that this necessarily means putting the brakes on a movement for justice that many Episcopalians and Anglicans believe is unbiblical, immoral, sinful, or simply untimely. This may be the bishops' role right now in this diocese and throughout the House of Bishops. They evidently believe it is. In this same ecclesial context, as a priest, however, I believe my primary vocation is to be pastorally, sacramentally, and liturgically present to lesbians and gay men who are seeking to be married by Episcopal ministers today in Massachusetts. With them, I believe the time has come.

6

Make Us Prophets and Pastors!
An Open Letter to Gay and Lesbian
Leaders in the Anglican Communion

In 2004, a special study commission within the worldwide Anglican Communion produced the 'Windsor Report' which concluded that gay men and lesbians ought not to be ordained nor have our relationships blessed by the Church. In response to the Windsor Report, authors Andrew Linzey and Richard Kirker commissioned and edited a book of essays, Gays and the Future of Anglicanism: Responses to the Windsor Report, O Press, 2005. *The following essay was included in this volume. In the Anglican Communion, a Primate (from Latin* Primus, *meaning* first*) is the chief bishop or archbishop of one of the 38 provinces of the Communion. The Presiding Bishop of the Episcopal Church is one of the Primates.*

When he saw the crowds, he had compassion for them, because they were harassed and helpless, like sheep without a shepherd.

Matthew 9.36

Dear sisters and brothers in Christ,

Ours is a special vocation in these times, one of accountability to God as She[1] is manifesting herself through the lives of lesbian, gay, bisexual, transgender, and other 'queer'[2] Anglicans, who are being

---

1 I tend often to use feminine pronouns for God as a tiny counter-balance to the massive weight of patriarchal Christianity, which as a matter of fact is the root of the Church's virulent homophobia (and, more generally its erotophobia – fear of the erotic).

2 I'm using the term 'queer' here to include not only 'homosexual' persons but all bisexual, transgender, and others derided by the Christian majority on the basis of our sexual/ gender identities and commitments and also those 'heterosexual' persons, who put themselves at risk in the Church and world by standing publicly in solidarity with us.

abandoned by the bishops of the Communion. We can look at the actions of the bishops in one of two ways: fearing major schism, the leading bishops of the Anglican Church are either 'buying time' by playing, for a while, to the patriarchal traditionalists on issues of sex and gender or they genuinely are willing to give up sexual and gender justice pursuits in order to preserve the unity of the Church.

We Anglican priests, deacons, and lay leaders who happen also to be lesbian or gay must step forward now to fill the breach created by the Primates' purposeful rejection of gay men, lesbians, and our allies. These bishops are barricading the doors against our participation, with them, in any genuinely mutual engagement and study of human sexuality. Despite their coy claims of 'care and friendship' toward 'homosexual people', the Primates' 'bonds of affection' do not, in fact, extend to gay people and our friends, and so we must take the place of most of our bishops in extending pastoral, sacramental, and liturgical care to our gay, lesbian, bisexual, and transgender sisters and brothers. Although few of us would have chosen this vocation, it has been cast upon us by the bishops' abandonment of the *whole* people of God, be it for merely pragmatic or more basic reasons.

A little personal and Church history may be helpful. In 1973, a week after my ordination as an Episcopal deacon – and five years before I realized I'm basically lesbian in my own sexual identity – I phoned the office of my bishop to say that I would be officiating several days later at the blessing of a committed 'holy union' between two women. After a brief pause, Bishop Stuart Wetmore spoke in his soft voice, 'Well, Carter, the Church blesses hounds and houseboats. I don't see why we shouldn't also bless committed, loving relationships between people. Thank you for alerting us. God bless you and these women – and we'd prefer, of course, that the press not get hold of this.' [3]

---

3 The Bishop of New York, Paul Moore, was unavailable, and so I spoke with Bishop Suffragan Stuart Wetmore. Some may find these comparisons offensive, and many are

Thirty-one years later, in May 2004, I solemnized the marriage of two women in Massachusetts who were among the several thousand gay men and lesbians married within days of the state's new non-discriminatory law going into effect, a law which permits the civil marriage of homosexual couples on the same basis as heterosexual. In between these two liturgical events, like many Episcopal deacons, priests, and bishops in the United States, I have officiated or participated in dozens of same-sex blessings and also scores of ordinations and consecrations of lesbians and gay men to Holy Orders in the Episcopal Church, including the 2003 consecration of the Rt Revd Gene Robinson as Bishop of New Hampshire, a holier man you'll never find.

I tell you these stories to illustrate that what is being portrayed by Anglican leaders as a sudden crisis in the Communion, something which seems to have taken the world of Primates by surprise, reaches back in history. In fact, the ordination and consecration of gay men is hardly a new phenomenon and those who pretend that it is are choosing to keep their heads in the sand.

Denial is, in fact, one of the Church's great sins. Denial is what enables Church leaders around the globe to imagine that homosexual bishops have not been attending the Lambeth Conference from its inception.

Denial is what allows any of us to assume that gay men and lesbians have not always been present in our common prayer and shared Holy Communion with us.

Denial is what allows bishops from the global South as well as the North to imagine that women who love women sexually and men who love men sexually are not seated in their own congregations, leading Bible studies, and singing anthems to the glory of God.

---

probably a bit taken aback by them and hear them as trivializing the love between people of the same sex. Today, 37 years later, a progressive bishop like Stuart Wetmore surely would not make such an implicit comparison of lesbians and gay men to houseboats and hounds. But at the time, I heard them as a sincere, positive mental stretch on the bishop's part to make sense of what I was talking about – a holy union between two women.

About 15 years ago, in one of my classes on a 'theology of sexuality' at the Episcopal Divinity School in Cambridge, Massachusetts, a young man – white, conservative, and earnest – rose to denounce homosexuality as a 'white Western phenomenon'. A moment later, a black Roman Catholic Sister from Kenya raised her hand. 'Actually, what you say is not true', she spoke patiently. 'We do not use the same language for these relationships as you do. But these relationships are present. Believe me. And how do I know? Because I was blessed to be raised by two mothers who loved each other sexually and were life-partners.'

But the Primates and most of our bishops, when they get together, tend to choose denial over such truth-speaking. Hear, for example, what they said in response to the Windsor Report:

> We wish to make it quite clear that in our discussion and assessment of the moral appropriateness of specific human behaviours, we continue unreservedly to be committed to the pastoral support and care of homosexual people. The victimization or diminishment of human beings whose affections happen to be ordered towards people of the same sex is anathema to us. We assure homosexual people that they are children of God, loved and valued by him, and deserving of the best we can give of pastoral care and friendship.[4]

My response to the Primates is this:

> With all due respect, dear bishops, and regardless of what may be your good intentions, you are fast putting yourselves, as a collegium, outside the realm of being able to respond pastorally to gay, lesbian, bisexual, and transgender Anglicans. You are increasingly unable to be pastors to us not primarily because most of you believe homosexual activity is sinful, or that gay

---

4 Communiqué from Primates' Meeting, Newry, Northern Ireland, 20 to 25 February 2005, Item no. 6, material accessed online from Anglican Communion website, 25 February 2005.

men and lesbians shouldn't be ordained, or that lesbian and gay relationships shouldn't be blessed by the church. These are, after all, important ethical matters to be studied and debated by people of good faith who hold different views about matters of human sexuality, people like you, people like us. Such debate and dialogue is what makes Anglicanism at its best 'comprehensive'. So it is not your lack of agreement with queer Anglicans that is the problem for us. It is your commitment to structures held in place to protect your own authority, structures like the proposed 'Instruments of Unity', that do not permit, much less invite, any genuinely mutual relation with those to whom you offer your 'care and friendship' that makes it impossible for us to take your spiritual or moral authority seriously. Where there is no room for mutual relation, there is no room for God.

Bishop Steven Charleston, former Bishop of Alaska and at this time President of the Episcopal Divinity School, counsels wisely that the current crisis in Anglicanism is 'a call to courageous self-reflection, careful historical analysis, and difficult cross-cultural dialogue'. 'It is', he writes, 'an opportunity for us to come in from the extreme edges of emotional conflict to find a common centre. It is an appeal to our leadership to lower the levels of invective and rhetoric so that the people of our Communion may listen to what others are trying to say.'[5] Unfortunately, most Anglican bishops are failing to demonstrate Bishop Charleston's openness to mutually sharing and studying our histories, theologies, politics, and cultures with one another – homosexual and heterosexual Anglicans alike, women and men from different parts of the world and Church, people of diverse cultures and traditions and Biblical hermeneutics.

---

5 The Rt Revd Steven Charleston, 'The Middle Way: A Congregational Resource for Discussing the Lambeth Commission Report', available on the website of the Episcopal Divinity School www.eds.edu.

I believe, dear gay brothers and lesbian sisters, that we should say clearly to our bishops and other Anglicans that the problem with the Primates' quaint offering of 'care and friendship' to us is not primarily that most of them are upset about Gene Robinson's consecration and the blessing of same-sex unions in the United States and Canada. The problem with their bid to care for us and other 'homosexual people' is that, as a group, the Primates transparently are not interested in any genuinely mutual journeying with us toward a 'common centre'. These men do not *want* a common centre with lesbian, gay, bisexual, or transgender Anglicans or, for that matter, with any Anglicans who show solidarity with us, like the scores of bishops, including Bishop Steven Charleston and Presiding Bishop Frank Griswold (USA), who participated in the Robinson consecration. The Primates, on the whole, seem frightened of women who openly love women, and they are probably terrified of men who openly love men. They do not want to get close enough to us to be touched by us, metaphorically or literally. Thus it is up to us, gay and lesbian, lay and ordained, to work closely enough together and keep closely enough in touch with one another to help the whole people of God work and pray their way through the fears and hostilities being set in place by the Primates of the Anglican Communion.

We can love only those to whom we are not afraid to listen and from whom we do not have to flee in fear. What, then, are we to make of the Primates' request, in February 2005, that 'the Episcopal Church (USA) and the Anglican Church of Canada voluntarily withdraw their members from the Anglican Consultative Council (ACC) for the period leading up to the next Lambeth Conference [2008]'?[6] What is this supposed to accomplish? Is this supposed to help 'restore bonds of affection' among Anglicans, asking two of its most controversial members to please go away long enough for everybody else to figure out what to do? And then, lo and behold, to suggest that these same two troubling

---

6 Communique from Primates' Meeting, Feb. 2005, Item no.14. Ibid. Item no. 16.

members be invited to the ACC as guests – as outsiders, people who do not belong – to defend themselves? That bishops in the United States and Canada would even consider going along with the Primates' request, justifying their compliance as necessary to preserve the unity of the church, shows how far removed they are pastorally from their homosexual and other queer constituents.

How can the message to US Episcopalians and Canadian Anglicans be anything other than that the Primates of the Anglican Communion really don't want us 'inside' the church? Of course, as good Anglicans, they can safely and politely invite us as 'outsiders' to explain ourselves without fear of their being polluted by our alien outsider ways. The message to 'homosexual people' from the Primates of the Anglican Communion is that queer people are alien, shameful, and wrong: Our lives are wrong – the ways we love, the relational bonds we form, the blessings we seek. Moreover, those who stand with us are wrong, and neither we nor those who stand in solidarity with us are welcome in the councils of the Anglican Communion. Still they ask us to 'be clear' that we are 'deserving of the best [they] can give of pastoral care and friendship'. Perhaps this *is* the best they can give, these Primates of ours. Nonetheless, it is a far cry from what 'homosexual people' either need pastorally or, if we have any self-respect, what we can accept from our bishops or from anyone else for that matter.

This is the context in which queer Anglicans are being called to take up the work of pastoral and prophetic leadership in the Anglican Communion. It falls to us, dear colleagues, to step in where our bishops are stepping out, to present ourselves as overseers of the wellbeing of gay, lesbian, bisexual, and transgender Anglicans even though it may be politically inexpedient. We must officiate at gay blessings and weddings, make ourselves available to queer Anglicans in other pastoral, liturgical, and sacramental contexts, and perhaps, from time to time, allow ourselves to be named and consecrated as bishops. In any case, to stand in every way we can with Gene Robinson and any bishops who may 'come out' and to be public and enthusiastic in our solidarity with 'homosexual people' and all others whom the Church oppresses and silences on the basis of their gender or sexual identity.

Stretching beyond what many of us may have assumed to be a ministerial vocation, we are called in these times to be community organizers. This means we share a vocation to help bring together other priests, deacons, lay leaders, the occasional brave bishop, as well as members of other Christian churches and faith traditions, in building a global movement which, for us Anglicans, can be faithful to the biblical witness, as informed by tradition and reason, and as illuminated by what Anglican professors Christopher Duraisingh and Kwok Pui-lan commend to us as 'postcolonial imagination'.[7] Such imagination requires not only that there be dialogue – more than one voice – in the search for theological and moral truth; but moreover that the dialogue be 'polycentric' and 'multi-vocal' – involving many voices speaking from many different situations and locations as partners in seeking to discover what may be most faithful to the Bible.

And this shared vocation requires us to be more than organizers. We must also be educators, not necessarily academics, but people whose special role at this time is, through our words and actions, to help educate the church through these turbulent, fear-based, hostile times. Good education is public instruction, education with implications for the whole community, not just a few. And so, we cannot hide our light under a bushel or go tip-toeing about our business, as if we gay-affirming Anglicans were called to live secret lives. This is no time to minister from the closet – unless, of course, we put ourselves or others at risk by coming out and ministering publicly as queer. For all of us, there are times and places when to be quiet, discreet, sometimes even secretive, is the better part of wisdom – and we need to pray that

---

7 See Christopher Duraisingh, 'Toward a Postcolonial Re-visioning of the Church's Faith, Witness, and Communion' and Kwok Pui-lan, 'The Legacy of Cultural Hegemony in the Anglican Church', in Ian T. Douglas and Kwok Pui-lan, eds, *Beyond Colonial Anglicanism: The Anglican Communion in the Twenty-First Century*, New York: Church Publishing Inc., 2001, pp. 337–67 and 47–70.

God will show us when we are in such situations and give us the serenity to maintain a quiet peace with ourselves and those whom we serve. Being able to discern different kinds and levels of danger and vulnerability and, therefore, how to conduct our ministries – publicly or privately, with fanfare or quietly, in each other's company or alone – can be especially important in the controversial arenas of sexual and gender identity, where emotions can be so explosive, psyches fragile, and possibilities of violence ever-present.

Nonetheless, as educators, we need to teach the Church by witnessing to the truths we are discovering through our ministries with the marginalized. For example, queer Anglicans, like all historically marginalized and outcast people, have much to teach the Communion about this 'unity of the Church', which the Primates are so eager to protect. 'With whom', we must ask, 'are the bishops of the Church seeking unity?' Unity with each other, which is fine, but at whose expense? How about unity with Nigerian women who love women and Zimbabwean men who love men, who must hide in fear for their lives? How about unity with the suicidal lesbian in London and the gay man who has been bashed and left dying on the fence at the side of the road in Wyoming? How about unity with Bishop Gene Robinson and his episcopal allies, such as the Primates of the Canadian and United States churches?

Pleading for 'the unity of the Church' has been, historically, a cry against justice movements that have threatened to change the Church and society. In the United States, movements such as those for the abolition of slavery, civil rights, and women's rights have met fierce resistance from Episcopalians worried about 'the unity of the Church'. Any authentic unity we can forge as Anglicans, any common ground, which will pass the test of time, will require the making of justice and compassion, both moral qualities rooted in mutual respect. Such mutuality can only be fostered through awareness and respect for cultural differences. In each location – in every town, county, diocese, province of the Anglican

Communion – we need to learn to share cross-culturally stories of how we have experienced justice and injustice, healing and liberation. Across the barriers which seem to separate us – walls of nation, culture, and experience – we need to come together to bear witness to our diverse lives, as the Spirit weaves us together.

Such a brilliant theological, anthropological, and sociological tapestry, woven boldly with diverse threads, patterns, and colours, would truly reflect 'the unity of the Church'. Our oneness in this Spirit would radiate an integrity and credibility that is probably unimaginable to most of the Primates who would abandon us instead to the reckonings of the Lambeth Conference and other 'instruments of unity' such as the Archbishop of Canterbury, the Primates' meetings, and the Anglican Consultative Council. Except for the latter, these so-called 'instruments of unity' are structured entirely around the authority of bishops.

It becomes our vocation as gay and lesbian Anglicans in this historical moment to be chief weavers of this tapestry of Anglican unity. But does it really matter that we are gay and lesbian? What difference does our sexuality make to our vocation as Anglican priests and other ministers? Being lesbian or gay matters because it signals a shared experience of exclusion and rejection, a common place of marginalization and silencing, in which the roots of our prophetic voices and pastoral sensibilities have been cultivated. Oppressed people can either identify with and mimic the oppressor or we can commit ourselves again and again to the struggles for liberation, for ourselves and others. Our choice, as lesbian and gay leaders today, is either to make a truce with oppression or to take on the mantle of the prophet.

Let me say also that we must never stop trying to help one another and other Anglicans make connections – moral and political links – between oppressive structures in the world and Church. Gay, lesbian, and other queer Christians must not be silent or passive in the face of racism and sexism, economic exploitation and imperialism, war and other forms of violence being waged against the poor by the United States of America more than any other nation on the face of the earth. There is no good excuse for gay and lesbian people to see ourselves as the only folks who suffer at the hands of a fear-based world and Church or as those who suffer most. Who suffers most varies from one context to another and, in the final analysis, is known only to God. We do know that any suffering laid on humans or other creatures in the name of Christ is too much. Christian leaders are morally obligated to help make this clear.

I am told that some of the Southern Primates – choosing to remain ignorant about who Gene Robinson really is – view him the same way they view George W. Bush, as a symbol of Western imperialism. Perceiving Bishop Robinson through the lens of such a superficial analysis of the very real complexities of neo-colonialism and imperialism enables these men not to notice the stunning difference between the Bishop of New Hampshire and the President of the United States, which we can summarize in an image of prayer: While George Bush does indeed offer the imperial prayer that 'God bless America', Gene Robinson prays that God bless all people, everywhere, Iraqis and Irish, Australians and Rwandans, homosexual and heterosexual, paupers and Primates, including those who distance themselves from him and judge him most harshly. The distinction between the two is almost as stark as that between Caesar and the poor man from Nazareth.

Finally, dear colleagues, we need each other's support and solidarity. Few of us may know many 'out' gay and lesbian priests and other ministers personally, and most of us are busy in this post-modern world doing too many things. May we be given the grace to slow down enough to take prayerful stock of this situation, this crisis in Anglicanism, and our place in it. May we be given the courage to publicly support one another in our justice-work, both those whom we know and those whom we don't know. May we hold one another in prayer morning by morning and day by day. Fortunately, many of us in the North have advocacy organizations in the Church, like Integrity and the Lesbian and Gay Christian Movement, to help us network. It is heartening to see bridges being built through these networks, between gay and lesbian people in the Northern churches and those in the global South who may not name themselves 'gay', 'lesbian', or 'homosexual', but whose same-sex love is real and vibrant, if often hidden. Never again should we neglect to search for ways to share in building these global bridges. We can learn together how to generate more fully mutual, polycentric, and multivocal relationships, through which God is always born again and gives rise to theological truths that none of us can discover simply on our own or among folks who are just like us.

So, let us pray, dear friends in the Spirit, that God will make us prophets as well as the pastors and overseers so desperately needed among those who are being abandoned, wilfully or inadvertently, by their own bishops. As Robert DeWitt, one of the bishops who ordained 11 women to priesthood in Philadelphia in 1974 – before the official Church was ready for us – often wrote to those of us whom he ordained: keep your courage.

In sisterly solidarity,
Carter Heyward

7

Some Violent Connections: Capitalism, War, Religion, Fear and Women

These reflections are taken from a presentation in Indianapolis, Indiana, on the evening of 27 October 2006. I had been invited to keynote a workshop on peacemaking and non-violence sponsored by several progressive groups in the Episcopal Diocese of Indianapolis and at the University of Indiana. The various themes in this piece provided foci for discussions in the workshop.

To help us think about violence and peace-building, I was asked to identify some links between the violence being waged by our country in Iraq and the 'cultural violence' being waged here at home against the good of the people. There are a couple of connections which we need to recognize here at the outset because they are basic to our life together and to everything we are here to consider:

Violence which targets the poor

1 *First, both military and cultural violence affect the poorest and most vulnerable with devastating consequences.* Those who suffer most chronically – those for whom there is no escape, no way out of poverty or harm's way – in the contexts of either military campaigns abroad or cultural battles here at home are the poor, especially poor women, children, and elderly people. Something similar could be said about violence to the land, air, and water at home and abroad; these natural resources are decimated, often with damage lasting for generations. In a few

minutes we'll examine some of the links between the violence against women in war and violence against women in our homes, workplaces, communities, and economy.

2 *Second, the same powerful people are waging battles on both military fronts abroad and cultural fronts at home.* As it happens, most of these powerful people in the United States are currently [in 2006] Republicans. This may or may not change in a couple of weeks. But whether or not the Republicans lose their hold on Congress, the forces we'll be thinking about tonight and this weekend will not be much altered. Because the problem of violence – military and cultural – is larger than either of our major political parties and their agendas. This is because so many who sit in the Executive, Legislative, and Judicial chambers of our national government are, despite their best intentions, first and foremost guardians of capital greed – wealth and profit – sometimes their own but always that of the corporate powers and lobbyists who thereby rule the military and cultural agendas that are hammered out in Washington.

The link between advanced global capitalism's apparent stranglehold on our President, Congress, and Judicial System and our national propensity for waging wars at home and abroad is, like addiction, so cunning, baffling, and powerful that we often don't recognize it until we 'hit the bottom'. Many of us wonder if we as a nation have bottomed out in these past few years, especially in the context of our war in Iraq. Whether we are in some sort of historical free-fall remains to be seen. Historians will be able to see more clearly than we can the extent of our national depravity, especially under the Bush presidency. But if we aspire to be informed citizens and responsible religious activists, we would do well to recognize the link between capitalism and the violence that threatens to undo this planet and its wonderfully diverse cultures and forms of life.

In a brilliant analysis of the significance of 9/11, Nafeez Mosaddeq Ahmed, executive director of the Institute for Policy

Research and Development in the United Kingdom, former Egyptian foreign minister and a highly esteemed political commentator in the Arab world, argues that 9/11 was a consequence of the convergence in modern times of global capitalist design and United States foreign policy (*The War on Truth*). That the targets of the attack – the World Trade Center and the Pentagon – represented capitalism and war-making made 9/11 shockingly emblematic of a global crisis that neither began nor will end with a 'war on terror' in Afghanistan, Iraq, or anywhere else.

Global capitalism and violence

One big question which we can begin to explore here is *how global capitalism and violence at home and abroad feed on each other*. I'm aware that a critique of capitalism can seem clichéd, like a bone over-worked by dogs, though it does not often seem so to leftist dogs like us, 'yellow dog democrats', as we're called in the United States South. But have no fear, my friends. I'm not going to launch into a major critique of capitalism as a global system of economic control. Such a critique needs to be made, and has been made, by political and economic thinkers, like Barbara Ehrenreich, Noam Chomsky, and others. What I want to do here tonight is to think with you theologically about advanced global capitalism as a system designed, implemented, and held in place by something other than human need. It was a good idea of Adam Smith's in the eighteenth century, but in the twenty-first century, the driving force of global capitalism is not human need but human greed – and *that* is a theological problem.

As an early capitalist aspiration, 'private enterprise' was not a theological or ethical problem. It was a good thing – humanizing, empowering, and liberating for the common person, more truthfully, for the common *man* whose well-being had been disregarded in European feudalism. Aspiring to continue the 'family business' is not a problem, theologically or ethically, but the problem we are facing today is that it has become less and less possible to own and operate a family hardware story or dress shop in the advanced capitalist network of Walmarts and Targets and Lowe's and webwork of online stores.

One of my life companions, Beverly Wildung Harrison, a brilliant Christian social ethicist, comes from a family in a small town in southwest Minnesota, where more than a half century ago her mother founded a small dress shop. I loved the Luverne Style Shop. Today, however, the store is closed, despite the energy, commitment and special love for this shop by the Wildung family. The Luverne Style Shop succumbed to rural poverty, as is happening in small rural towns throughout the United States. More and more, women must travel to cities, big chain stores, or shop online to get clothes made in China or Thailand. It is increasingly hard, often impossible, to make enough to support a family, raise children, help care for ageing parents, pay for gasoline, food, medicine, health care, education and even a home, by owning a small business or holding down a job.

I'm talking here about capitalism and how far removed we are today from Adam Smith's early vision of a chicken in every pot. People in the United States of America revere something called 'capitalism'. We look upon capitalism as if it were God, when in fact the goods we tend to associate with capitalism – especially the ability to make a living, to work hard for a buck, to support a family – no longer really exist for increasing numbers of hard-working people. Karl Marx was wrong about communism's future, but he was dead on about capitalism's trajectory. He saw, correctly, that capitalism, left unfettered, would grow and grow until, finally, it devours itself. Marx anticipated that the greed of capitalists would turn on them, generating more and more social injustice, pain, and trouble, to the detriment of the whole society.

Under capitalist control – the control of the corporate, global, capitalism embodied by Halliburton and emblematized by Enron – all wars, all public policy, all elections, all communication systems, all religions would eventually 'conspire' in the perpetual, 'unfettered', generation of greater capital – wealth – for those who have it. And let's be honest, folks, most truly wealthy people are not social visionaries like Warren Buffett. Most people, period, do not share Mr Buffett's assumption that others can do more with his money than he himself, or his own family, can – and that others need his money more than he, and his heirs, do. I don't know Warren Buffett or his family personally, but I do know that his decision to give his billions away to another foundation, larger than his own, for the purpose of helping solve global hunger and other problems baffled large numbers of very wealthy people. Not that he would want to use his money to help people – rich people do that all the time – but that he would give it away to others to make decisions over which he and his family will finally have no control. *That's what capitalists cannot comprehend: giving up control of their wealth.*

I submit that two of the most durable connections between advanced global capitalism and the waging of violence are *greed* and *control*. When we want more and more and ever more, when we believe that we have a right to get more if we can, then we are likely to do everything in our power to get our hands on more of whatever it is – oil, land, airspace, machines, and more control over whatever it is. How can we not see the intrinsic link between advanced global capitalism and violence, between greed and the desire for control – politely if possible, by force if necessary?

Nafeez Mosaddeq Ahmed, the Egyptian political analyst, who has done so much interesting research on the meanings of 9/11 from different perspectives, makes links between United States foreign policy – which has for at least a century been shaped by US economic interests – and all that has transpired in the Middle East during the last several decades. It's important to note here, especially among those of us critical of the Bush Administration, that Bush did indeed inherit the situation in Afghanistan, as well as Iraq and elsewhere in the Middle East. George Bush did not create the mess; it was passed on to him – and not simply by his immediate predecessor, but also by Clinton's predecessors –

especially, in the case of Iraq, George Bush the First and, in the case of Afghanistan, Ronald Reagan. Always leery of the Soviet Union, which he dubbed 'the Evil Empire', Reagan helped arm and support Afghanistan in its struggle against the Soviets during the 1980s.

As we surely are aware by now, one of the young warriors whom we helped arm and train was Osama bin Laden, who had come as a freedom fighter from his native Saudi Arabia to Afghanistan. Following the Soviets' withdrawal from Afghanistan in the late 1980s and the Taliban's rise to power in the mid 1990s, the Clinton Administration (along with Saudi Arabia and Pakistan) befriended the Taliban, even though Clinton and his cabinet understood that the Taliban was a brutal fundamentalist group committing atrocities against their own citizens, especially women.

And why would the United States have done this under Clinton or anyone else? Professor William O. Beeman, an anthropologist who is director of Middle East studies at Brown University specializing in Islamic Central Asia, concludes that the answer to this question 'has nothing to do with religion or ethnicity – but only with the economics of oil'. Writing in 1998, three years before 9/11, Professor Beeman pointed out that to the north of Afghanistan, 'on the eastern shore of the Caspian Sea in republics formed since the break-up of the Soviet Union', is one of the world's wealthiest oil fields. This oil needs to be transported out of the landlocked region through a warm water port. And Beeman noted,

> The simplest and cheapest pipeline route is through Iran . . . [but] the US government has such antipathy to Iran that it is willing to do anything to prevent this. The alternative route is through Afghanistan and Pakistan. Beeman pointed out, in 1998, that this 'would require securing the agreement of the powers-that-be in Afghanistan – the Taliban. . . . Therefore, as far as the United States was concerned, the solution was for the

anti-Iranian Taliban to rule Afghanistan *and agree to the pipeline through their territory*. (1998, p. 17)

This is not intended to be an historical overview of our flirting business relations with Afghanistan prior to 1999, when the relationship came apart, and when we first began to talk to Iran and the Soviet Union about joining us in a military assault on the Taliban – two years prior to 9/11. What I am attempting here is to help us see the connection between the United States' global capitalist aim – in this case, to secure oil – and the wars that were to follow. The terrorist attacks of 9/11 gave the United States a pretext for the war it was going to make regardless. As many commentators and analysts have noted over the past several years, the wars with Afghanistan and Iraq were not – and are not – about 'terrorism' but truly about the lust for wealth and control, about who will control the oil. Concerns about the location of Osama bin Laden have served as a smokescreen to validate this so-called war on terror.

Osama bin Laden and Al Qaeda's hatred of the United States and their desire to hurt us would have been just as ferocious if the Democrats had been allowed to take the White House in 2000, an election most observers believe they won. 9/11 had been in the works for a long time and might have taken place under anyone's watch. From the perspective of Al Qaeda, I imagine, the difference between Republicans and Democrats in early twenty-first-century USA is negligible in all except one important respect: the Republicans make Al Qaeda's work easier, because, like Al Qaeda, most Republicans in the United States today see the world in dualistic terms: good versus evil, us versus them.

Every time I hear a broadcast by Zawahiri, Al Qaeda's intellectual voice, I'm reminded of how important it is for Al Qaeda to keep the Republicans in the White House and preferably in control of Congress as well. Since bin Laden and Zawahiri are no fools, surely they know this. But whether or not *they* do, we should. Bush and Tony Blair are making it easier for Al Qaeda and other terrorist groups to make *jihad* than a more measured response to 9/11 would have elicited, a response less unilateral, less militaristic, and more respectful of human rights.

I recently saw *All the King's Men*, the contemporary remake of the film of Robert Penn Warren's stunning book about power exercised as absolute control over others. What interested me about this story, which I had not read since college, was that Willie Stark (a fictionalized Huey Long, Governor of Louisiana) was a man who wielded political power politely where he could and coercively – violently – where he had to. He told himself and others that his control was always on behalf of 'the people of Louisiana'. And listen to this – Willie Stark acknowledged his own abuses of power, his own corrupt appointments, his ethically dubious shenanigans, but because he was using his power on behalf of the common people of his state, he declared passionately and publicly that *his* uses and abuses of power were far less damaging to the people than the uses and abuses of power by the corporations, oil companies, other big-monied interests. As I left the theatre, I found myself thinking that Willie Stark had a point – his greed and lust for power, undeniable and sleazy as they were, had done less damage than the oil companies and big corporations. Willie Stark had provided very real relief for the people. He had built bridges, schools, hospitals, and public places for the working poor and common people, and they had loved him for it. Of course, like many of us, Stark justified his behaviour by claiming that he had chosen the lesser of evils. Certainly it's how the United States, or any nation's, military understands its violent activities, and it surely must be how our fundamentalist Islamist enemies – 'the terrorists' – understand the violence they have inflicted upon us and will continue to direct toward us.

Willie Stark, a greedy man, used violence to fight the greedy corporations. Osama bin Laden, as much a product of global capitalism as George W. Bush, uses violence to fight the greedy capitalist imperialists. In order to begin to comprehend this 'war on terror', we need to realize that it's not at root about virtuous defenders of either side fighting off the evil people on the other side. It is not simply a matter of 'good guys' fighting 'bad guys'. It is, more fundamentally, a matter of greed fighting greed, one lust for power fighting another lust for power.

The United States' *public* position – and what, as individuals and perhaps collectively as well, our soldiers believe they're fighting for – is to counter terrorism by bringing freedom and democracy to the world. As a nation, we present ourselves, to ourselves as well as the world, as a force for good: 'freedom and democracy'. We present our enemies – Al Qaeda, other 'terrorists', and those who support them – as a force for evil that must be eliminated. Of course, from the perspective of our critics in the Arab world and elsewhere, we as a nation are not a force for good. In the eyes of our enemies, Halliburton, Cheney, and Rumsfeld represent the greedy capitalists fighting for more and more capital. Of course, even among most Arabs, Al Qaeda and Osama bin Laden are not considered 'holy people', given the wretched violence they bring down upon innocents, including their own people. Nevertheless, to much of the Arab world, including its own critics, Al Qaeda represents an underdog, a feisty force waging violence – *jihad* – against the evil capitalists who control the world.

Violence and religion

The religion used to inspire 9/11 was a fundamentalist Islam, a gross distortion of the religion of Mohammed, which teaches neighbour love as a basis of a holy life. From within the United States, the religion used to exploit that day has been a fundamentalist Christianity, a distortion of its spiritual roots in the life and teachings of Jesus.

Sociologist of Religion Nancy T. Ammerman describes 'fundamentalist movements' as 'organized efforts to shape the future of a people in light of a past that is seen through the lens of sacred texts and authorities traditionally available in the culture' (1994, p. 151). James Piscatori, a Fellow at the Royal Institute of

International Affairs in London during the 1990s, wrote of Islam that, 'from the perspective of the fundamentalist, the stakes are high: the faith must be protected from assault and preserved from heterodoxy' (1994, p. 363).

One enormous, predictable consequence, therefore, of the United States' ousting of Saddam Hussein has been the rise of a fundamentalist Shi'ism in Iraq that has more in common with, and stronger allegiance to, fundamentalist Iran and its current leaders, including Ahmadinejad, than it can, or will, have with the United States. Saddam Hussein evidently understood that religion could be a powerful social force and, perhaps for that reason, did everything he could to suppress it, especially fundamentalist Shi'ism, in Iraq.

The Islamic fundamentalist leaders of Iran (Shi'ite) and Saudi Arabia (Sunni), like Christian fundamentalist George W. Bush, realize the power of advanced capitalism to shape and use religion toward capitalism's ultimate goal: the control of wealth. What this means concretely is that political and economic leaders 'encourage' (by persuasion if possible, coercion if not) the promulgation of religious traditions that will keep the masses under control. Marx's 'opiate of the people' indeed! As far as the political and economic leaders of either the United States or any predominantly Muslim country are concerned, whether people are really 'good Christians' or 'good Muslims' is likely to be of much less interest than whether we are good citizens, willing to obey without questioning, and supporters of the government (its laws and its wars). We are to be compliant pawns in the organization of the political economy – that is, of how money 'works' among us, of how it shapes the political landscape, and of how we interpret our religious traditions.

We need to be clear that the role of religion as an instrument of social control is by no means limited to fundamentalisms. In fact, until recently in United States history, the powerbrokers of this nation, through war and peace times, have used mainstream religions – the major Protestant denominations as well as the

Roman Catholic Church in the United States – with greater consistency and effectiveness than fundamentalist Christianity. In fact, until the last quarter of the twentieth century, fundamentalist Christianity was pretty much ignored as a major social force by most political and economic leaders. We don't have the time here to trace the history of either fundamentalist Christianity in the United States or its manipulations by the state into 'right wing' religion – but these are fascinating topics. So let's return to the way the fundamentalist branches of Islam and Christianity use social control to both inspire and exploit violence.

If fundamentalisms are '*organized efforts to shape the future of a people in light of a past that is seen through the lens of sacred texts and authorities traditionally available in the culture*' and if [fundamentalist] '*faith must be protected from assault and preserved from heterodoxy*' – including everything and everybody that is not a like-minded fundamentalist – then what governs this 'war on terror' here and around the world? What one characteristic do fundamentalist Christianity and fundamentalist Islam share at their core?

Fear: the root of fundamentalism

A demonic spiritual force, fear is the primary spiritual energy of fundamentalism, used both to inspire such terror as 9/11 and to exploit it in retaliation, such as the invasion of Iraq on the baseless charge of the non-existent weapons of mass destruction. If people in the United States can be frightened into believing that the 'war on terror' is more important, and more urgent, than anything else, the Republicans stand to gain, not only because fear is a centrepiece of their platform – fear of terrorists, fear of feminists, fear of lesbians and gay men, fear of immigrants, fear of 'the other' – but also because, in the United States, fear is *the* centrepiece of the Christian fundamentalism that has taken over much of the Republican agenda. Fear of a merciless God who smites his enemies. And who are his enemies? Well, everybody except those Christians who believe and practise the same things in relation to the headship and absolute authority of God the Father, the universal claims to salvation made by Jesus Christ His Only Son Our Lord, the Bible as the inerrant Word of God, Christ as head of the family, men as head of women, women as head of children, obedience of children to their parents, rightness of sexual expression only in marriage (by definition heterosexual), the rightness of holy wars (militarily against fundamentalist Islam, culturally against such social evils as the 'homosexual agenda') and the importance of such wars in bringing on Armageddon and the end times, when Christ will return.

We could debate, I suppose, whether fear has created fundamentalisms or, conversely, whether right-wing religion has made us afraid, but the question is moot, because in fact each generates more of the other. From a spiritual as well as psychological and material (economic, political, and social) perspective, fear shrinks us. It makes us spiritually smaller, the antithesis of what many spiritual seekers believe we are created to be: open to one another in our differences, stretched and enlightened through mutual involvement, and able to be most fully ourselves when we are rightly – mutually – related to one other. If this is so, then what are we to make of fear-based religion? What kind of a god does such religion require that we submit to?

Let me speak for myself here and, perhaps, for many other Christian and post-Christian women. This fear-based god is false. He is an idol that feminist Christians and folks from other liberation spiritual traditions have rejected. We feminist Christians believe that the deity constructed through patriarchal religious traditions – a patriarchal power which Christianity has in common with Judaism and Islam – is not the Creator, Liberator, or Sustainer of this or any world. This false god was born in the minds of men and has been sustained through their religious traditions which have served as powerful instruments of social control. It is not that this god is 'unreal' or doesn't 'exist'. To the contrary, he is a powerful global force, based largely in men's fear and their need to control forces that seem, and often are, beyond their control – plagues of locusts and tsunamis, hurricanes and disease, planes that fly into skyscrapers and gun-wielding teenage assailants at Columbine, the simple teachings of an itinerant preacher named Jesus and the ecstatic, erotic spirituality of Rumi, the real power of women's sexuality and child-bearing capacities, and the ubiquitous presence of gay kids, gay parents and gay families. Patriarchal religion is always born and sustained in the fear of dynamic social forces.

To what extent must, or should, our fear shape our spiritualities, for Christians our understandings of God, Jesus Christ, Bible, and Church; for Muslims, their understandings of Allah, Mohammed, and the Qur'an? And how can we, those of us who do not wish to be held spiritually in the bondage of fear, engage one another, across our religious traditions to offer mutual encouragement and learning, which is respectful of our various traditions, spiritualities, and perspectives? In a recent article in *Newsweek*, Anna Quindlen, writing as a mother, laments the extent to which fear has captured our young people and is holding them hostage, making it increasingly difficult for children to grow up loving life. 'The drumbeat of danger becomes persistent white noise, unremarked, unheard, unheeded' (14 September 2006, p. 72). Her concern echoes the lament voiced a week earlier in *USA Today* by Canadian freelance writer Patricia Pearson:

> According to a study done in 1933, American children at that time were most afraid of the supernatural and the dark – what you might call normal childhood fears through the ages. Now, apparently, there is no normal. Everything is frightening. (5 September 2006, p. 11A)

Fear of women

I would add that, in hetero/sexist, patriarchal cultures, whether in North America or the Middle East, most people, women as well as men, are frightened of the power of *women. Fundamentalism is steeped in the fear of women's power.* As I was writing this presentation, I heard a terrible report on CNN about women and girls horribly gang raped, then cast out of their homes, in the Democratic Republic of Congo. And, of course, this could be any one of many countries and cultural situations in which women's lives and bodies are simply disregarded and routinely violated. Take the United States. In a period of one week this fall, violent men singled out girl schoolchildren in two different states and murdered them, chillingly reminiscent of the murder of the women engineering students in Montreal in 1986, and a reminder that twisted misogynist demons lurk among us, often invisible and unrecognized (and maybe unrecognizable?) until they let loose their rage – against wives, daughters, sisters, girlfriends, co-workers, and neighbours. In this violent context, which many Christian and Muslim fundamentalists take in their stride as simply the way it is, women and our male allies need to press the question that feminist biblical and theological scholars have raised.

Whose voices are missing from the sacred Christian texts of our traditions of violence, such as the near-sacrifice of Isaac by his father Abraham; Jephthah's murder of his daughter as an offering to God in thanksgiving for his victory over his enemies; Lot's offering of his daughters to appease the gang-rapists seeking to have their way with his male houseguests; and the invisibility and irrelevance of women's lives, voices, and stories throughout so much of the sacred texts, both Hebrew and Greek? Drawing connections between the invisibility of women's bodies (and silencing of women's voices in Christian tradition) and the perpetuation of violence in the name of Christ has been founda-tional in the work of such Christian feminist biblical scholars and theologians as Phyllis Trible, Beverly Wildung Harrison, Rosemary Radford Ruether, Delores S. Williams, Rita Nakashima Brock, Susan Thistlethwaite, Joanne Terrell, Marie Fortune, Mary Hunt, and Frances Kissling, to name just a few of the activists, scholars, and teachers who have addressed these issues.

These theologians put before us the question: How, in our still overwhelmingly patriarchal religious situations, can we women 'hear each other to speech'? It is a wonderful metaphor coined by Nelle Morton, an early feminist theologian and Methodist minister prior to her moving, along with Mary Daly, into a more post-Christian spirituality in the last years of her long and creative life (see Morton 1985).

Earlier this fall, I attended a national conference for ordained Episcopal women, the first such meeting ever. In some ways it was a fine gathering – nearly 200 strong women coming together to share our stories and look toward the future, an environment full of enthusiasm, of hope, and of celebrative rejoicing in the election of Katharine Jefferts Schori as the next Presiding Bishop of our Church. Katharine's presence at the conference added to the delight and expectation among the gathered women. In another way, the conference was more challenging, highlighting a growing generation gap, a widening gulf, in the Episcopal Church between those women who 'came of age' fighting sexism and those women, often younger, who don't see what the fuss is all about today and who aren't especially interested in thinking about women's history, including our shared suffering. One proudly feminist woman priest quoted the Reverend Alison Cheek, 'Women shouldn't seek ordination unless they want to change the church'. But a younger woman priest, born the year Alison Cheek and I were ordained 'irregularly' in 1974, said that she's frankly not all that interested in listening to the stories of 'older women'. She continued, 'We younger women aren't as hurt and angry as you are. We don't have a critical agenda with the Church. We didn't get ordained to change it.' This lack of critical consciousness on the part of a younger generation of women church leaders, to the extent that it extends beyond the Episcopal Church, and I imagine it does, reflects a similar 'post-feminism' at work in the larger society. By that, I mean an 'equal rights' feminism to which only the most outrageous misogynist could object.

So then, how do we create movements for change? Movements

for peace building and gender justice, movements to en-courage women and men to speak out and act on behalf of generating a more genuinely just and compassionate economic system here at home and around the world? How do we break through the apathy that festers in our senses of impotence and ignorance when we ponder these connections between economic greed and control, the manufacture of war, fear-based religions, and violence against women? We are gathered here tonight to begin to explore some of these connections, lift up other connections, and imagine together what we can do to help build justice and peace in this nation and world.

8

Strong Faith: Martin Luther King Prayer Breakfast

Every year the Human Relations Council in Brevard, a small town in the mountains of western North Carolina, remembers the life and legacy of Martin Luther King, Jr, with several public events, including a Prayer Breakfast. On 14 January 2006, I addressed this gathering.

On the front of a card I received recently were words I offer as a text for this splendid occasion: 'Those who believe that something can't be done should not interrupt those who are doing it.' I want to speak this morning about faith and not just any faith but *strong* faith in the power of God to help us do what many folks, liberal as well as conservative, say can't be done: the creation of a deeply just and truly compassionate world, beginning here in our own communities, in our own lives, our own love, our own work, our own relationships.

As a child of four or five growing up in Hendersonville, right down the road, I have memories of being distressed about the disparities I saw between the conditions in which the white people I knew lived and the conditions in which the 'coloured'[1] people I knew lived. My beautiful justice-loving mother tells me I came to her and my dad a number of times to express my distress: 'Why is it like this? Why does Bessie, our coloured maid, come to

---

1 Throughout the United States South during the first half of the twentieth century, the word 'coloured' was the most commonly used term by which white people referred to African Americans. Not until the Civil Rights movement in the 1950s and 1960s did the terms Negro, followed by black, Afro-American, African American, and people of colour supersede 'coloured' as language more acceptable to people of African and European descent.

our house and we not go to Bessie's house? Why can't William, Bessie's little boy, and I play together? Why does God let things be this way?'

My mother says that they responded with something like: 'Honey, it's not God's will. God doesn't like it this way.'

And I would press on, 'Well then, why doesn't God do something about it! and why don't we?' Recalling these conversations that took place some 55 years ago, my mother says that she remembers being totally perplexed about how to respond to such questions from her child.

About five years after my little inquisition of my God-loving baffled parents, somebody did do something about it. On 1 December 1955, Rosa Parks refused to give up her seat on that bus in Montgomery, and in that moment God was born again, as God is always born whenever women and men, children and adults, regardless of race, religion, or culture sit down, stand up, or speak out on behalf of a more justice-loving, compassionate and non-violent world.

But let's get the story right here: This is not the story of a nice little lady who was too tired to get up from her seat, though that's the way the story has been passed on among most white folks and probably a good many black folks too, because it's such a simple, sweet, and non-threatening story. Mrs Rosa Parks was not just a seamstress at the Montgomery Fair Department Store, and she was not just 'tired' on that December day. Rosa Parks was a savvy political activist. She was trained at the Highlander School in Tennessee. She was secretary of the Montgomery branch of the National Association for the Advancement of Colored People. She was a community organizer working primarily with young people. And, indeed, she was tired, but it wasn't simply about being at the end of a work day.

Like the man whose life we are gathered to celebrate today, a man who would follow Rosa Parks as the leader of the Civil Rights movement, Mrs Parks was tired in her body and soul of the injustice, oppression, and indignities of being black in America. The sister was worn out by the cost of being alive in a racist society and she was bone weary of the excuses and the indifference and the violence. Many of us will recall the murder of the young boy Emmett Till. He had been lynched in Mississippi just four months earlier, and he was one among many, before and after. Rosa Parks was sick and tired of this, she was fed up with white racism, and she was politically savvy enough to realize someone needed to do something that most folks said couldn't, or shouldn't, be done.

She was not the only one who knew this. Nine months earlier, a fifteen-year-old girl, Claudette Colvin, had been arrested for refusing to give up her seat on a Montgomery bus. But Rosa Parks' act of civil disobedience became the spark of the Montgomery Bus Boycott, a movement waiting to happen. And here is how it happened.

The boycott was organized by the Women's Political Council, a group of several hundred black women,

> working against the mistreatment of Blacks in Montgomery. The Women's Political Council had been planning a bus boycott for some time and jumped on the opportunity to use Rosa's arrest as the trigger to launch their planned protest. They contacted Rosa's lawyer Fred Gray, who agreed to help by soliciting the support of two black clergy in the area. (Culbertson 2005, p. 72)

These men, together with the Women's Political Council, called a meeting of black people in the Montgomery area. About 5000 folks showed up. Out of this meeting on 5 December the Montgomery Improvement Association was formed directly in response to Mrs Parks' arrest, only four days earlier. This Association chose two young, local Christian pastors as its officers: Martin Luther King, Jr as president and Ralph D. Abernathy as vice-president.

All of this happened because people were tired – of injustice and oppression, and because some people believed that, against the odds, something *could* be done. It was the strong faith of these people that launched the Civil Rights movement – people like Rosa Parks, Claudette Colvin, the Women's Political Council, the NAACP, lawyer Fred Gray, pastors King and Abernathy, the 5000 folks who came to the meeting that launched the bus boycott, and the thousands of black people who refused to ride the buses for 381 days. The boycott ended four days before Christmas 1956 following a ruling from the US Supreme Court that the segregation laws, in Montgomery, and the state of Alabama, were unconstitutional.

But that was in many ways, as we know, just the beginning of hard times for people with their minds set on freedom. The structures of oppression do not give way easily and injustice does not die without a fierce struggle.

In the spring of 1963, six and a half years after the Montgomery Bus Boycott and about six months before the great march on Washington, Martin Luther King would write to his fellow clergy – white and black – from his cell in the Birmingham City Jail:

I must confess that over the last few years I have been gravely disappointed with the white moderate. I have almost reached the regrettable conclusion that the Negro's great stumbling block in the stride toward freedom is not the White Citizen's Councillor or the Ku Klux Klanner, but the white moderate who is more devoted to 'order' than to justice; who prefers a negative peace which is the absence of tension to a positive peace which is the presence of justice; who constantly says, 'I agree with you in the goal you seek, but I can't agree with your methods of direct action'. . . who lives by the myth of time and who constantly advised the Negro to wait until a 'more convenient season'. Shallow understanding from people of good will is more frustrating than absolute misunderstanding from people of ill will. Lukewarm acceptance is much more bewildering than outright rejection. (King, 'Letter from Birmingham City Jail', in Washington 1986, p. 295)

I feel sure that Dr King, like Mrs Parks, like Jesus of Nazareth, knew deeply the gospel truth that those who believe that something can't be done should not interrupt those who are doing it.

These times of ours today, decades after the Civil Rights movement, continue to be challenging times, do they not? These times are surely testing the spirit of Martin Luther King, Jr. We are a long way from racial justice in the United States of America, in North Carolina, and here in these mountains and this county. Yes, we've made gains, but we are yet a long way from that Promised Land, and we are fast going backwards, as Hurricane Katrina revealed for the world to see. Can you not hear the lamentation of Dr King's spirit? Listen sometime to his widow Coretta Scott King who continued to critique racism and other forms of injustice in our society. How horrified King would be today – as we wage a war that ought never to have been conceived in the first place. As we witness a Supreme Court nominee who has over the years made a point of belittling and denying the justice-claims of racial ethnic minorities and women.[2]

We are a nation whose horrific racial and economic fault lines are exposed not only by hurricanes and the recent mining disaster, but also by the constant clamour among the rich for more tax cuts and economic breaks. Here we ourselves are in a county in which the three major employers of our people have disappeared in the past five years, leaving sisters and brothers, fathers and mothers, out of work, without ways to make ends meet, and few safety nets being provided by local, state, or national powers.

Today those in power are proudly threatening to reverse the gains made slowly over the last 50 years by black and other people of colour, by women, by the poor, by the earth and sky and waters. Affirmative action. Public education for our children. Health care for all people. Environmental protection. A right to

---

2 Reference is to Samuel Alito who was confirmed as an Associate Justice of the Supreme Court on 31 January 2006.

fair trials, in public view, with juries of our peers. A right not to be tortured, whoever and wherever we are.

Sisters and brothers, today we are at a crossroads in the history of this nation. We, the people, we black and white and Hispanic and Asian and Native people, will either be marched to our separate lonely graves – or we will rise and shine together for justice! We women and men, we adults and kids, we gay and straight, we Christian and Jewish and Muslim and Buddhist and Hindu and Pagan and others, we either will be among the walking-dead, or we will be working together, learning to make our voices heard, taking heed of the lessons we can learn from such mentors as Rosa Parks and Martin Luther King, Jr.

And so, what advice would they give us – Mrs Parks and Dr King? They would counsel us to *be prepared*. Remember that Rosa Parks was a shrewd woman who was trained to do what she did. They would counsel us to do something. None of us can do it all, or even most of it. But all of us can *do something*. They would tell us to stand for something, not to sit around waiting for someone else to do our justice work! Mrs Parks and Dr King would counsel us to *work together,* to hold hands and share resources in the struggle, not to let ourselves get isolated or fall into believing that we, and we alone, can wage a struggle for any lasting justice. Martin Luther King and Rosa Parks would also counsel us to *make connections* between and among the many movements for justice being waged. King himself connected the war in Vietnam with racism, and he saw the connections between the Civil Rights struggle and the garbage workers' strike in Memphis. Parks spent much of the last decades of her life working in Detroit with US Representative John Conyers, one of the most justice-minded people in Congress. Martin and Rosa both understand that we ignore others' oppressions and trouble at our own peril. They realized that it's the same powers that be, the same rulers of the nation, who work against racial, sexual, economic, and environmental justice.

Working along these very lines, making connections as I am

wont to do, I picked up the *Asheville Citizen-Times* this past Wednesday and the headline read, 'Gay Couple: We were fired after getting married – incident stirs discrimination issues'. It seems that two Asheville women, Laurel Scherer and Virginia Balfour, went to Massachusetts to get married in October and ran a wedding announcement in the *Citizen-Times* in November. And, evidently, for this reason Ms Scherer has lost her contract as a photographer at the Wolf Laurel Ski Area in Madison County.

Now, this is tricky territory for us, isn't it, because the 'gay issue' is being exploited by the powers that be in this nation to drive a wedge between communities of colour, especially African–Americans, and those progressive movements for justice which include justice for lesbians, gay men, bisexual, and transgender people. When I speak to predominantly gay groups about anything, I always insist that my gay and lesbian brothers and sisters get involved in anti-racist work, as well as the struggles for women's well-being, including procreative freedom. And when I speak to groups about racism and anti-racism, I urge folks – like you, like us all – to be mindful of the roll-backs in gender justice, of this Administration's broadside against Roe v. Wade, and of the ongoing blatant attacks against the bodies, dignity, and well-being of lesbian, gay, bisexual and transgendered people in our communities.

I urge you, I implore us all, people of faith and our friends here in Transylvania County, not to allow wedges to be driven between us on matters of race, sex, gender, or anything else. If we commit ourselves to working together – for liberty and justice for all – we can model how folks can struggle together: for affordable housing for all of us, non-discrimination employment practices for all of us, for resources for all of us to be able to experience good lives and good work and good love. We can do it here in Transylvania, and the Christian churches and other religious communities should lead the way, as they have very effectively in the past on matters of race in particular.

Sisters and brothers, like Rosa and Martin, we can confound the nay-sayers, those who say it can't be done. It *is* possible, it's the way of Jesus, the way of Shalom and Salaam, the way God calls us to be people of *strong* faith, acting in love, as the prophet Amos implores us, 'to make justice roll down like waters and righteousness like an ever-flowing stream!' (Amos 5.24). It's seldom an easy way, but it's the only way to live faithfully in relation to God. So, may we go forth from this place today, a people of *strong* faith: 'to do justice, love kindness, and walk humbly with our God' (Micah 6.8). And may we walk always in confidence that Jesus is with us, morning by morning and day by day. Amen.

9

The Dream Continues: Martin Luther King, Jr, Day Celebration

After the Prayer Breakfast speech [Chapter 8], the Human Relations Council in the small town of Brevard, North Carolina, invited me to address the Martin Luther King Day Celebration at Brevard College the following year. In response to this presentation, on 15 January 2007, the mayor of Brevard wrote me a letter decrying what evidently some in the audience had heard, and reported to him, as the anger and divisiveness of my words. The difference between the two settings was that those who attend the annual Prayer Breakfast are, for the most part, justice and peace activists and civil rights leaders, whereas those who attend the larger celebration come together as an audience more representative of the general population.

A year ago, I was pleased to speak at the Prayer Breakfast honouring Martin Luther King, Jr, here in Brevard. At that time I called us to four tasks, if we are serious about the work of helping 'make justice roll down like water and righteousness like an ever-flowing stream' (Amos 5.24). I said, first, that like Rosa Parks and Martin King, we must 'be prepared' and not let ourselves be taken by surprise by either the forces of injustice that rage against us or opportunities to resist these devilish, cunning forces. Second, I called us to 'do something' – not to sit around waiting for someone else to do our justice work for us, passively wondering what on earth we can do. Third, I counselled us to 'work together', not to fall into believing that we, or we and only those who agree with us, can mount any creative, or lasting, efforts for justice, healing, and liberation. Finally, I urged us to 'make connections' between and among the many movements for liberation from oppression that may greet us in any given historical moment, not to assume that any justice matter is unconnected to other struggles for fairness, equality, and liberation. In an effort to sharpen this call to all of us, I want to take this occasion tonight to clarify several of the connections we need to make, we who believe that justice, peace, and compassion are among the greatest spiritual gifts and material goods we humans can share.

In a fine book on the subject of white supremacy (Harvey, Case and Gorsline, 2004), the editors suggest that 'white supremacy' is often a more helpful term than 'racism' in the long-term struggle for racial justice in the United States because it much more clearly lays the responsibility for the problem on white people – those with the most to gain by perpetuating this historical and ongoing structure of social, economic, and psychological oppression. This is deeply different from suggesting, much less contending, that every white person is a racist. The term 'white supremacy' denotes the reality that all people classified as 'white' in our society have some unearned, and undeserved, 'privilege' – a 'free pass'. A 'pass', for example, to browse in a department store without having a suspicious eye kept on us, a pass to get a lower mortgage rate and therefore to have more money in the bank, a pass to be treated with some respect if we're stopped for speeding, a pass to pull out our wallet and not get shot by a police officer of any colour who imagines we're pulling a gun. Happily for all of us, white people don't have quite as much of a free pass as we used to, but white supremacy is still very much at work in our society. It's just that those of us who are white, even here in this place tonight, have a 'free pass' not to notice.

The editors of *Disrupting White Supremacy* go on to make two assumptions about white supremacy: 'that it has its own [roots] and internal logic' and that 'it interlocks with other systems of domination to reinforce itself and create complex patterns of benefit and exclusion' (Harvey, Case and Gorsline, 2004, pp. 25–6). Among the other systems of domination cited by the editors are patriarchy, capitalism, colonialism, heterosexism, Eurocentrism, and able-bodyism. To these I would add militarism, environmental degradation, and age-ism, especially the systemic violence being perpetuated in our society against children and elderly people.

Every one of these structures of oppression is linked to all the others, and each enforces and reinforces the others. For example, an African–American woman with some economic resources is usually less likely to be treated disrespectfully by an employer than a poor African–American woman. If the black woman, rich or poor, is blind or disabled in some other way, she will come up against able-bodyism and the fear and ignorance which accompanies it among people across colours and cultures. If the disabled black woman is also poor, sick, or elderly she will likely be subjected to even greater humiliation and disrespect – including white racist responses – than if she had more money and a personal 'style' more acceptable in a white supremacist society like ours.

In our justice work, it is important both to realize and respect the integrity, and uniqueness, of each structure of oppression – such as white supremacy, or white racism. Each structure has its own unique history and internal logic. At the same time it is imperative that we recognize and take seriously the interlocking character of race, gender, sexuality, class, and all the other forces in our common life that we use to define ourselves and others: usually too tightly, and way too often, to exploit one another.

This 'making of connections' is something that Martin Luther King did brilliantly and boldly, especially in the last years of his short life. I have no doubt, and neither did his widow, the late Coretta Scott King, that were Martin King still walking this earth, he would be calling this nation and its people, you and me, to account for many forms of bondage and oppression, which he would understand as profoundly linked with the stubborn structure of white supremacy.

'Continuing the dream' is our theme tonight. But how seriously do we want this dream to continue? And more to the point, how seriously do we wish to count ourselves among those struggling to embody Martin Luther King's dream? If we are serious about continuing the dream, we're going to have to help each other realize that this dream of social justice was – and continues to be – *more radically persistent, stubborn and 'in your face'; more radically inclusive; and way more controversial than most of us in the United States, including most Christians, are comfortable with.* This means we must help each other find, and keep, our courage.

One white Southern woman who kept her courage was Lillian Smith, best known for her 1949 book *Killers of the Dream.* Lillian Smith was a writer and the kind of white person the Ku Klux Klan labelled a 'race traitor' way before most white folks in the South or elsewhere had begun to awaken to the problem of white supremacy. She was born in 1897 in Jasper, Florida, to a 'prosperous, civic minded, Methodist' family and, from her earliest years, was haunted by what she called the 'collective madness' (1949, p. 222), the 'ruthless games' (1949, p. 11) of white supremacy. Furthermore, Smith understood the ways Southerners and Christians connected race, sex, and God. Here's a passage from *Killers of the Dream*:

> When we as small children crept over the race line and ate or played with Negroes or broke other segregation customs known to us, we felt the same dread fear of consequences, the same overwhelming guilt we felt when we crept over the sex line, and played with our body, or thought thoughts about God or our parents we weren't supposed to think. Each was a 'sin', and deserved 'punishment', each would receive it in this world or the next. Each was tied up with the other and all were tied up with God . . . The lesson of segregation was only a logical extension of lessons on sex and white superiority and God. (1949, pp. 84 and 90)

In this way, feminist theologian Sally MacNichol notes,

> Smith dared to put forth the taboo issues that Ida B. Wells had brought to public attention half a century earlier. She was

relentless in her analysis of the intimate intertwining of race and sex in the psyche of the white South that was the cause of such unspeakable violence. (2004, p. 208)

In reading Lillian Smith and reading about her, it's clear that what disturbed her deeply about the civil rights struggle, in which she had been an early forerunner, was not only the outrageous, explicit white supremacy of the Klan and others who stood fiercely against integration and in favour of maintaining a segregated public world. What also troubled her was the resistance of white liberals in pushing hard for social change. Later, Martin Luther King would lament the 'lukewarm acceptance' of 'white moderates' in his 1963 'Letter from Birmingham City Jail'. In the 1950s, Lillian Smith decried the insistence on moving slowly and not pushing too hard for integration on the part of such civic leaders as newspaper editors Hodding Carter and Ralph MacGill, both of whom had won Pulitzer prizes for their writing against racial violence.

Throughout her life, Lillian Smith was scorned as a psychiatric case by white moderates and liberals for being too pushy on behalf of black people, integration, and racial justice. Here was a white woman, a lesbian (which surely frightened lots of white liberals), whose mind was set on freedom for black people way before most white people noticed there was even a problem. When Smith received an honorary doctorate from Howard University in 1950, the award came with the following declaration: 'You are a dangerous revolutionist. There is enough dynamite in what you say to blow up the very foundation of segregated society.' Lillian Smith was an 'in your face' social radical, who believed that the time had come – 'now is the time', she wrote in her 1955 book by that title; now, not later, when white folks are ready, but now. Eight years later King would publish his book, *Why We Can't Wait*, as a response to the race violence that was escalating in the United States South. Lillian Smith. Rosa Parks. Martin Luther King. Each embodied a dream that was – and is – radically persistent, in your face, and stubborn in pursuit of justice.

Even more difficult for most of us, here and elsewhere in this nation, is the radicality of the dream's inclusivity. It didn't stop with the granting of basic civil rights to black Americans. The integration of schools, restaurants, hotels, buses, and other public accommodations was, for Martin Luther King, Jr, the beginning, not the end of the dream. What would Dr King make of efforts in Michigan and elsewhere to reinterpret Brown v. Board of Education so as to suggest that, in 2007, affirmative action is actually a mode of discrimination, a means of segregation rather than integration? All we can be sure of is that Martin Luther King would be a proponent of liberty and justice for all, and that his dream would be evolving to include rather than exclude the poorest, the most excluded, the most disregarded among us. It is interesting to imagine, and to call upon his spirit, in these times in which demands for equal opportunity, fairness, and justice challenge us with confounding complexities.

Many of King's most liberal critics, then and now, black as well as white, were disturbed by his linking what they saw as other issues to the urgent matter of civil rights. Liberal critics, even those who agreed with him on matters of economic justice and the war in Vietnam, urged him to keep matters separate so as not to confuse people and drive them away from the Civil Rights movement. To his liberal critics, Dr King responded: 'I have worked too long and hard now against segregated public accommodations to end up segregating my moral concern. Justice is indivisible' (King in Washington 1986, p. 636). King is saying that the dream grows as it continues, reaching not only to secure and deepen justice and human rights for African Americans but also to include those we may not even have realized were left out.

Two of the most controversial 'groups' seeking basic human and civil rights in the United States today are Hispanic, or Latino, immigrants and persons who are gay, lesbian, bisexual, or transgender. Most of us, maybe all of us, including those of us who are either immigrants or GLBT, get nervous and uncomfortable when these matters of basic dignity and decency are brought out into the open and turned into a public struggle for justice. And yet that's exactly what needs to happen here in Brevard and throughout North Carolina, as it does everywhere else in the United States. We who believe in freedom and justice, we who wish to continue the dream, cannot close our hearts and minds to the well-being and basic rights of GLBT people to work, love, form families, and live with the same social privileges and responsibilities granted to heterosexual people among us. And do not imagine that Dr King would ever have used the Christian Bible as a weapon to beat up on anybody the way white people have used it as a bludgeon to keep black people down and subservient. He understood well that God's Word lives through us, in community building, in putting out the welcome mat, in opening our minds and hearts to new peoples and new occasions; and that the Bible is a welcoming manifesto, not a book to be read literally, verse for verse, in order to keep folks down, out, silent, or hidden.

Similarly, if we intend to carry the dream forward, we cannot close our communities, our healthcare system, our schools, our opportunities to live and work and build families; nor can we close off the possibility of receiving public assistance to our brothers and sisters who come from Mexico, El Salvador, or other parts of the Americas and the world. And please, do not chat on about how expensive it is to support all these people, about how we can't even afford the poor among us now. We seem to be able to find five billion more dollars to drop into the military escalation in Iraq being sought by our foolish President. As journalist JoAnn Wypyewski wrote in response to the health care crisis in our nation, 'It's hard to hear about the government spending 1.5 billion a week wreaking havoc for four years and then to [be told] that comforting the afflicted is simply beyond our collective means' (2007). Whether the issue is healthcare or immigration, we have the money. We as a people, we as a nation, are simply choosing to spend it on bombs rather than bread and housing and medicine. You and I can imagine what Martin Luther King would think about this state of affairs, but let's hear what he actually wrote about the war in Vietnam in his last book, *Where Do We Go From Here: Chaos or Community?*

> The stages of history are replete with the chants and choruses of the conquerors of old who came killing in pursuit of peace. Alexander, Genghis Khan, Julius Caesar, Charlemagne, and Napoleon were akin in seeking a peaceful world order, a world fashioned after their selfish conceptions of an ideal existence. Each sought a world at peace which would personify his egotistic dreams . . . So in this day, I take fearful pause. (1967, p. 627)

At about the same time, late in the year 1967, Dr King preached a sermon that was broadcast in December of that year by the Canadian Broadcasting Company. Here are several excerpts from this sermon:

> Since the spring of 1967, when I first made public my opposition to my government's policy [in Vietnam], many persons have questioned me about the wisdom of my decision. 'Why *you*?' they have said. 'Peace and civil rights don't mix. Aren't you hurting the cause of your people?' And when I hear such questions, I have been greatly saddened, for they mean that the inquirers have never really known my commitment, my calling, or me. Indeed, that question suggests that they do not know the world in which they live.' (p. 634)

King continued:

> In 1957, when a group of us formed the Southern Christian Leadership Conference, we chose as our motto: 'To save the soul of America'. Now it should be incandescently clear that no one who has any concern for the integrity and life of America today can ignore the present war. (p. 636)

And what does it involve – saving the soul of America? Forty years later it involves the same Spirit, the same dream that Martin Luther King preached then:

> We as a nation must undergo a radical revolution of values. A true revolution of values will soon cause us to question the fairness and justice of many of our past and present policies. A true revolution of values will soon look uneasily on the glaring contrast between poverty and wealth. With righteous in-dignation, it will look across the seas and see individual capitalists of the West investing huge sums of money in Asia, Africa, and South America only to take the profits out with no concern for the social betterment of the countries, and say, 'This is not just.' A true revolution of values will lay hands on the world order and say of war: 'This way of handling differences is not just.' A nation that continues year after year to spend more money on military defense than on programs of social uplift is approaching spiritual doom. (King in Washington 1986, p. 640)

You see, Martin Luther King's dream was controversial during his life. Remember that he was seldom in favour with the leaders of the nation or with the leaders of the white mainline churches or with most white folks during his lifetime. If we here share his dream, we will be controversial, often at odds with the leaders of the nation and also with elected leaders of our local communities as well as within our own families and groups of friends and loved ones.

Having these kids here tonight from Brevard and Rosman, singing their tributes to Dr King, is very moving to me – and says a lot about how far we've come! I was reflecting, as the middle school kids performed, that when I was in junior high school, in Charlotte, in 1958 and 1959, it was almost unheard of for white kids to admire Martin Luther King. Doing so publicly opened us up to being perceived 'communist', 'traitors', and of course 'unpatriotic'. Please be clear that Dr King was not popular with most white folks during his lifetime!

But so it goes, my friends. The 'revolution of values', of which Dr King spoke, never ends and it's always controversial. In every generation, every new occasion, sometimes it seems almost every new day, we realize that there are folks among us who do not have access to the same rights and responsibilities shared by many of us. And of course we realize now, more clearly than 40 years ago, that our planet home, this earth, also needs our advocacy and attention.

What do we do about these matters? Especially now, in this critical moment, in the history of our country so deeply beloved among us, as we are being hurled by a foolish, arrogant, and out-of-control Commander in Chief into a valley of dry bones – us and the Iraqis with us, not to mention the rest of the Middle East and much of the world? What are we, our elected represent-atives, and our religious leaders going to do about this?

We are waging the war in Iraq on the basis of fear and greed, not on the basis of any sane or strategic plan to diminish terrorism or defeat Al Qaeda. We are on a misconceived and misguided military adventure, and we are indeed approaching, in King's words, our 'spiritual doom' if not outright military defeat. Much of the military has come to see this. Most of Congress, across party lines, knows this. Many of our religious leaders realize this. Many people in the United States and around the world know this. This madness must stop! Senator Chuck Hagel of Nebraska has called President Bush's management of this war, especially his deter-mination to escalate it at this point, 'the worst foreign policy blunder since Vietnam'. We who are committed to the continuing dream must become a movement for peace in these critical times and this urgent situation. When you leave tonight, may you carry in your hearts and minds a pledge to do something together about this!

I close with a statement from Martin Luther King, Jr, in which I am substituting the word *terrorism* for *communism*, the place

Iraq for *Vietnam* and the concept of the *Middle East* for the *developing world*. There are significant differences between communism and terrorism, Vietnam and Iraq, the Middle East and other parts of the so-called 'developing world', but the similarities between what King was facing then and what we are facing now are profound. We can learn from King's response to the crisis facing his generation 40 years ago. Listen to what he had to say:

> Terrorism is a judgment against our failure to make democracy real and follow through on the revolutions that we initiated [such as the Civil Rights movement]. We [who believe in freedom and justice] must move past indecision to action. We must find new ways to speak for peace in Iraq and for justice throughout the Middle East, a world [close to us]. If we do not act, we shall surely be dragged down the long, dark, and shameful corridors of time reserved for those who possess power without compassion, might without morality, and strength without sight. (King in Washington 1986, p. 640)

> Somehow this madness must cease. We must stop now. I speak as a child of God and brother to the suffering poor of Iraq. I speak for those whose land is being laid waste, whose homes are being destroyed, whose culture is being subverted. I speak for the poor of America who are paying the double price of smashed hopes at home and death and corruption in Iraq. I speak as a citizen of the world, for the world as it stands aghast at the path we have taken. I speak as an American to the leaders of my own nation. . . . We [the people of America] are at a moment when our lives must be placed on the line if our nation is to survive its own folly. (p. 639)

Of course we are so busy, aren't we? As for me, I have to find ways of somehow juggling the heightened demands of peace-and-justice work with my time spent with Free Rein [therapeutic work with horses], visits with my elderly mom and family in Charlotte, shared care for sick friends here in Brevard and elsewhere, various opportunities for writing as a theologian and priest, participation in a worshipping community, and of course daily life and recreation with my beloved family and friends, including my horses and other animal-companions, here in these magical hills.

What will it mean for *you*? What must *you* find ways of juggling that will allow you to help carry the dream forward and help move our country in directions of spiritual liberation and healing? May we find our ways to continue the dream, together.

God bless us one and all.

God bless America, God bless Iraq, God bless the whole created earth.

Shalom. Salaam. Peace, my friends.

10

The Wisdom to Lead:
Why I Support Obama

I planned to, but did not, submit this 'op ed' [opinion editorial] to The Charlotte Observer, a daily newspaper in the United States, shortly before the 2008 United States Presidential election. My hesitancy in publishing it in the United States South reflected two concerns: (1) As an openly lesbian theologian, I did not want my sexuality to be used as a foil against Obama among folks already agitated by his blackness; and (2) as a white person, I did not want to fan flames of racism by talking about race so close to the election. I passionately hoped that we would come together across the historic race divide if Obama were elected. In fact, my hope was so strong [see the fourth paragraph below] that it muted my fears that, to the contrary, racism would be awakened and our society would be shaken by anger and chaos, for at least a while. I kept this little essay on file, and offer it here, as a record of some idealistic musings about the election as it neared.

I'm a white Christian woman in my 60s, an Episcopal priest, an ardent feminist, and a Charlotte, North Carolina, native who spent most of my childhood in the mountains of western North Carolina. The first child of a politically conservative salesman and a more liberal housewife, I became a Democrat at age seven, when I took the role of Adlai Stevenson in a second-grade debate at Rosa Edwards Elementary School in Hendersonville, North Carolina. Today, retired after three decades of teaching theology and ethics, I live in Brevard. I was a strong supporter of Hillary Clinton and now am enthusiastically for Barack Obama.

A friend of mine, an intelligent white woman in her 40s, admitted the other day that, as an Independent voter, she'd come to realize that her problem with Obama is that he's black. 'I'm ashamed to admit it,' she said. I confessed to her that, several years after my ordination in 1974 as one of the first women priests in the Episcopal Church, I gasped as a woman pilot welcomed us aboard a flight! It took me a good ten or fifteen minutes in the air to take hold of myself instead of the arm rest and begin to relax. It takes most of us a while to begin to realize the fears we harbour toward anything 'different'.

Obama gave a compelling speech on race in Philadelphia during the primary in which he called us across race and party lines to join in a national dialogue on race. For a couple of weeks, many liberal and mainstream media were so enthusiastic about this speech that the public might actually have imagined such a dialogue would begin during the primaries and extend into the general election. Instead, any mention of race in the campaign, especially by Obama, has been rejected as 'divisive' and 'negative'. Even to suggest that race might be playing an invisible hand in this election – which it is – is to 'play the race card' rather than be heard as an opportunity to learn something about ourselves and others.

If Obama is elected – and probably only if he is – people beyond the halls of liberal universities and religious groups might begin to actually talk about our experiences of race and racism in America. Bearing the authority of the Presidency, an Obama administration would signal permission for us to begin to relax together across lines that historically have kept us apart. Our lives might become less segregated, because we might begin to see each other through less fearful lenses. President Obama and all that he would represent, simply by being sworn in, would help set the stage for people of all races and ethnicities to get used to ourselves and one another as sister and brother Americans rather than as alien tribes, people divided by race, culture, and language.

During the primaries, most folks also pretended that sex, like race, was not important and shouldn't be talked about. Yet public antagonism to Clinton in her run for the White House was rife with sexism. Even progressive newsmen like MSNBC's Keith

Olbermann and Chris Matthews ranted about Clinton in ways all too familiar to women who've tried to break glass ceilings.

With Sarah Palin's nomination, as Anna Quindlen pointed out in *Newsweek* (2008), the Republicans have suddenly learned the word *sexism*, which they mostly don't connect to historic injustices imposed upon women such as unequal pay for equal work, unavailability of adequate child care or health care for poor women and their children, and ongoing efforts to limit women's reproductive freedom. To Palin's fans, *sexism* seems to mean putting a Republican woman candidate on the spot. Most feminists, by contrast, view McCain's selection of Palin as a sexist manipulation – the exploitation of a woman for his own political gain.

As a matter of fact, although she is bright and 'a breath of fresh air' to many socially conservative Republicans, Sarah Palin stands against much of what many of us, including most feminists and most men and women who take women's lives seriously, have struggled toward for more than a century. Although I've always imagined that I personally would not have chosen to have an abortion if I'd been faced with an unwanted pregnancy, abortion rights are sacred to me. I will never cast a vote for anyone, like Palin or McCain, who would reverse Roe v. Wade, because I am adamant that every woman and girl in the world, including the United States, should be respected as custodian of her own body, relationships, and reproductive choices.

More generally, I am troubled by Palin's anti-scientific, narrow view of the world. I have nothing against small town or rural America. I moved to Brevard for that reason. I love living in the woods myself. But does Palin understand the world beyond the state of Alaska? Moreover, can Sarah Palin separate her values and priorities from the constitution and laws of a government by and for all the people, not just those like her? And be very clear – it's not 'sexist' to press her on these questions. Sarah Palin lacks the wisdom crucial to leading the United States of America and, God forbid, the world. It is precisely what we have so sorely lacked in

George W. Bush. The same could be said of the erratic John McCain, whose lack of wisdom gave us Palin.

And where does McCain actually stand on sex and gender issues, on women's wellbeing? His votes on women's rights and gender justice have been consistently among the worst in the US Senate, and he has promised to appoint Supreme Court justices like Antonin Scalia and Clarence Thomas. That promise is gender-coded, and feminists know it. It tells us that, if elected, Mc-Cain will try, through his court appointments, to overturn Roe v. Wade. Not only women, but also gay men and lesbians, working people, prisoners, and the environment would suffer under McCain's judges. Moreover, the United States would be in grave danger internationally with McCain as President because we would be perceived even more than we are already as a nation indifferent, if not downright hostile, to those who don't look, think, speak, and act like the leaders of the Republican Party.

In recent days, McCain has presented himself as a maverick. Beneath his mask of fury at Wall Street, John McCain is a pre-dictable party man who has voted with Bush 91 per cent of the time during the last eight years and 95 per cent of the time during the past two. On the economy, John McCain's leadership cred-ibility is limited not only by his temperament but also his longstanding allegiance to the Republican Party's mantra: the deregulation of Wall Street! Change, he says? Senator McCain must think we're all fools. A McCain Administration would find us splashing around in the same seas of economic distress that the Bush Administration has generated.

Senator Obama's supporters are probably energized more by his moral compass than by his political affiliation, though many of us are delighted he's a Democrat. Obama points beyond the wealthy toward diverse communities of people and ideas. These communities, including quite a few rich people – Warren Buffett and Oprah Winfrey being notable examples – have helped Obama see the extent to which our nation is increasingly divided between rich and poor, black and white, *us* and *them*. When he talks about 'change', this is what he means. These great chasms must be bridged. Obama believes that the President of the United States must help bring about this change. Working with other organizations as well as the private sector, our government must wage sustainable struggles for social justice in this nation and world.

So while feminists like me would love to vote for a woman as President or Vice President, a large majority of us assess the McCain–Palin team as contemptuous toward most women, children, and marginalized people, as well as the earth and its many varied creatures. An Obama–Biden Administration, by contrast, will open doors to the possibility that, yes, we can build that nation envisioned by our fathers and mothers in which there is liberty and justice for all, not just those near the top of the pyramid.

11

Feminism and Love

On 28 June 2009, Holy Ground, a feminist spirituality resource centre in Asheville, North Carolina, closed after 15 years. Founded by two recent seminary graduates, Sandra Smith and Dorri Sherrill, Holy Ground offered lectures, retreats, workshops, and networking in such areas as feminist and womanist theologies, evolving understandings of marriage and partnering, lesbian and bisexuality as justice matters for women, economic and racial justice, sexual abuse and violence, prayer and spiritual formation, care of the earth and environment, organic gardening, opportunities for artists and musicians, and understanding the Enneagram as a resource for spiritual growth. I was asked to give a presentation in the closing ceremony, which took place on a beautiful riverside farm in the mountain town of Swannanoa, North Carolina.

This is a bittersweet moment – Holy Ground drawing to a close as a creative small organization, remarkable community resource, much beloved by hundreds, more likely thousands, of us near and far. But sadness is only one of several strong emotions – like gratitude and joy – which have brought us to this place, because, like at all commencements, we come to acknowledge not only an ending but many beginnings as well, moments and movements in our lives that have taken tenacious root in Holy Ground. Roots of friendship, spiritual integrity and transformation, ways of organizing community, deepening experiences of self-awareness, and ongoing processes of healing and moments and movements of both personal and transpersonal/social/political courage and liberation. Think of how many of these gifts, and others, you have received in small or great measure from being involved over the years with Holy Ground.

It's hard for me to believe that it was fifteen years ago that

Sandra, Dorri, and I sat over dinner in their home and discussed this emerging adventure. Recently graduated from seminary, bursting with energy and hope, Sandra and Dorri yearned for Holy Ground to be a resting place for women tired in the struggles for liberation and healing; a resource for empowerment for women and men seeking to further the work of justice-love; and a welcoming space for everyone seeking to love God and neighbour in ways that build community and change the world.

One of the things Sandra, Dorri, and I had in common was that all three of us were women without a church. As lesbian women, we were unwanted by the churches, because we were not celibate and we were not repentant and we had no intention of bending ourselves out of shape, spiritually and professionally, in order to squeeze ourselves into the tiny gender boxes that the churches have historically prepared for every woman, and every man, to either fit into or pretend to fit into. Well, for Sandra and Dorri and me, this was not to be, and so all three of us (and many others of you) have had to build our vocations and generate sacred spaces around the edges of organized religion, drawing from the Christian tradition, where we have been able, and letting go of the parts that trivialize or violate those whose questions are too honest, and whose lives too challenging, for most religious institutions to tolerate, much less celebrate. Holy Ground was born in Sandra and Dorri's yearning to generate such sacred space for women and men like themselves, sojourners seeking spiritual and social liberation and healing.

That was 15 years ago, and here we are still, joined by that same yearning, even stronger today, thanks to Holy Ground.

Several months ago, Sandra phoned and asked if I would reflect for a few minutes today on 'Feminism and Love'. Of course, I said YES (Y'all know how it is when Sandra asks you to do something), but as I was thinking about it last week, I said to Sandra, 'Now you know this topic "feminism and love" could be about ANYTHING almost! It's so huge!'

And she said to me, 'Carter, what I really meant was that you should talk about "feminism" being about relationality, not about dogma or rules or political correctness.'

'Indeed!' I responded. And that's what love is – right relation, mutual relation, in which both or all parties benefit in important ways. Right, mutual relation – that's what love means. That's what justice means, in the deepest sense. That's why the Presbyterian Church's Study Commission on Sexuality, whose gay-affirming report was rejected by the denomination in 1991, coined the term 'justice–love' – meaning right, mutual relation, in the larger and smaller arenas of our lives, as individuals, partners/spouses, families, communities of all sorts, nations, and religions (1991).

From the beginning, this radical love, this justice–love, has been the basis of the feminist vision of who we are at our best, respecting and calling forth the best in one another and experiencing those dimensions of ourselves in relation to the whole. As the old saying goes, it's as good as it gets! That's what feminists have been seeking, and struggling for, all along – and, yes, that's what anti-feminists and so-called 'post-feminists' have been struggling against.

Make no mistake, the forces that murdered Dr George Tiller last month,[1] those who inveigh against women's rights to choose, women's reproductive freedom, those who threaten women seeking abortions and the health care providers who serve them, those voices speak volumes against radical love through which all lives, women's lives and men's lives, LGBT /Queer lives and 'straight' lives, are treated with respect, justice, and compassion.

President Obama articulates an inclusive vision of human and environmental justice – a great vision which this great man has yet to actualize fully, of course, but which many of us believe he will in time. Given the horrendous and precarious mess he stepped into, a mess we're all in together, those of us who support an inclusive vision of human and environmental justice, need to

---

2 Dr George Tiller, who ran a health clinic in Wichita, Kansas, where late-term abortions were done, was murdered in his church as he was ushering on 31 May 2009.

exercise some 'revolutionary patience' (Soelle 1974). In order to love the world, one another, and the earth, in order to further the feminist vision – which many of us believe is also a powerful spiritual vision – we need to both PUSH and SUPPORT our leaders, like Barack Obama. We need to affirm what he is trying to do and criticize when he seems to be downplaying or ignoring commitments he previously made, like those involving LGBT Queer justice. We need to keep in front of him his promises to eliminate the Defense of Marriage Act and the Don't Ask Don't Tell policy,[2] for maintaining the absolute sanctity of abortion rights and the safety of abortion providers. Feminism is a call to keep things in perspective – that is, to learn to see issues and conundrums and challenges in a larger view than simply our own and, at the same time, to struggle passionately for what we believe.

Unfortunately for the women of the earth, women's issues are often sacrificed, by parliaments, presidents, and popes, to so called 'larger issues' like war and peace, poverty and the economy, racism and cultural imperialism. Feminism reminds us that right at the centre of every 'larger issue' stir the daily lives and deaths of women, deaths by bombs and death squads, deaths by poverty, death by race hatred; death by misogynist (woman-hating, woman-fearing) religious customs such as honour killings and, usually a little closer to home for most of us in the United States, domestic and intimate violence. Feminism is the Love that names these things. As James Baldwin, radical gay black poet and essayist, once wrote, 'If I love you, I must make you conscious of the things you don't see' (1989, p. 156). This is actually a great slogan not only for black radicalism but also for feminism: A Love that makes us conscious of what we don't see, a Love that names

---

2 The Defense of Marriage Act [DOMA] was adopted by Congress on 21 September 1996 and states that for the purposes of Federal Law (including those upheld by various administrative bureaus and agencies of the United States) marriage means a legal union between one man and one woman. Don't Ask, Don't Tell, a military service policy, went into effect in November 1993. Don't Ask, Don't Tell was instituted by the Clinton Administration as a compromise between banning gays, lesbians, and bisexuals from military service and allowing them to be honest and open about their sexual identities and relationships.

rather than avoids reality. Feminism is about loving women and naming those things that hurt and break women's lives and bodies. Those nay-sayers who caricature feminism as man hating are trying to scare women away from feminism and to discredit feminism as a social and spiritual movement rooted in the love of women and to frighten those men who respect and love women as people, as spouses, sisters, daughters, friends, colleagues, lovers.

Now from all reports, feminism is a thing of the past. Is this true? Is feminism dead? It seems to me that, as a high profile social movement, feminism is taking a little rest these days in order to be stirred again in forms that, even now, are being prepared to grow out of contemporary cultural, social, and historical priorities. I enjoy the bumper sticker that reads, 'I'll be a post-feminist in a post-patriarchy'. So, although taking a little rest from high public profile, as its new leaders are born and raised and trained to lead, feminism will be a thing of the past only when male domination of women's lives and of the world is behind us. Because no revolution is ever fully won, movements for justice of all forms have to go through transformations over time in order to re-emerge as social movements when the time and place are right.

Certainly, the on-going struggle to secure safe, legal conditions for women's reproductive options; the movement for LGBT Queer justice; and efforts throughout the world for women's well-being bear witness to the constancy of feminist movements often known by other names, or by no names at all, so frightened are so many women and men of the term *feminism*. But don't be fooled. The fear is not really of the word. The fear is of the reality that women throughout this nation and the world will live empowered lives, will have choices, will be able to live free of violence. And so the scary words like *feminism* will be spoken when women are ready to speak them – *women's suffrage, women's liberation, feminism, womanism*, whatever words may come along next will come, when women are ready to speak out loud of their public struggle for the love of women – love of themselves and other women, love of their mothers and grandmothers, their daughters and nieces, love of their friends, love of their lovers and, yes, women's love of their spouses, male or female! And to speak publicly of their love of men who share their strong, respectful love of women.

This on-going, historical process will provide the social context in which Holy Ground will be born again someday, in Asheville and elsewhere, as a 'daughter' to the small, wonderfully creative Christian feminist 'love-child' of Sandra Smith and Dorri Sherrill. Like feminism itself, and like Love, the heart and soul and work and play of Holy Ground is not gone. It is simply changing, and we have to let it go. We have to let it go like the leaf that must fall and die so that new leaves will appear in due season.

When the time comes, by whatever name and in whatever form, Holy Ground will be drawing us together again, because this is how it works, how feminism works, how love works, how God works. Our Sacred Energy for making right, mutual relation, building and strengthening our communities will make justice rise again. This is the energy that gave us Holy Ground 15 years ago, thanks to the wisdom, courage, and willingness of Sandra and Dorri and to so many others who have joined them over the years, including many of you right here today. This feminism, this love, this God, will bring Holy Ground back when we, and those who come after us, are ready.

Part 2: Remembering Who We Are

Introduction

The fifteen chapters in Part 2 focus on our spiritual identities as sisters and brothers and our common vocation to love our neighbours as ourselves. These pieces are intended to draw us toward compassion and forgiveness as foundations of our shared humanity and shared divinity. They are also meant to present our participation in God as a spiritual foundation we share with other creatures. As in Part 1, these chapters, with the exception of the last one, appear in the order in which they were written.

The first entry in Part 2, Chapter 12: 'Compassion and Enemy Love', was a sermon at the Episcopal Divinity School in a 2000 celebration of Dr Martin Luther King, Jr. In it, I used Harry Potter, the wildly popular imaginative creation of J. K. Rowling, as a literary vehicle to explore our need to become 'bi-cultural' in order to live responsibly, as justice-makers, 'in the world, but not of it'. The small Chapter 13 which follows, 'Pentecost and Harry Potter', is taken from a sermon also given in 2000; and, as in the previous chapter, attempts to lift up the possibility, and wisdom, of looking beyond what we can see with our eyes if we hope to really experience, and come to know, the Sacred.

Chapter 14: 'Godbearing in Hopeless Times' was preached in May of 2001 at the Commencement ceremony of the Bangor Theological Seminary, a small theological school of the United Church of Christ, in Bangor, Maine. Presenting several Christian virtues – mutual presence, advocacy, and resistance – I draw from three different sources of my recent experience: teaching Christology to my seminary students, helping care for a sick and dying friend, and the healing energy being offered to me by my horse (I was 56 at the time and learning about horses in order to help initiate a therapeutic horseback riding centre).

The next two chapters, 15 ('God of All, Not Just Humans') and 16 ('The Horse as Priest') are adapted from my 2002 response to the September 11, 2001 terrorist attacks, *God in the Balance: Christian Spirituality in Times of Terror*. These two essays are included here because they reflect my heightened awareness and interest in the whole of creation, and other creatures, as sacred, as embedded in our divine life as we humans are. This earth/creation-based theological perspective has been increasingly present in my life and work over the past decade.

Chapter 17: 'Good Friday', (2003) and Chapter 18: 'Forgiveness' (2004) focus on forgiveness as a foundation of life in God. 'Good Friday' is excerpted from a sermon at the Episcopal Divinity School during Holy Week in 2003. The essay 'Forgiveness' was published by the progressive Christian magazine *The Witness* early in 2004. I wrote it in the context of the debate raging in Massachusetts about 'gay marriage', which had only recently been approved by the highest court in the state.

In my 2004 homily 'Stubbornness in the Spirit' (Chapter 19), I am happily making a virtue out of what is usually considered, by Christians, to be a vice. This short sermon was given in a service celebrating several women's rights activists – stubborn, and effective.

Chapter 20: 'Queer Conspiracy!' was my sermon at an ecumenical 'Welcoming Church' Conference held in Chicago in the summer of 2004. The Welcoming Church movement in the United States was founded as a queer advocacy network by gay, lesbian, bisexual, and transgender Christians and our allies. In this piece, I am speaking directly to other queer folks about community-building through advocacy, courage, compassion, and the healing of the splits that divide us and also keep us separate from other oppressed people.

Gender and Sexual Diversity is the theme of 'A Path Wide Open' (Chapter 21), my presentation at the 2006 'Love Welcomes All'

Conference in the mountains of western North Carolina. Love Welcomes All is an interfaith LGBT advocacy organization in North Carolina. In this piece, I discuss a few of the special tasks shared by queer Christians and people of other spiritual traditions. Acknowledging the interfaith character of the gathering, I discuss ways in which the Christian Bible can be used creatively, but is too often badly misused, in theological explorations of gender and sex. The title of this piece, 'A Path Wide Open', is an image for God offered by Jewish theologian of liberation Marc Ellis in his 1997 book, *Unholy Alliance: Religion and Atrocity in Our Time.*

Chapter 22: 'Remembering Who We Are' was a sermon given in the summer of 2007 at the Myers Park Baptist Church, a progressive church in Charlotte, North Carolina, renowned for its justice commitments. The title is taken from my sister Ann Heyward's gentle urging of her children to 'remember who you are', as they were growing up. In this piece, I weave together lessons from the Bible, the Harry Potter series, the theology of Jewish mystic and activist Martin Buber, Anglican theologian Frederick Denison Maurice, and my sister Ann in exploring what it means to be a people of soul.

The next two chapters, 23 ('But How Do We Love?') and 24 ('Humility'), were published by the moderately progressive journal, *The Christian Century,* in the fall of 2008. In the first of these essays, I explore the moral conundrum of how we love our enemies. In the second, I present humility as a sense of radical connectedness with others, a quality of being that enables us to see ourselves and others through the eyes of God.

'God's Fierce Whimsy' (Chapter 25) was preached in 2008 at Myers Park Baptist Church in Charlotte, North Carolina. My focus here is the whimsy, or light-heartedness, of our life in God and God's life in us. I draw on lessons from Bishop Robert L. DeWitt, one of the Episcopal bishops who 'irregularly' ordained the eleven women priests in 1974. Among his greatest gifts to me, and the other women priests, were his laughter, guitar picking and jamming, lightness of heart, and sweetness of spirit. I also lift up experiences of the MudFlower Collective, in which seven of us feminist theologians wrote *God's Fierce Whimsy: Christian Feminism and Theological Education* (1985). In our book, we named whimsy, God's and our own, as a spiritual good.

The whimsy and playfulness of God is also the theme of the final piece of Part 2, Chapter 26: 'Light as a Feather'. This chapter is adapted from my 2005 book, *Flying Changes: Horses as Spiritual Teachers*, in which I reflect on lessons learned with the horses in my life. During the last ten years (2000–10), horses have become a wellspring of healing energy and spiritual clarity for me, introducing me to dimensions of the Spirit I had only imagined during the first five decades of my life.

12

Compassion and Enemy-Love: The Hope of the World

During the first decade of the new century, I found much delightful inspiration from J. K. Rowling's remarkable Harry Potter *books. The piece below and the next brief excerpt (Chapter 13) were presented in 2000, early in the* Harry Potter *series. This homily was given at the Episcopal Divinity School in Cambridge, Massachusetts, on 6 April 2000 during a celebration of Dr Martin Luther King. In this piece, I invite the listener/reader to imagine a world in which justice and compassion are real and vibrant forces. I am using the* Harry Potter *series here as a literary vehicle to help my audience take an imaginative leap into a 'bi-cultural' reality where we have to live simultaneously in two worlds: the world as it is and the one Dr King called us to create. See Chapter 22 in this book for some reflections in 2007 on* Harry Potter *during the time I was reading one of the last volumes in the series.*

A literary phenomenon in this and other parts of the Anglo-dominated world has been the rapid, mind-boggling success of a series of children's books. I am speaking, of course, about the story of Harry Potter, the young orphaned boy, being raised by an abusive aunt and uncle, who finds himself transported by friendly forces to the Hogwarts School for Witches and Wizards where, with dozens of other boys and girls, he learns to live in a magical universe. This adult reader, still early in my Harry Potter experience, suspects that, in our post-modern language, Harry is learning to be 'bi-cultural', being schooled to navigate daily life among regular earthlings ('Muggles') and, simultaneously, among others who can generate happiness or despair by the skilful application of a wand and carefully crafted spells and incantations. Children and adults alike are being charmed by the wildly imaginative powers of J. K. Rowling, the young English woman, single mom of a young teen daughter, and author of *Harry Potter*. But I think more is going on here than simply a good story. Fiction is, after all, not about falsehood but rather about truth in disguise. Harry Potter is not simply an imaginary character. He is, as his critics on the Religious Right are quick to point out, potentially subversive of our social order. According to the American Library Association, the Harry Potter books were the most challenged books of the years 2001 and 2002 and the second most challenged in 2003.

Think about it. These are times of economic prosperity, we hear, and some of us, depending upon our earned and unearned privilege, probably experience this growth personally. Yet, as we surely realize, this prosperity for the few is systemically connected to poverty for the many. In this nation alone, as our friends from the United for a Fair Economy organization pointed out at the seminary community meeting Tuesday, 10 per cent of the people in the United States possess and control 70 per cent of the wealth and, throughout the world, the poorest among us are becoming poorer. In a market economy, unparalleled prosperity is completely dependent upon unparalleled greed – and un- paralleled greed breeds unparalleled competition, unparalleled desire to come out on top, and unparalleled possibilities for lies, betrayals, and violence. We cannot practise greed and nonviolence at the same time, nor can we teach the distinctions to our chil- dren. In this context, Harry Potter may be for many kids and adults an icon of hope. For here is a child who, with other kids and the mentoring of some wise adults, helps create alternative ways of seeing things, doing things, being human.

I bring this up on this day in which we celebrate the life and witness of Martin Luther King, Jr, because I believe that, in its own playful way, the imagination of Rowling is spiritual kin to the vision of Dr King. 'How so?' you might wonder. To begin with, each is dreaming an alternative to the dominant culture, a differ- ent mode of being human. Each is urging us to stay fully present in life and to accept rather than deny reality with its racism, sexism, greed and violence. Each is encouraging us to struggle toward transformation. We cannot settle for a dream; we have to work together to make it real, while realizing that we'll always fall short, to some degree, of fully realizing it.

Baptist minister and university professor Michael Dyson argues that our society has largely missed the point of Dr King's dream. As a society that is still racist, we have chosen to dwell upon the idealism conveyed so powerfully in Martin Luther King's 1963 'I Have a Dream' speech rather than wrestle with his more radical message. 'I have a dream', King preached, 'that my four little children will one day live in a nation where they will not be judged by the colour of their skin but by the content of their character' (King in Washington 1986, p. 219). But Dyson warns, 'The overvaluing and misreading of [this dream] has skilfully silenced a huge dimension of King's prophetic ministry' (2000, p. 16). It is this 'huge dimension of King's prophetic ministry' which pushes hard against the principalities and powers of our present social order.

Today, many of the progressive churches and other producers of cultures in this nation have been doing to the memory of Dr King what generations of Christians have done to Jesus: We have raised him high above us in order to tame him. We have done this, in both cases, to strip these brothers of their prophetic power so that we don't have to deal with either their most challenging voices or to take responsibility for our own. It is after all easier ethically, pastorally, and liturgically to pray to Jesus than to follow him; and it is easier politically and socially to grant Martin Luther King, Jr a holiday than it is to translate his words into action and policy. This is Michael Dyson's point. We have whitewashed Martin Luther King, sanitized his memory and spiritualized his dream. This is exactly what we have done to Jesus, and it is what we do all the time to folks whose presence casts too bright a light on our present condition.

The Exodus story (Exodus 14.5–31) recounts the journey of a

people to freedom from slavery. But is this journey to freedom, whether from bondage to Pharaoh in Egypt or to white people in the Americas, ever simply about the flight from oppression into a morally neutral space in which former slaves can start from scratch, as if they had not been imprinted by the values of their oppressors? And what of the former oppressors? Are we ever able simply to wash our hands of the brutality and violence of the past, in this case the historic problem of chattel slavery, and the structures of racist, sexist, and classist oppression which held it together, structures of oppression that continue to distort our life together?

King, as Dyson and others have pointed out, understood that Civil Rights for African-Americans depended not only on radical changes in how white people and black people regard one another, but also on the dismantling of the structures of economic injustice in the United States, which themselves generate militarism and other forms of systemic violence. King saw this. It's what led him to denounce the War in Vietnam and it's what took him to Memphis to the garbage workers' strike and to his death. Martin Luther King was killed in 1968, not because he was a safe black man, but because he was a dangerous subversive, a threat to the principalities and powers of racism and capitalism and militarism.

King's dream of a colour-blind, race-blind society was not an easy and harmonious dream. The longer he lived, the more clearly he himself realized that this dream was of a Promised Land not unlike the Realm of God – a community of equals, a commonwealth of justice and peace, a Sacred Realm that is both here (seen dimly, in Paul's language) yet always coming, wherever we are struggling for justice. Human struggle usually involves more than a hope or a dream or a prayer, as vital as these may be.

So then, does this struggle lead us unavoidably into bitterness, resentment and frustration about that which is not yet? Or can we help one another see that the most radical social transformation – that which will move us toward ending white racism and male gender supremacy, heterosexual privilege and global capitalist exploitation, and the reckless domination of animals and the earth – can only come about through compassion? We must be clear that compassion is not simply a nice soft feeling, not a warm comforting emotion. Rather, like love, compassion is a purposeful leap of faith into solidarity with the other, including the enemy. Compassion is the root of the 'enemy-love' which is grounded in faith not only in God but also in one another's humanity. In the Gospel reading, Luke's famous passage about enemy-love (Luke 6.27–38), Jesus sees that solidarity with one's enemies, irrespective of how we may feel about them, is our only hope. Could it be that compassion and enemy-love offer us a bright, vivid image of God with us?

Like Jesus, and in his Spirit, Martin Luther King, Jr saw his enemies through the eyes of God, as his brothers and sisters. Like Jesus, and in his compassionate Spirit, King realized that the only way out of the vicious spiral of violence, of racism and gun mania, of monopoly capitalism and greed and fear, was to put down the weapons, tone down the rhetoric, and step back – to study war no more.

To love our enemies, regardless of how we may feel about them, is the most radical act in the realm of God. It was for Jesus, it was for King, it was for Gandhi before him and Mandela after him, the most powerful tool in the world for social change. Visiting here at the Episcopal Divinity School, Dr Pumla Gobodo-Madikizela of South Africa's Truth and Reconciliation Commission has suggested that the capacity of victims to forgive those who have violated them enables victims to help restore not only the fullness of their own humanity but also the fullness of their enemies' humanity. This is the enemy-love of which Jesus speaks in Luke, and it was the staying power that sustained Martin Luther King, Jr.

As we learn to view the world, one another, ourselves, and God through lenses of radical politics and enemy-love, we become better able to live a day at a time, to let go when we've done what we can, to rest and play and love and enjoy one another and ourselves. For such a transformative and compassionate dream emerges from our faith that none of us has to do it alone, or do it all, or do it perfectly – whatever 'it' may be. There's room for mistakes, for unlearning, for learning more fully what we do not yet know. We are partners in a team sport, a line dance, in which some step forward as others step back, in which sometimes we go faster and sometimes more slowly, in which sometimes we sit it out and sometimes we get in over our head and need help, just as sometimes we don't know what we are doing or we are afraid to do what we know we need to do, requiring encouragement, compassion, solidarity, and good humour to help us be ourselves at our best.

I suspect this is where Harry Potter's author, J. K. Rowling, is leading us – into places where we will meet our own possibilities for love, compassion, and empathy through the struggles of her magical characters. In the Martin Luther King, Jr story, it is real characters who are plunged into the struggle to embody compassion and enemy-love. And so, what for Harry Potter and his friends is possible through a spell or incantation becomes for us possible through prayer and strategizing, organizing and acting on behalf of justice and kindness. And whereas Harry Potter is introducing us to the astonishing world of owls that carry messages and cats transfigured into human teachers, Martin Luther King, like Jesus, is introducing us to the astonishing realm in which the blind see and the lame walk and the oppressed are liberated and we are able to live as daughters and sons of God.

But where Harry Potter has the most in common with Jesus and Dr King is in their awareness that we are surrounded by a cloud of witnesses, powers that can help us, ancestors to strengthen us, a communion of saints to give us courage. For Harry Potter it's by magic; for Christians, it's by the grace of God that Martin Luther King lives among us today, just as Jesus and other prophets and wise men and women of all generations continue to live and act among us. Encouraged by their example and inspired through their company, we move along toward that great day on which we will be free at last!

Blessed be! Amen!

13

Pentecost and Harry Potter

This small piece is from a sermon I preached at Los Gatos United Methodist Church, in Los Gatos, California, on 11 June 2000. Rather than attempt to combine it with the previous chapter, which also uses Harry Potter imagery, I prefer to let this excerpt stand on its own because it focuses on Pentecost.

In real life, when economic security for a few is being secured by unabashed greed and violence against many, I ask you: Might J. K. Rowling's imaginary, whimsical character Harry Potter be an icon of possibility for a better way? Here's a kid who, with his buddies and mentors, is learning to embrace an alternative way of seeing things, doing things, and being human. Harry is learning to be ethically bicultural – able to live in two different worlds, charting his way through two very different sets of values and priorities for his life. What might we learn from this?

Perhaps Harry and his friends are not unlike those early friends of Jesus who, we are told, while gathered together to receive the law seven weeks after Passover, heard a rush of mighty wind and saw tongues of fire and began to speak in foreign tongues because they were filled with the Holy Spirit. If receiving the Holy Spirit means being filled with a powerful, palpable sense of God's presence, then surely it draws us into a 'bicultural experience' through which, like Harry Potter, we learn to navigate the spaces of two worlds at once – the world as we know it, our daily lives spilling over with opportunities and problems, excitements and sorrows, and the realm of the Spirit which permeates and shapes our lives. And to the extent that we do indeed help create the realm of God here on earth, we generate alternatives to the greed, violence, and systemic evils such as racism, sexism, and hetero-sexism which continue to shape our life together.

Like Harry Potter, the early Christians on Pentecost and we Christians today are being invited to a different mode of human society, and human being, than the ones we have been born into; at the same time, we are being asked to live, with humour and courage and compassion, where we are in this world at this time. To be fully present in life, in this world, accepting reality, even as we struggle toward its transformation. This is the bicultural call of Pentecost, learning to live in this world but not of it.

But what could this possibly mean? To live in this world but not of it, to be genuinely Spirit-filled people, a Pentecost community, creating norms that run against the dominant culture's greed, violence, and apathy? Harry Potter looks at a broomstick and sees a flying machine. He looks at an owl and sees a messenger from his friends. The magic of Harry Potter, and of any spiritually bicultural worker, is to be able to look at something, anything, and see more than any of us can see with the naked eye.

Consider this story from Scripture:

> Jesus sat down in the temple opposite the treasury and watched the multitude putting money into the treasury. Many rich people put in large sums. And a poor widow came and put in two copper coins, which are worth a penny. Then Jesus called his disciples and said to them, 'I tell you, this widow has put in more than anyone . . . for they contributed out of their abundance, but she, out of her poverty, has put in all she had, all she had to live on'.   Mark 12.41–4

You and I have a spiritual opportunity to notice in this story more than we might ordinarily see in our daily lives. We have a chance to notice systemic poverty and personal generosity, through which – contrary to what the dominant capitalist ideology teaches – the poor can, and often do, give more than the rich. And so, just as Harry Potter looks at the large black dog and sees his godfather, so too we can learn to look at the world around us and see and hear God with us in an infinite variety of shapes and sizes and sounds and languages. That is the excitement of Pentecost. Could it also be one reason the Harry Potter books are stirring such enthusiasm among kids and adults in our world today? Could it be that Rowling, the author of these books, is inviting us to imagine the possibilities which await us, if we can see beyond what is visible to the naked eye?

14

Godbearing in Hopeless Times

This was the Commencement Address, on 25 May 2001 at Bangor [Maine] Theological Seminary, a small liberal theological school of the United Church of Christ in the United States. My colleague and long-time good friend Marvin Ellison is Professor of Christian Ethics at Bangor and is also one of the leading gay male voices in Christianity in the United States. By the term 'Godbearing' in the title, I am referring theologically to our giving birth to the Sacred, making the Spirit incarnate among us, as we love one another.

> *An ancient rabbi once asked his pupils how they could tell when the night had ended and the day was on its way back. 'Could it be,' asked one student, 'when you can see an animal in the distance and tell whether it is a sheep or a dog?' 'No,' answered the rabbi. 'Could it be,' asked another, 'when you can look at a tree in the distance and tell whether it is a fig tree or a peach tree?' 'No,' said the rabbi. 'Well, then when is it?' his pupils demanded. 'It is when you look on the face of any woman or man and see that she or he is your sister or brother. Because if you cannot do this, then no matter what time it is, it is still night.'*
>
> *(Source unknown)*

If we cannot look on the face of our brothers and sisters and recognize them as our family, it is still night. If we cannot behold other humans and other creatures as well as our sisters and brothers, what hope is there?

Hopeless times are 'cannot' times, in which we cannot see who we are, cannot recognize one another, cannot experience the power of the sacred thread connecting us one to another and each to all, cannot imagine that such power is ours to share, cannot really believe that this power is God.

Hopeless times, in which we cannot easily believe that the God whom Jesus loved, the one who presumably has called us to seminary and to ministries of one sort or another, is not only inviting us to change the world but moreover is empowering us to do it! You and me, every one of us here, not only our happy and grateful graduates, are being empowered by the Spirit of all Life and Love to change the world, to make history. And we are being invited to believe that we *can* do it.

Over the last few months, since late January, my life has been divided into three parts woven together, I have no doubt, by the Spirit of God. Let me say something about each and then tell you a little about what I've been learning through them about ministry. First, Sue Hiatt, one of my best friends for more than 30 years, has been dying of a fast-acting and terrifying cancer. Some of you may recall that this same Sue Hiatt was the leader of the movement for the ordination of women in the Episcopal Church. She was the one who actually organized the first ordination of women priests in this country – two years prior to the Church's authorization of the ordination of women. Over the next decades, Sue became known among us as 'bishop to the women' because she was the one to whom women of all ages, classes, races and sexual identities, women seeking ordination, often turned for counsel and encouragement when, more often than not, these women were being shut out and turned away by their own bishops. The Revd Sue Hiatt was the woman priest who spent her life helping other women 'make ways out of no ways', to borrow a strong affirmation from womanist (black women's) spirituality.

In early February, Sue was diagnosed with an 'anaplastic thyroid tumour'. I was with her in the doctor's office, on that occasion, as a second pair of ears to hear this terrible diagnosis and prognosis. The doctor told her that he had 'unmitigated bad news' for us; that, even with treatment, she would be dead by summer; and that the situation was 'completely without hope'. And although we both told the doctor that even such a grim situation as the one he described would not be 'completely without hope' for us – thinking as we were of the power of friends and loved ones to rally and pray – we did indeed walk down the hall of Boston's Brigham and Women's Hospital on that cold winter day feeling pretty hopeless. Between this past February and today, Sue has had three surgeries, four or five hospitalizations, one two-week stint in a rehab centre and, for the last two months, has been living in a small apartment adjacent to mine on the campus of the Episcopal Divinity School in Cambridge. Since late March, a Hospice programme has been working with us to help Sue have as peaceful a transition as possible. About a week ago, she said to me, 'I've always known that it takes a village to raise a child, but I've learned recently that it takes a community to say goodbye.'

Another part of my life over this semester has been working with my students at the Seminary. As it happened, one of the courses I was teaching was my favourite course, 'Introduction to Christology', which I've taught at least a dozen times. Each time, it's a new course for me as well as the students, since what we bring to the course from our lives provides much of the energy and material for our work on who and what this Jesus/Christ character was and is all about, not only for us but for the larger world. For me, during this particular period, the Christology course provided a theological framework within which I could struggle, alongside my students, with the dynamics of living and dying, losing and grieving, suffering and peace being stirred through Sue Hiatt's illness. It was not that I actually said much in class about Sue's illness and my relationship to her, but I did tell the class, at the beginning, that this process of death and grief was underway. At the end of the course, I told the students that they had been brother and sister pilgrims with me on a journey that is close to the heart and soul of what the Jesus story is all about.

The third part of my life since January has been spending time with my horse 'Red', who came with me to Massachusetts this year. Red and I spend most of our time in the mountains of North Carolina, where I live with several other folks and where we have begun a therapeutic horseback riding centre. With me in Massachusetts this semester, along with Red, has been my horse-riding companion and friend Sister Angela, a 75-year-old Anglican Poor Clare nun from Australia who is part of our community in North Carolina (see Chapter 31). A remarkable horse trainer named Linda Levy has been working with Red, Sister Angela and me. Linda's talent is rooted in her deep knowledge that it is from the horses themselves that we best learn how to relate to them, how to ride them, how to treat them – and that there is much we can learn from horses about how to relate to one another. Being mentored by Linda has been opening me to a whole new realm of 'our power in mutual relation', a power which I have long experienced as the power of God. Throughout this period of grief and stress, with Linda as our guide, Red the horse has been a priest to me, offering me as a resting place, a healing place, a place of confidence, her big body with a big heart and a soul as close to God as yours and mine.

A dying friend, my seminary students, a quarter horse mare and our mentor have stood out for me in bold relief these last few months against the backdrop of a nation and world and, too often, a Church that seem increasingly hopeless. I want to sketch briefly this afternoon, especially for the graduates of this good school, a few lessons I've been learning about ministry through these experiences in this world. *Lessons about presence, advocacy, and resistance.*

Mutuality of Presence. Something that has come home to me repeatedly through sitting with Sue Hiatt, teaching Christology, and learning how to connect with my horse is the value of a shared authenticity, a mutuality of presence, a willingness and ability to be ourselves – in silence as well as speech, in fear as well as courage – with one another, making space for one another in what is a sacred relational place. It is a relational place without pretence, guile, or self-absorption because by its very nature it makes space for everyone in it. Relational space for the real presence of each person or, in the case of Red the horse, each creature.

About a week ago, I asked Sue Hiatt what she had learned through her ordeal of sickness and dying. The first thing that popped out of her mouth was that 'clergy are inept in dealing with death'. What she has experienced over these months is that many clergy have come around briefly, maybe said a prayer, maybe done something liturgical, maybe quoted the Bible, but primarily they have made themselves scarce. I think clergy are often unable to be authentically themselves, really present, in pastoral situations, and whenever this is the case, it cuts the heart and soul out of our capacities to minister.

It has been clear to me this spring that the most meaningful ministry with Sue has been consistently offered by nurses, home health aides, hospice workers, and personal friends (many who are clergy but who have been with her, more basically, as friends). I am speaking of the companions who have taken her to the doctor, sat silently beside her bed, read her mail or the newspaper to her, talked with her about a recent film or play, sung an Emily Dickinson poem to her, helped her with her medication, prayed with her, sometimes shared holy communion with her, washed her hair and arms and legs, held her up when she has been too weak to stand on her own, cried with her, laughed with her. I am thinking even of Rubyfruit, the seventeen-year-old cat, who has laid on her bed day in and day out for weeks, purring as Sue, with her eyes closed and the bare hint of smile on her face, has stroked her. It has been friends like this, none of us primarily in our professional roles, who have been Sue Hiatt's ministers, those who have accompanied her most faithfully into the borderlands of eternal love. And we, of course, have been led by Sue and one another, throughout the process of her dying, more fully into our own confidence in the power of love, friendship, and real presence as the healing and comforting power of God. No question it has been a mutual journey for those most involved in it, including the nurses and health aides.

My seminary class on Jesus has borne witness to the same lesson about mutuality of presence. As a teacher and priest, I had some fleeting moment of doubt about whether I should talk with my students about Sue's illness, our friendship, and my grief. 'Professional boundaries' have a pastoral purpose which we need to be mindful of. But good boundaries are always lines of connection, not just separation, and good common sense often can tell us when we need to step back and when it is well and fine to step forward. In the case of my class on Jesus Christ, it was clear to me that not sharing with my students that one of my best friends, who also was one of the seminary's legendary icons of prophetic power, was dying of cancer right in our midst would have been in some real way untruthful and unfaithful to Sue, to myself, to my students, and to God. 'Christology' is, after all, about the passion – the life and suffering and death and resurrection and on-going real presence of Jesus and the rest of us, too.

So the question for me was not whether to share this but how to do it in such a way as to help open space for the students to experience and express their own spiritual questions and theological discoveries. I have not yet read their final papers or evaluations of the course, but my sense of the class is that it became a spiritual pilgrimage as much as a theology class for all of us – and that, even though Sue Hiatt's name was not mentioned at all except at the beginning and at the end of the course, we all *knew* that we were being guided by the same christic power of mutual presence that was shepherding her to her peace.

Throughout this same period, I was learning some important lessons about mutual presence from Red, my horse, and Linda, our teacher. These lessons have had to do with paying attention to what's actually happening around us and respecting the particularity of those with whom we relate. One day in early February, I got on Red's back and merrily took off around the covered arena, paying no attention whatsoever to the feel of Red's body, or her mood, or what was going on around us. I was perched on top of the horse, happy in my own daydreaming, as she jogged along at a nice slow trot. Then, before I knew what was happening, we had ridden right into the middle of some commotion involving three other horses. Quick as a flash, the normally easy-going Red spooked, shot out from under me like a bat out of hell, and I went over her shoulder and came out in one piece only because I was wearing a helmet. On another occasion, when I was having a particularly hard time getting Red to do something I wanted, Linda said, 'Carter, you're not communicating with your horse. Communicate with her!' So, good Euro-American theologian that I am, I began *talking* to Red as if she were one of my human theological colleagues. At this point Linda yelled across the arena to me, 'I didn't say *talk* to her! I said, *communicate!*' For a moment I was completely baffled – communicate without talking?

It took me some time to see that in neither case was I relating to my horse in a spirit of mutuality. I was failing to respect Red in her particularity by not taking her seriously in her 'horse-ness'. As fear-based animals, most horses need not to be ridden into the midst of commotion and certainly not by riders who aren't paying attention to what's going on. And every horse needs to be communicated with by its person's whole self – back, seat, legs, arms, voice, the whole of who we are physically, emotionally, and spiritually, not simply talked at with words like *whoa* or *trot* or *good girl*.

So, too, with ministry. We are called to be present to others not primarily with words but with the fullness of our human being – able to wait, in silence, rather than filling the air with words; as ready to listen as to speak; as able to be still as to busy ourselves with things to do; as ready to receive others' perspectives as to offer our own; and as open to meeting others in their particular uniqueness as to hope that we ourselves will be met in this spirit. This mutuality of presence is a basis of good ministry and one too often devalued or dismissed in our efforts to be professional.

Advocacy. One of the truisms of our time and place in history here in the United States is that our health care system is not user-friendly. Let us be clear about it: The problem is not incompetent professionals, bad doctors, or uncaring nurses. In fact, Sue Hiatt has been cared for by many competent, compassionate nurses, doctors, and other health care professionals. The problem is much larger; it is a systemic problem. Our medical *system* is a little fish which has been swallowed by a larger fish, big insurance, which has been swallowed by the largest fish of all, global capitalism – and none of these 'fishes' is patient friendly, poor friendly, or friendly to most women or people of colour anywhere in the nation or world. Morally, our system of health care is a shambles, and it is precisely the business of our religious institutions and religious people to call the medical establishment to account for this deplorable situation. If you don't believe it's really so bad, try it.

Again and again, during these past months, Sue Hiatt and her companions have been appalled by how little good attention – real presence – is available in the professional health care arena, especially in hospitals and other institutional settings such as rehabs and nursing homes. In hospitals, doctors' offices, and rehab, I'd say Sue spent about 80 per cent of her waking hours waiting to see the doctor; waiting for a hospital bed; waiting for pain medication requested thirty minutes or even an hour or two earlier; waiting to meet the social worker assigned to her case the week before; and too often snapped at by tired and overworked personnel for asking a second or third time for some attention.

Throughout this ordeal, Sue needed advocates – people to speak for her when she had no energy to speak for herself; people to go for the nurse when Sue's calls were unheeded; people to track down the doctor through various electronic and human inter-mediaries when she needed a medical opinion; people to point out to rehab aides that no one had served Sue dinner; and so forth. Had Sue not had a bevy of good friends surrounding her and taking care of her, we all agree that she probably would have died through neglect many weeks ago. We are aware that this is happening all the time, throughout the medical institutions of this nation, to poor people, homeless people, uninsured people, most people of colour, women, children and elderly people who are ill, people without advocates, unless they are lucky enough to be surrounded by good friends who like the prophet Isaiah will 'go for them'.

I tell you graduates about this because I can think of no higher calling in church and society today, no greater ministry, than for clergy and lay leaders to be advocates, much in the lineage of our prophetic ancestors, including the brother from Nazareth. Our seminaries and churches need to be teaching advocacy skills to all who are thinking about chaplaincy or parish ministry. Without advocacy skills – beginning with the ability to analyse the social power in any situation – our ability to pastor will be, as Sue Hiatt noticed, 'inept'. But not just clergy, all of us – teachers and counsellors, parents and children, friends and colleagues, lay people and clergy – need to be sharpening our advocacy skills. This means we must notice who is being neglected or marginalized, which is the core of a power analysis. We must learn from neglected and marginalized people what they need. We must be willing to go for them, speak up on their behalf, speak truth to power, make no peace with the neglect and marginalization of our sisters and brothers. We must be willing and able to raise the roof on behalf of those left standing outside the gates of the privileges enjoyed by those of us with wealth, health, or in Sue Hiatt's case politically savvy friends with some social power and plenty of advocacy skills. Sue Hiatt, herself a community organizer as well as a priest, had taught us well that all pastors must be advocates.

Resistance. The last of the three lessons for ministry I will mention today is the vitality of resistance to oppression and injustice that I have been learning from Sue Hiatt, my own students, Red the horse, and our mentor Linda. It's important to realize that all of these relationships have been happening against the backdrop of the greed and violence that are crushing us, and shaping us, as humans, as other creatures, and as a world. Electronic communication connects the world, and too often enabling an insatiable, all-consuming global drive for profit and economic power. We are all being distorted by these death-dealing forces. We may not realize this. We may sort of realize it but not be able to imagine what it really means for us. Or we may disconnect ourselves, mentally and emotionally, from all of this stuff and live as if none of it matters much to us anyhow. We just try to get on with our own lives, doing the best we can.

And surely this detachment isn't an entirely bad thing! In fact, it is spiritually and psychologically vital to do our best, step by step, one day at a time. It is important to our souls and sanity to be as really present as we can be, in our own personal, interpersonal, and professional lives. We need to care for ourselves so that we do not become overwhelmed or otherwise undone by the scope and complexity of the problems of our larger communities, nation, and world. We need to encourage one another to take care of ourselves in whatever ways we can – a walk on the beach with a parent, a picnic in a meadow with a lover, a good book with a cup of coffee. Or back in North Carolina, a square dance for the whole town and white-water rafting on the Nantahala River. In Maine, a hike up Cadillac Mountain followed by tea and popovers at the Jordan Pond House. These are a few examples of how folks take care of ourselves, our souls as well as bodies, which is something we all must do if we hope to minister effectively in this world because the world will wear us out. So we must go easy and be gentle with ourselves and others.

But we must also cultivate among ourselves the wisdom that knows the difference between the things we can't change (the fact that a friend lies dying of cancer) and the things we can change (the fact that the health system in which she and we find ourselves is geared more to profit than people). We may not often be able to change a diagnosis or prognosis of an individual, but there is no institutional structure or system on earth that we need to accept as simply the way it is. It is important that we understand the fact that none of us, by ourselves or simply on our own, can bring about systemic change. This is a peoples' project, not simply a personal one. This is also where the Church, as an institution, comes into play in a major way because what more biblically based, Jesus-centred role can the Christian Church today possibly have than to resist oppression and injustice in its many forms?

And so, I must ask us today, as Christian women and men:

- Where are our voices, as the Church, in response to our profit-driven health care system?
- Where are our voices today as the Executive, Legislative, and Judicial branches of our federal government conspire to ignore or undo much of this nation's and this world's efforts toward sustainability of the planet itself – its water and land and air?
- Why are we, as a Christian community, not rallying publicly, like the feisty Harvard students recently, on behalf of underpaid workers?
- Where are we, Christian advocates for justice, as the attacks mount in Church and society against women's reproductive options and basic civil rights for gay-lesbian-bisexual-transgender sisters and brothers?
- Why are we Christians, most of us, so quiet these days in the face of an increasingly privatized prison industry and a death penalty which is being used primarily as a weapon against the poor and those left out of most social benefits?

And where, I must ask, were the Christian voices of outrage last November and December, when our democracy was further unravelled by the travesty that passed itself off for an 'election'? What do you suppose we as a nation would have done if, in any other country in the world, countless people had been blocked from voting for President and the ballots of unknown numbers more thrown out on various technical grounds and, after any number of other astonishing events of intimidation and efforts at justification, the Supreme Court of this other country had reversed the pattern of most of its rulings and declared the winner to be the candidate most politically compatible with the Court's majority?

Jesus said, 'Those who have ears to hear, let them hear.' Do we not hear? Do we not see? Do we not care? Why do followers of Jesus who, we believe, are empowered by God to speak truth to power find ourselves so mute in the face of such moral disgraces? As individuals, you and I may perhaps be pardoned for throwing up our hands and pleading ignorance or confusion. But as institutions, our various church denominations and most of our parishes have no such excuse. Our churches are peopled, after all, with folks who hold our society together, folks who work (or know those who work) in government, medicine, law, insurance, managed care, pharmaceuticals, commerce, communication, banking and finances, education, as well as many other good and bright folks who, as individuals, are seldom bad people. Indeed, we who have learned to recite and live by profit-driven professional and political scripts, can – together, as Church – *unlearn* these death-dealing scripts, in the name of a Holy One of healing and compassion, a God who makes 'justice roll down like water and righteousness like an ever-flowing stream!' (Amos 5.24). We, as Jesus people, can be what we are called to be as ministers – people committed to challenging the world, not placating it; agents of social, not just personal, transformation.

Yes, you graduates and all of us committed to ministry are called to the barricades of resistance today. We are being called by Jesus and led by the Spirit to resist silence where voices are needed, to resist apathy where advocacy is required and action is mandatory, to resist using ignorance as an excuse when, together, we are smarter than the principalities and powers realize. We are called to resist pleading confusion, when, truth be told, we know something bad is the matter and, with a little reflection together, we can figure out what. We are called to resist letting fear run our lives by encouraging one another to drink deeply from the wellsprings of the Spirit that is always with us, ever a source of power and hope and even joy and humour! My students always teach me this, year after year, helping me make connections between the public life of the Church and our more personal commitments; helping me see, through their own lives and faith, that strong personal commitments, wisely organized, can build great churches led by ministers of courage and compassion.

My horse has also been teaching me about resistance. As a survivor of abuse, Red was trained early in her life (before she came into my own) by a woman known as 'the trainer from hell'. Red bears witness to an incredible tenacity to resist violence. She survived not with a broken or bitter spirit, but rather with a strong resistance to violence and coercion. She will not attempt to hurt anyone. She simply refuses to cooperate with harsh or punitive relational dynamics. She will not move. She will have nothing to do with a person whom she senses will attempt to treat her roughly. Anyone who wishes to work with Red the quarter horse has to meet her where she is, as a survivor of violent training, and convince her that she will not be subjected to harsh, coercive treatment. Only when Red is confident that her rider is willing to meet her in a spirit of mutuality does she become willing to move her feet and let me, or anyone, ride her.

About mid-way through his ministry, Jesus says to his friends that the realm of God is coming among them, with power. Many interpreters over the years have assumed that Jesus was referring to himself as the initiator of God's realm among us and himself as the sole bearer of God's power. But others, myself included, have long believed that God was revealing through Jesus what God always reveals in ministries of mutual presence, advocacy, and resistance. God was revealing through Jesus the hope of the world, a power that is sacred because we share it.

Dear graduates, my beloved friend of many years, Marvin Ellison, your esteemed and cherished professor of Christian Ethics, tells me what a remarkable, godbearing graduating class you are, and how much you will be missed here at this seminary. It sounds to me like the school's loss will be the larger community's gain. May you go forth from this celebration into the various communities that await you as bearers of hope in this world of broken hearts and shattered dreams. And may God bless you with fertile fields for ministry, open minds, compassionate hearts, good humour, and good friends.

15

God of All, Not Just Humans

This essay is excerpted and adapted from my book God in the Balance: Christian Spirituality in Times of Terror, *which I wrote shortly after the September 11, 2001 terrorist attacks in New York City and Washington DC. It's included here because, along with Chapters 16 and 26, it reflects an expansion of theological interest beyond the human–divine relationship. This interest is the basis of my 2005 book,* Flying Changes: Horses as Spiritual Teachers, *in which I explore what has become a new source of theological learning in my life over the past decade: my work with horses, both through teaching therapeutic horseback riding and my personal relationships with the horses.*

Beyond a personal God

We monotheists are inclined to personalize God as both creator and destroyer and to assume that God acts like we do, except on a much larger scale. We wind up creating 'God' in our image and then justifying our behaviour, even to ourselves, by assuming and insisting that we are doing 'God's will' – whether it is bombing terrorists or ministering to the sick and the homeless.

A more honest spiritual reckoning is possible when we realize that God really is not a person like us or anyone else. God is a spiritual presence that we, like Jesus, can experience in deeply personal ways. But God really is not simply a larger, better version of a human being. God is more like the air we breathe and the ground we walk on. To be sure, the Spirit that is God takes human shape through our lives – and creature shape through the lives of all living beings. But that does not mean that God can be pinned down as 'more' in Jesus than in the Buddha, or more in Gautama than in Mohammed, or more in Mohammed than in Mary, Jesus' mother, or Peter, Jesus' friend, or you or me, or the sea bass or the locust tree.

Jesus and other prophets and saints of God may indeed have embodied and, as such, loved God in very special ways. Indeed, we Christians believe that something like this happened in Jesus' life. We believe that Jesus was rooted and grounded in God in amazing ways. But this does not mean that God loved Jesus more than us; or that God loves any person more than others or that God loves people more than fish and birds and cattle. The Spirit of God does not discriminate in this way by choosing some creatures to love more and others less.

For many Christians, it is at least thinkable to struggle with theological and ethical nuances about the sadness, and often the evil, of killing human enemies.[1] It is much more difficult for most Christians to even imagine sustaining serious reflection on the ethics of killing other creatures and destroying the creation. The spiritual trivialization of creatures and creation is steeped in the long-standing Christian assumption that only humans have souls – intrinsic spiritual value, a 'meeting place' with the divine, a dimension of creaturely being that seeks and can receive salvation. This arrogant anthropocentrism – human centredness – sits close to the core of all patriarchal religion, not only Christianity. It is rooted in scientific and spiritual ignorance, and it reflects and out-of-touchness with our own most soulful possibilities. Split off from right-relation with the rest of creation, we humans are unable to make right-relation with one another or with God, the root/source of our spirituality. We humans are in need of help.

Turning to the animals and earth

One thing about the other animals: they teach us not to idealize

---

1 A theological discussion of violence and non-violence can be read in the original, longer version of this essay in *God in the Balance: Christian Spirituality in Times of Terror*, Cleveland: Pilgrim Press, 2002, pp. 73–91.

life and death, violence and peace, and the Spirit in which it happens. Like humans, most animals kill. They kill to protect themselves. They kill to eat. They kill because they want more of a good thing, such as land, food, or sex. It is not true that we humans are the only species that kills without good reason. So it would be unwise to adopt the rest of creation as a teacher of relational ethics and it is nonsense to look to nature to teach us much about non-violent resistance, for the rest of creation evidently is as fiercely violent as we humans are.

Looking to the animals and the earth for help in making mutual relation is not a matter of turning to morally superior or innocent beings. We turn to the earth and its creatures not because they are better than we are, but because they are our sisters and brothers. They, no less than we, reflect God's image. They, no less than we, have soul – a dimension of relational being in which each creature, in its particular identity, and the Sacred Spirit, touch and are mutually transformed. We look to animals and earth not simply because they need us, because we need them as much as they do us and, in many cases, much more than they need us. We turn to animals and earth because, perhaps, with these others, we can experience new dimensions of mutuality and come to life together in fresh, surprising, ways. As we get to know these other creatures, our brothers and sisters – woodpecker and redbud, jelly fish and lupine, volcano and barrier reef – we may begin to notice that we are more alike than different in both spiritual and scientific ways. Interconnected and interdependent, we are creative and destructive and we bear in ways we may not necessarily see, much beauty and also terror throughout our lives.

Sadism: the difference between humans and the rest of creation

In the realm of violence, however, there is one significant difference between humans and the rest of creation. The violence wrought by humans is often not merely to destroy but to humiliate and increase suffering. It is more than cruel. It is sadistic – pain and cruelty imposed at least partially for the pleasure of the torturer. How is this different from a cat torturing a mouse? I think it's fair to suggest that the cat doesn't enjoy the mouse's pain and suffering per se but rather the pleasure of the sport of doing battle with a living – squirming, squealing – opponent.

By contrast, sadism is the emotional enjoyment of another's suffering and is probably unique to the human species. Sadism is a perversion or distortion of God's image, in which the sadist takes pleasure in the painful effects of dominating some person or creature. If God is our power in mutual relation, we can surely assume that the enjoyment of domination is not an aspect of divine power. To be in God's image, and to share sacred power, in this world involves struggling to transform, not take pleasure in, systems of violent domination and dynamics of coercion.

As sadistic as human beings often are toward one another, the cruelty we continue to inflict on the rest of the created world – animals and natural resources – is beyond our capacity to imagine. This is because so many of us regard animals, earth, and water as our possessions, and ourselves as their owners. We assume a divine right to do with them as we please. More often than we admit, we humans take pleasure in hurting and destroying our brother and sister creatures.

Litany of terror

We chase the animals. We trap them. We terrify them. We enjoy the hunt. We set them up. We shoot them down. We cook them and eat them. We enjoy eating them.

We raise them in small crates. We do not let them move around. We look at them and see 'things'. We deny there is any serious moral issue here. We pump their bodies full of chemicals to make them attractive to the human eye and taste-buds. We frighten them. We buy and sell them. We cook and eat them. We enjoy our meals.

We raise them. We tie them up. We brand them. We beat them. We chain them. We agitate them. We sell them and eat them. We enjoy the taste.

We look for more 'humane' ways of raising and killing them. Regardless, they are ours, and we enjoy our meat.

We breed them to race, to run faster and faster. We make them run to make our money. We do what we must – whip them, feed them, drug them – to make our money. The winners enjoy the glory, the owners enjoy the money, and it's sad there's no place for the losers.

We breed them to fight. We kick them and beat them if they won't obey us. We chain them and starve them to make them mean. We like watching them fight to the death. We are sorry – we know it's cruel, but we enjoy the sport, and we take pride in the killers.

We tell ourselves they are doing what they are born to do. Regardless, they are ours, and we enjoy our sport.

We devastate the forests. We poison the waters. We drive the animals away from their homes. We run over them on our roads. We leave them dead or dying. We are sorry about the animals, truly sorry, but we enjoy our good roads and fine new homes.

We deplete the soil. We desecrate the land. We rip down the trees, we strip the mountains, we pollute the rivers, we foul the air, we break the earth's body, and we call other people 'terrorists'.

Elephant God, forgive us

Human beings need to bow down before the One who meets us through the other creatures, and confess:

We have sinned against Thee in thought, word, and deed, by what we have done and by what we have left undone. We have not loved the other creatures as we do ourselves – and we do not love ourselves all that well. We have not loved the Spirit that meets us in the chickens and the cows that we eat, the horses and dogs that we train, the wolves and sea turtles whose habitats we have claimed for ourselves. We have regarded animals and earth primarily as resources for our human food, human sport, human pleasure. We have not loved the animals, the earth and water and air, as our sisters and brothers. We have not realized that God lives in each blade of grass, grain of sand, snail and ant. Amen.

We do not know how to live on this planet without killing other humans in order to protect ourselves from violence and harm. We do not know how to live on the earth without destroying other creatures, often mercilessly, for our own use – to eat, enjoy, or stay safe from whatever harm or disease we fear they may bring us. It may be that the human species is not far enough evolved to know how to live safely and peaceably on this planet with all of creation, human and other. Or perhaps such a notion reflects an unrealistic and unwarranted fantasy about where we humans are headed and what may become of us.

May the day come on earth when Christians and people of other spiritual traditions will realize that what Christians have called the Incarnation was not the birth of the Sacred simply in Jesus of Nazareth and the religious tradition generated in his memory. May we see on that day that God is, and always has been, *really present* throughout the whole created universe, including this planet and its many, varied species, including humans. May we see that, just as God has many human faces and not just one, so too does She/He have the faces and bodies of many creatures, not only humans. May we see that we humans and other creatures 'god' (verb) together.

In the meantime, may we find and keep our balance between an ever-deepening respect for human beings – ourselves and others – and what, for many of us, is a more recently cultivated respect for other creatures as they are in themselves, not simply as we can use them for food or pleasure. There's no question in my mind that, for reasons of both morality and health, most humans in the so-called 'developed' world should eat less meat, and in many cases none at all. Of course such questions of morality and health, which are always connected, vary in shape and size from culture to culture. The questions I am raising here about food and sport among affluent, urban citizens of the United States, Britain, and other Western nations cannot be simply 'translated' into ethical questions for people in other parts of the world.

However, while ethical questions about what food to eat, and how to raise and harvest food, vary significantly from place to place, the same cultural variance cannot apply to matters of animal cruelty or earth devastation. Certainly, the differences among religions and customs require careful and respectful acknowledgment, and attempts to transform practices of morality and health, in these and other matters, need to be home-grown insofar as possible. But in the end, it is simply the case that we humans, whoever and wherever we are, share a moral obligation and opportunity to do something on behalf of the well-being of other humans and of our animal and earth partners. Cruelty, wherever it occurs, is never right or permissible among those who are striving to live in God, the Sacred Spirit of mutuality.

Elephant God, forgive us.
Holy mountain, shelter us.
Sister spirit stream, carry us on.
Tiny sparrow, sing to us
your favourite hymn.
Pelican brother Jesus,
cover us with your wings.
Bid us goodnight
and raise us in the morning
in your christic power
to recreate the world.
Amen.

16

The Horse as Priest

This piece was excerpted and adapted from my 2002 book God in the Balance *(2002, pp. 92–5) to illustrate a spiritual experience and enlarged theological understanding of the place of animals and the rest of creation in our salvation history. Having been involved in therapeutic horseback riding and education since 2000, I wrote the original version of this piece in 2001, just as I was beginning to realize how remarkably true it has been that our horses have served us as priestly companions. This piece is framed around traditional Christian interpretations of the priesthood. See my* Flying Changes: Horses as Spiritual Teachers *(2005) for a much less conventional and more extensive and (to me) more exciting theological discussion of the horse–human relationship.*

Shortly before I began working with therapeutic riding, as the founder of a centre and an instructor, a former seminary student of mine who had worked in therapeutic riding told me that I would discover that the horse is the priest. In that moment her words struck me as a lovely poetic commentary on the power of therapeutic horseback riding. But, as I began to work in this area, and to spend time every day with my own horses as well, I realized more and more the power and truth of this affirmation: the horse is the priest.

Traditional interpretation: mediator of God's power

Even from a traditional Christian perspective, to assert that the horse is the priest is not simply to lift up a poetic image. It is theology, good theology, the kind rooted in a living spirituality. If God is the creative wellspring of all that lives and breathes and loves, and if God meets us through those who offer us occasions to drink from this healing spring, then surely it is this same Holy Spirit that a horse offers to the child or to the adult who comes seeking strength. The priest in the Catholic tradition is, after all, fashioned theologically as a mediator, one who stands at the altar for both God and humanity, in some way representing each to the other. This is what the horse is doing at the altar of the therapeutic arena – bringing together the human rider and her, or his, restorative, healing power. The horse is helping open the rider to this sacred energy and, we can prayerfully imagine, helping open God to the embodied yearnings and needs of a particular human.

From this Catholic perspective, therapeutic horseback riding, like the Eucharist, can be an occasion of thanksgiving, in which creatures and our divine life are united through our mutual participation in the holiest of sacrifices – God's giving up of omnipotence (control) in order to be there with and for those in need. The horse represents God in this transaction, giving its body over to the human's need for strength and health. The horse also represents our creaturely moral capacity to give ourselves over to another – in this case, a human rider – so that, together, the horse and human can 'walk on', working together to generate more mutuality in the relationship.

At the same time, like all who share in the Eucharist, the human rider, empowered through the relationship with the horse, represents all humans and other creatures who need to draw strength, sacred power, through struggling for compassionate connectedness with one another. This right relation is forged through our willingness, following Jesus, to give up our spiritually ignorant claims to autonomy and independence in order to be there for one another in an authentic holy communion. The building of such community – like the creative relational connectedness between horse and rider and those who accompany them – generates sacred space in which miracles can happen. (*Note: Within several years after this piece was originally published, two different therapeutic riding students, ages eight and five, had spoken their first words on, and to, the horse they were riding.)*

Beyond Catholicism: priestly riders, radical mutuality

This is a fairly traditional Christian interpretation of the horse's role as priest. But it pushes beyond Catholic understanding in one way and beyond Protestantism in another. Both of these movements beyond our theological heritage are significant.

Moving beyond Catholicism, the images offered here assume that the human rider as well as the horse can be priest. The autistic child, the teenager at risk, the addicted woman or man not only represents our humanly/creaturely need for one another's presence and solidarity. These priestly riders, male and female, old and young, offer images of Sacred Power, which can touch and change not only human life but the rest of creation as well.

At its best, therapeutic riding is a mutual endeavour in which the horse as well as the rider is affected – empowered, brought to some new sense of him/herself. For many feminist Christians, this radical mutuality rings deeply true in the Jesus story as well, in which the brother from Nazareth is not the only agent of Sacred, Healing Power. Like the horse, Jesus receives healing energy even as he offers it. Indeed, his power is 'sacred' precisely, and only, because it is shared – a powerfully *holy* Spirit because it belongs to no one, but to us all.

In the Jesus story, in the Eucharist, and in therapeutic riding, God is not simply represented by Jesus, the ordained priest, or the horse. God is the Power, the Sacred Healing Energy, which sparks between and among all the characters in the drama – Jesus and the rest of the people; the priest and the whole congregation; the horse, the rider, and other creatures with them. The horse is the priest – and so too are those with special needs who come to the horse for help.

Beyond Protestantism: sacred creation

This theology pushes us beyond Protestantism as well, specifically in its affirmation here that other creatures have as much to do with God's healing, liberating work as we humans do. Is it sacrilege or revelation to affirm that the horse, like Jesus, is our priest? Does it move us outside the bounds of Christian faith and worship, or does it deepen our witness, to claim that therapeutic horseback riding – like many other realms of human and creaturely efforts to bring healing and help – can be as filled with the Sacred Power and Real Presence of God as any place of Christian worship?

As a Christian priest, I have no doubt that our worship and understandings of sacrament historically have been patronizingly male-centred and arrogantly human-centred. In realms of both gender relations and the rest of creation, we have been woefully ignorant and unfaithful to God as well as one another. Realizing this more and more, I'm grateful now to be able to turn to the horse and rider as my priest and to be open to whatever God may be trying to reveal at this time.

Or perhaps we – the horse, rider, you, me – are being called to witness something God has been offering us from the beginning – an ancient Wisdom, sometimes we call her Sophia, which some of us late learners may be hearing, seeing, or simply recognizing for the first time. In the sanctuary of therapeutic riding, I believe my vocation today is to become an acolyte to the horse and rider.

17

Good Friday: The Ones at the Foot of the Cross

This homily was preached at the Episcopal Divinity School in Cambridge, Massachusetts, during Holy Week in 2003.

'Abba, forgive them, for they do not know what they are doing.'
Luke 23.33–4

But, sweet Jesus, what if they *did* know what they were doing when they hung you on the tree? What if the leaders of this nation know *exactly* what they are doing in Iraq? And what if *we*, too, no less than these public figures past and present, know what we are doing, not only in Iraq, but throughout the world, and here at home? Flexing our economic muscle, strutting our military stuff in the streets for God and everybody to admire. I'd like to think that more likely most of us here are trying to figure out what, if anything, we can do to curb the violence and vengeance being wrought by others. What if those who crucified Jesus – the Roman Empire – knew, as we know, that violence pays? And what if those at the foot of the cross, the ones who stood there watching knew, as we know, a sense of helplessness?

We can't know to whom Jesus was referring when he asked God to forgive those who didn't know what they were doing. Igniting sparks of anti-Semitism, many Christians over the years have insisted that Jesus was talking about the Jews. Others have assumed he was referring to the Romans which, if we accept this, suggests an easy, if chilling, analogy for our own time and circumstances, bogged down as we are today in violence, vengeance, and greed that would seem to be spinning evermore out of control.

Let's imagine for a few minutes this afternoon that Jesus was perhaps referring also to his own friends and family who were standing at the foot of the cross on that Good Friday. His own community, a band of disciples, bonded together in this terrible moment by a shared sense of powerlessness. Let's imagine their friend Jesus glancing down at them, then lifting his eyes, 'Abba, forgive them, for they don't know what they're doing.' Could Jesus have possibly been thinking of people like us – not only the murderers, not only the executioners, not only the Secretary of Defense, Secretary of State, or the Commander in Chief – but *us*: the ones standing at the foot of the cross? 'Abba, Father/Mother, forgive them'?

Let's look for a minute at 'forgiveness'. What is it? Forgiveness is a psycho-spiritual, social, and political leap out of the past toward the future. Forgiveness is the letting go of resentment over what has been done in order to get on with life. It has at least as much to do with the capacity of those who've been wounded to move forward as it does with those who have inflicted the injury. Was Jesus asking God to forgive them, and us, at least in part for his own sake – in order to be able to step into eternity at peace with his brothers and sisters, a peace that eludes those who do not forgive?

But what on earth would Jesus have been forgiving his community, his friends and family, for? What had his band of disciples done that needed forgiving? What had they not done? What have we done, and what have we not done? (*Book of Common Prayer*, p. 360).

Could Jesus have been asking God to forgive folks like us for falling into the spiritual abyss of believing that we are powerless and helpless? And not only us, but the leaders of the nations as well? Was Jesus suggesting that our *sin* – our alienation from God and one another – is our stuckness in the spiritual lie that, without wealth and weapons, we are powerless, helpless, unable to do much about anything of great importance – and that, with wealth and weapons, there's nothing we can't do? Is this the great lie that leads us to crucifixions of many kinds – either as the executioners or as the on-lookers?

'Abba, forgive them, because they don't know what they are doing.' Let us imagine that Jesus got it right: They didn't know what they were doing, not really; and neither do we today.

Forgive them, because they fell into assuming that without crucifixions and crowd control, they couldn't build a better world.

Forgive us, because we too fall into believing that without soldiers and bombers, without wealth and prominence, without big names and big guns, we can't make much difference anyhow.

Mother/Father, forgive us, because we don't realize who we are: your daughters and sons infused with the Spirit to bear hope to a despairing planet, faith to a disbelieving people, love to a world torn apart by fear of differences and 'otherness', courage to a society that is hiding behind big budgets and 'smart bombs', and joy to depressed and sorrowful human and creaturely communities. Grant us your power to move the struggle, alter the course of history, and change the world.

18

Forgiveness

This piece appeared as an Epiphany reflection in The Witness *magazine, 16 February 2004.*

Then Joseph said to his brothers, 'Come closer to me.' And they came closer. He said, 'I am your brother Joseph, whom you sold in Egypt. And now do not be distressed, or angry with yourselves, because you sold me here; for God sent me before you to preserve life.'   Genesis 45.4–5

But I say to you that listen, Love your enemies, do good to those who hate you. Bless those who curse you, pray for those who abuse you. . . . Do not judge, and you will not be judged; do not condemn, and you will not be condemned. Forgive and you will be forgiven.   Luke 6.27–38

Listening this past week to the debate raging in Boston over same-sex marriage, a national and international 'conversation' that is still young and building its strength as a serious public debate, I felt alternately euphoric and furious. As a lesbian Christian priest who's been 'out' for about 25 years and teaching theology courses on sexuality for even longer, the content of the debate is hardly new to me. Biblical, traditional, historical, psychological, personal, political arguments all feel like old worn-out slippers, and yet I found this debate as riveting as ever and was emotionally exhausted when it came (temporarily) to an end the other night so that the Massachusetts legislators could go home to sleep for awhile.

What turns me on and shakes me up about the gay marriage

conundrum, as well as the response to Gene Robinson's consecration, is the depth of the passion stirred on all sides of 'the gay issue',
a passion generated by real life experiences of love and joy, fear
and confusion, violence and hatred, loss and grief. And it's no
simple thing. It's not as if we queer Christians have all the love and
joy and God on our side and those 'others' have the fear and
confusion and hatred. The making of justice–love (a term coined
about a decade ago by Presbyterian ethicists Marvin M. Ellison
and Sylvia Thorson-Smith, 2003) is always more complex than it
appears to be to either the target group (in this case, gay, lesbian,
bisexual, and transgender people) or the oppressor group (those
struggling against gay marriage, gay ordination, gay civil rights,
gay love, and gay justice).

It's more complex than it seems because none of us, on any side
of any issue, is a stranger to fear which is often irrational and
crazy-making. None of us on any side of any issue is a stranger to
the sort of anger that festers into rage against forces we feel, or
have come to assume, will hurt us. Few of us, truth be known, are
strangers to our own fear-based capacity to violate others if we
think it will keep us safe from harm of whatever kind. And we all,
yes even we queer folks, are violent, collectively and individually:
We inflict physical wounds upon those we have come to fear
or hate (remember that hatred is fear's first cousin). We exploit
others economically. We batter one another, often those closest to
us, emotionally. And we alienate, push away, drive out, those who
are different from us spiritually. Churches, good old Episcopal
parishes and countless other churches and spiritual communities,
do this all the time. In a word, we all sin, and we need forgiveness
from one another, forgiveness in the Spirit of the One who
forgives us before we ask, before we even know what we have
done.

The gay issue provides us an occasion to get spiritually a little
clearer about our own sin – defined, let us be clear, not as sexual
behaviour (which, in gay and straight situations, may or may not
be sinful) but as alienation from God. In the context of the

struggle for gay rights, folks like me are the target group, and we have every reason to be angry at the fear and bashing, indeed the sin, that passes for love and justice, and we have good reason to be euphoric at the love and solidarity we tap among ourselves and friends and allies everywhere. But in a gazillion other contexts, white privileged folks like me and my people carry banners of sin – fear, exclusivity, indifference and exploitation – without batting an eye.

This moral conundrum which we share on planet earth – often as the target/victim of injustice, often as the oppressor/perpetrator of violence – is the context in which Jesus invites us to practise forgiveness: 'Judge not, and you will not be judged. Condemn not, and you will not be condemned. Forgive and you will be forgiven,' he tells his disciples in Luke 6.37.

In the story of Joseph (Gen. 45), we see a man who forgives his brothers for having sold him into slavery. In every situation, before we can understand what forgiveness involves, we must understand who has the social (political, economic, physical) power in the story, the power to direct the outcome of the story. In this case, Joseph is in the power-position when he encounters his brothers. He has power over them and can treat them as he wishes. Throughout history, in all situations, this is an easier, privileged, position from which to forgive those who have wronged us – when we ourselves, at last, have the power no longer to be violated by them. In this power-position, not only does Joseph welcome his errant brothers back into his life; he tells them not to be angry at themselves.

It's much like the now legendary story told to groups of North Americans in Nicaragua when we visited in the 1980s and 1990s. We heard this story many times, in barrios, churches, on the road, throughout the country. It was about a meeting between Sandinista Minister of the Interior Tomas Borge and a man who had tortured him when he, Borge, had been in prison during the rule of Batista. Following the 1979 Sandinista victory over the Batista government, the new Interior Minister Borge came upon his torturer, who was now in prison himself. The prisoner is said to have trembled upon seeing Borge approach and to have asked him, 'What are you going to do to me? What is your revenge?' Borge is said to have offered the man his hand and said, 'I forgive you. That is my revenge.'

Such stories as these, about Joseph and Tomas Borge, convey a stunning spiritual strength. But they don't give us much help in understanding how we might forgive those who wield power over us, whether they be the leaders of a nation or a terrorist movement or those who fight against making justice–love for queer people. Whenever we are in a relatively powerless position – and gay people seeking the civil right to civil marriage exemplify this – our forgiveness requires several 'steps':

1 *Humility.* We need to be mindful of our own capacity to sin, to violate others, and of our actual ongoing participation in the sins of the world. Humility is what brings us down to earth, and we see that we share this planet with many humans and other creatures.

2 *Willingness to forgive.* This may be the hardest part for most of us because it requires us to imagine making right relation with those who are violating us and others. Like an alcoholic's willingness to be open to the possibility of not drinking today, our willingness to be open to forgiving those who someday may seek our forgiveness is often a stretch, psychologically and spiritually. It is also a major, critical step in the long process of learning to forgive our enemies.

3 *Patience.* Dorothee Soelle spoke of 'revolutionary patience' (1974), a trait we certainly need in order to wait for the Spirit to soften the heart of the enemy, if not in this generation, then in the next, or the next. We need the patience, willingness, and humility to be ready to welcome our brothers and sisters home. However cruel they may have been, whatever violence they may have generated, they are our sisters and brothers in God and we are theirs.

19

Stubbornness in the Spirit

This homily was given at Episcopal Divinity School in Cambridge, Massachusetts, in the Lenten season of 2004. On this day, the school was celebrating the lives of four women abolitionists and women's rights activists: Sojourner Truth, Harriet Tubman, Elizabeth Cady Stanton, and Amelia Bloomer.

Wisdom is more mobile than any motion; because of her pureness she pervades and penetrates all things. For she is a breath of the power of God. In every generation she passes into holy souls and makes them friends of God, and prophets, for God loves nothing so much as the person who lives with wisdom.   Wisdom 7.24, 25a, 27b, 28

And Jesus said to them, 'Suppose one of you has a friend, and you go to him at midnight and say to him, Friend, lend me three loaves of bread; for a friend of mine has arrived, and I have nothing to set before him. And he answers from within, "Do not bother me; the door has already been locked, and my children are with me in bed; I cannot get up and give you anything." I tell you, even though he will not get up and give him anything because he is his friend, at least because of his persistence he will get up and give him whatever he needs.'
                                                                Luke 11.5–8

Not through friendship but persistence – stubbornness in the Spirit – is justice done. We don't often hear stubbornness professed as a Christian virtue, but that's what we're hearing today. Not only are we met by Jesus' suggestion, through Luke, that a refusal to be brushed off may be what it takes to follow Jesus; we are also met with the possibility that such stubbornness may be a strategy of Wisdom – a pastoral strategy, a way of helping us become better friends of God, and prophets, like the four women of God whose prophetic lives we remember today:

Sojourner Truth, go with us! Harriet Tubman, lead on! Elizabeth Cady Stanton, speak! Amelia Bloomer, ignite our imaginations! These four brave women – abolitionists and women's rights activists all – like Jesus and the saints before and after them, embodied lives of persistent annoyance to the principalities and powers of their generation. They knew, as does anyone who has been seriously involved in justice work, that friendship and good intentions are not enough.

It's easy for us to look back and say, what great lives! What courage! What sacred stubbornness in the lives of these four women. But this Lenten season is an occasion for us to look forward into the possibility that we ourselves, no less than they, indeed in the same Spirit, are called by God to live stubbornly in the Wisdom of God. Perhaps this is part of what it means for us to keep a Holy Lent: to cultivate spiritual resources for sacred stubbornness.

Now we don't often hear our Ministries Commissions, bishops, priests, mentors, and seminary faculty call us to become more stubborn or persistent in our justice–love. And yet, we at this seminary are proud to be hosting and celebrating the ministry of our brother Desmond Tutu, whose life has been radiant with the spiritual stubbornness of one who refuses to be silent when the world and God are crying out for advocates and voices; songs to be sung and dances to be done on behalf of justice; human rights and respect for the whole creation; compassion, nonviolent resistance, and peace.

Archbishop Tutu asked my class the other day, 'Why are you [Americans] so vindictive?' This he asked us in the gentlest way. He was speaking to us, collectively, as United States citizens and as Christians. And before we here get too defensive (pleading that we're not in favour of capital punishment, don't like this so-called war on terrorism, and didn't even vote for our current President), let us remember that we're all in this together – this world, this nation, this mess. As Gretchen Grimshaw reminded me yesterday, quoting a marvellous song, 'We may have come here on different ships, but we're in the same boat now!' Indeed we are. And we share a spiritual opportunity to refuse to be silenced when a strong public voice of dissent is needed against the foreign and domestic policies of the United States that are being forged as necessary for 'national security' and vital to the 'war on terrorism'.

It is one thing to stand, sit, or kneel quietly in the Spirit and pray, as we must, for humility and serenity and senses of perspective and humour. Prayer and silence are wonderful gifts of the Spirit. And Lent is surely a season to deepen our acceptance, with gratitude and relief, of these gifts. But it is another thing altogether, and a spiritually twisted and wicked thing, to allow ourselves and one another to be silenced by a fear of how we will be regarded by others if we speak truth to power. This is the state of affairs that has afflicted us, collectively, since September 11.

This morning's Gospel passage is clear in offering us a sharp, challenging Lenten discipline: We are called by God to put our ethics above our etiquette. We are called by God to value human and creature need over politeness, which for many Episcopalians is often quite a stretch! We are called to realize why actual impact really is more significant than good intention in the work of justice-making with compassion. We are called by the Spirit to practise cultivating a 'revolutionary patience' (Soelle 1974) with God, ourselves, one another, and the world. We are called to resist letting ourselves be spiritually deflated by a wicked combination of fear and the seduction of being well liked for a fleeting moment in history. We are called to speak, preach, and write as patriotic critics of the 'war against terrorism' that threatens to go global in its devastating impact.

Sisters and brothers, the increase in racial profiling is disfiguring us all spiritually. The popularity of the death penalty is poisoning our soul. The growth of the prison industry is breaking our collective spirit. The building up of the United States war machine is tightening our spiritual defences. The popularity in the polls of vindictive leaders is shrinking this nation's moral stature. And the acquiescent silence of Christian communities in all of this is yet again nailing the Prince of Peace to the tree.

In the context of this mighty challenge, may this Lent be an occasion for us to cultivate among ourselves the courage that will strengthen our stubbornness in the Spirit, so that we too can become better friends of God, and prophets. Amen.

20

Queer Conspiracy!

This sermon was preached at the ecumenical 'Welcoming Church' Conference for gay, lesbian, bisexual, and transgender Christians in Chicago, Illinois, in the summer of 2004.

A man named Ananias, with the consent of his wife Sapphira, sold a piece of property; with his wife's knowledge, he kept back some of the proceeds, and brought only a part and laid it at the apostles' feet. 'Ananias,' Peter asked, 'why has Satan filled your heart to lie to the Holy Spirit and to keep back part of the proceeds of the land? While it remained unsold, did it not remain your own? And after it was sold, were not the proceeds at your disposal? How is it that you have contrived this deed in your heart? You did not lie to us but to God!' Now when Ananias heard these words, he fell down and died. And a great fear seized all who heard of it. . . . After an interval of about three hours his wife came in, not knowing what had happened. Peter said to her, 'Tell me whether you and your husband sold the land for such and such a price.' And she said, 'Yes, that was the price.' Then Peter said, 'How is it that you have agreed together to put the Spirit of the Lord to the test? Look, the feet of those who have buried your husband are at the door, and they will carry you out.' Immediately she fell down at his feet and died. . . . And great fear seized the whole church and all who heard of these things. Now many signs and wonders were done among the people through the apostles. . . . None of the rest dared to join them, but the people held them in high esteem.

Acts of the Apostles 5.1–5, 7–13

Brothers and sisters, welcome to this homiletical response to what is surely one of the least preached texts in Christian scripture. Here we have Ananias and Sapphira, Christian husband and wife, straight as arrows we may assume, who drop dead when confronted by the Holy Spirit's displeasure with their selling of land and keeping some of the profit. What is this word of God? That unless we're socialists, we die? That unless, like those early Christians in Jerusalem, we 'hold all things in common', we're doomed? That unless those Republicans wrapping up in Philadelphia, those Democrats meeting soon in Los Angeles, and we gathered here now, offer all that we have into a 'common-wealth', we are dead meat? Welcome to this very queer homily on the least favourite text in the Christian Church, which is being shaped increasingly by global capitalism.

How on earth can this be good news to any of us who attempt to live responsibly and sanely in capitalist America today? How, in particular, can this text be good news for the building of queer community, by which I mean not only lesbian, gay, bisexual, and transgender sisters and brothers but, moreover, everyone in public solidarity with us?

My friends, these early passages in the Acts of the Apostles, which offer images of Christian community, constitute a moral indictment of all economic arrangements, systems, and structures which foster inequality; systems in which poverty and wealth are inextricably bound up in each other. Here we are, two thousand years later, participants in a global system that exists for one primary purpose: to increase wealth and grow it, and grow it, and grow it. As for the poor, well, somebody will tend to them.

It's time for a very queer response to this moral conundrum. It's time for us to struggle as a Christian movement with a question: What keeps us from really showing up for each other as a human race? What keeps us from struggling to hold all things in common? Why do we, like Ananias, want to hold back 'our portion' rather than share all that we have with one another? After all, we already have all that we need. Keep in mind that Peter was speaking to a man and woman who did in fact have what they needed. Ananias and Sapphira might well be stand-ins today for 'middle America'. Folks like you and me, folks called, as Peter, John, and earlier apostles called our forebears, to burn with a passion for a God whose nature is community – and not just any community, but one with fire in its belly, burning for the Spirit that 'makes justice roll down like water and righteousness like an ever-flowing stream' (Amos 5.24).

Sisters and brothers, social justice, economic, racial, sexual, gender, environmental justice, justice in its many forms, is the queerest notion in the world! There could be nothing odder, nothing more out of synch with dominant cultural motifs today, than the image of a just world in which we actually share with one another from our abundance, whatever our abundance may be – money, time, talent, knowledge, or simply willingness to be present, willingness to show up for one another.

Think back to the dismissal of Joan Clark by the Women's Division of the United Methodist Church in 1979, because she was a lesbian and, two years earlier, to Ellen Barrett's ordination as the first openly lesbian priest in the Episcopal Church. These two events were pivotal in my decision to come out in solidarity with my sisters in June 1979. I thought then what I have come to believe even more strongly over these past two decades: that the struggle for sexual and gender justice in Church and society is something much more than simply an effort to secure 'rights' to participate in the perpetuation of unjust structures and systems. The Church doesn't need women to be patriarchal priests. Neither the church nor the society needs to cultivate lesbian recipients of heterosexist privilege, women who can be ordained or blessed provided we don't try to undermine assumptions about what is most holy or most moral or question assumptions about what constitutes an ideal relationship: that is, heterosexual monogamy.

Moreover, the churches and our society do not need white lesbian leaders to act as if we are oblivious to the violence of the modern racisms that are ripping through communities of colour in this nation and also damning the spiritual and moral soul of white people. I refuse to make peace with the savaging effects of racism and global capitalism on human and other creatures, and that is why I am here in this 'Welcoming Church' movement.

To be queer, my friends, is to refuse to collude with injustice, refuse to participate in our own or others' oppression. We do this by learning to conspire – that is, breathe together. Let me say a little about this queer conspiracy into which you and I are being invited by the Spirit. What does it mean, to conspire?

First, it means that we are advocates for one another. Every one of us is here on this earth to call forth the best in others and to help pave the way for people to live more freely and fully in peace and dignity, recipients of whatever we need to live well and love well, able to care for others as well as ourselves. Those who make the best teachers, pastors, parents, partners, neighbours, and friends are ones who believe in us and are committed to helping us learn to believe in ourselves. A conference like this is an advocacy event. The singing, drumming, dancing, conversation, and other gifts we are giving and receiving are ingredients of our conspiracy – our learning to breathe together as one queer and lively body!

Second, our conspiracy gives us courage to dispel the fears that cause us to hold back who we are and what we have to offer. Fear is our chief demon. Fear is the enemy that tears us apart and tells us that all talk of 'conspiracy' is nonsense and impossible anyway. But as we practise advocacy of one another and become recipients of others' advocacy, our fears begin to dissipate – our fear of differences and of the unknown and of what could happen to us and indeed our fear of ourselves at our best . . . and of the God who is our power for building mutuality and justice. We cast out our fears as we learn to breathe together. It is a process that requires patience and steadfastness.

Third, queer conspiracy gives us energy to heal splits that have broken our common body. Our conspiracy empowers us to reach across our divisions. It gives us courage to begin to understand

and dispel the animosities between our races, classes, genders, cultures; between able-bodied and disabled sisters and brothers; between older and younger people among us; and between humans, other creatures and the earth itself. It is, and will be, a long time coming and a laborious process. To learn to conspire is to take the time we need. It is to become aware that, because there are many of us, and many who will follow after us to pick up wherever we leave off, we ourselves don't have to do it all, or do it now, or do it by ourselves.

One of the most interesting verses in the biblical text we have read is this: 'Now many signs and wonders were done among the people through the apostles. . . . None of the rest dared to join them, but the people held them in high esteem' (Acts 5.12–13).

Does this not ring deeply true for many queer folks, especially those like Janie Spahr, who are such powerful advocates; and Irene Monroe, such an effective exorcist of fear; and John McNeill and Virginia Mollenkott who are compelling healers of our split and broken places?[1] How few dare to join them, and how many held them in high esteem!

So a fourth commitment of our queer conspiracy is to practise compassion not as a sweet feeling, but as an act of solidarity. Solidarity involves practising humility in relation to those lesbian and gay men who, out of fear or disapproval to be 'political', refuse to join us – and yet are grateful for what we are doing here in this 'Welcoming Church' movement. We are learning to see our sisters and brothers more clearly as God sees them – vulnerable, afraid, maybe overly-busy. For whatever reasons many brothers and

---

1 The Reverend Janie Spahr, a lesbian Presbyterian minister, has been one of the most vocal and charismatic leaders in the LGBT movements in the Christian churches in the United States for several decades. The Reverend Irene Monroe is a public theologian and one of the most outspoken lesbian activists in the Christian churches. She is also a leader among African American women and among Christian feminists and womanists across culture and religious affiliation. John McNeill and Virginia Ramey Mollenkott are two of the 'elders' among gay and lesbian religious leaders, authors, teachers, and theologians in the United States. Their books rank among the contemporary 'classics' in gay and lesbian religious texts.

sisters are unable to conspire with us, just as we ourselves so often have been. Realizing this, we see that we are called in the queer community to be a conspiracy of compassion with and for one another.

Some years back, at a folk music festival, the great Pete Seeger was teaching the audience a song. He worked with us and worked with us until we finally got it. Then he smiled and said, 'Trouble is, once you've learned it, the song's almost over. A lot like life!' It is a lot like life, which we learn by living! We learn this queer conspiracy by living it. This is also how we learn to love God, through godding, conspiring, breathing together with and in the Holy Spirit.

Finally, conspiring, we discover that what we own or possess matters less to us. We seek ways of sharing what we have. It is such a queer notion in this world – to share what we value and love, to pass it on, to let it grow for others, not just for ourselves.

So let us pray now. O God, help us speak your word boldly, while you stretch out your hand to heal. Season our compassion. Grant us your peace. And may we keep our courage, by the power of the Holy Spirit. Amen.

21

A Path Wide Open: Sexual and Gender Diversity

'Love Welcomes All' is a religious organization in the mountains of Western North Carolina founded to support gay, lesbian, bisexual and transgender people. This was the keynote address at the annual Love Welcomes All Conference, on 1 April 2006, held at Trinity Presbyterian Church in Hendersonville, North Carolina.

Mutual blessing

We're gathered here today to celebrate the lives, talents, and courage of gay, lesbian, bisexual, and transgender women and men in our religious communities and throughout our society. Let there be no question that we here are a very queer gathering indeed, and that we are proud to be! By 'queer', I mean not only lesbian, gay, bisexual and transgender but also others who stand publicly in solidarity with us. I often point out that my ninety-year-old heterosexual, happily married, now widowed mother who lives in Charlotte is probably the 'queerest' member of my family, because she is so proud and unapologetic about her lesbian daughter (that's me) and, as she is discovering, all the other gay and lesbian friends in the lives of her straight kids (my siblings) and her grandchildren.

The fact that we hereto represent a controversial matter – justice for GLBT men and women in our religious communities and in our society – places us in the prophetic movements of our various religious traditions: Christian, Jewish, Unitarian Universalist, pagan, and perhaps others as well. This means that we queer folk do not stand 'outside' our religions. We are not outsiders looking in. We are not knocking at the doors of our traditions asking to be 'let in'. We are inside, our lives rooted and grounded in our religious traditions, members of the family. Like all prophetic voices that rise up from within community, we are lifting up our voices to affirm the presence of LGBT people within our churches, synagogues, and other places of prayer and worship. Our religious communities have always been blessed by our presence and talents, just as we have been blessed by the gifts that have come to us through our traditions. We are here this morning to affirm this mutuality of blessing – that we have been blessed by the God we have come to know through our religious and spiritual traditions and that we ourselves are blessings to our churches, synagogues, and religious communities.

Seen through queer eyes, this historical moment is, as Dickens would have it, the best and the worst of times. After all, who would have guessed, even five years ago, that any state in the union would in the foreseeable future legalize civil unions, much less marriage, between persons of the same sex? Or that nation upon nation would be taking the same step – Netherlands, Belgium, Sweden, Canada, Spain, Britain, South Africa. . . ? Who would have imagined that mainline Christian churches – the Unitarian Universalist Association and the United Church of Christ – would affirm the presence and leadership of LGBT persons in their midst; that Reform Judaism would move in the same direction; and that the Episcopal Church in the United States would consecrate as Bishop of New Hampshire an openly gay man who is in a committed relationship with another man?

In these 'best of times' for queer people, should we be either surprised or disheartened by the force of reaction against us? Are we surprised that states are clamouring to 'defend marriage' by outlawing gay and lesbian marriages and civil unions; that politicians right and left are hastening to add that *they* believe marriage is between one woman and one man; that many social progressives are trying to avoid dealing with LGBT issues because they're just too hot right now; or that communities of colour are being stirred politically by a homophobia that reflects the fear and ambition of those who hold the power in place? We need to be clear that this climate of fear and reaction in the United States, in which queer people have become scapegoats, is part and parcel of the Bush agenda to scare folks to death. What could be worse than life in a world overrun by terrorists and homosexuals! Never mind that most of the terrorists would, if they could, quickly dispose of the homosexuals!

In these 'worst of times', the most prominent religious voice, as we know, has been that of the so-called Christian Right, whose widely hailed marriage to the Republican Party has produced several deeply troubled offspring: ignorance, fear, and hatred, all of which tend to generate scapegoats and stir violence as they spread. In the guise of 'patriotism' and 'family values', these unholy siblings – ignorance, fear, and hatred – go about their messy business and believe it to be 'the work of the Lord'. They initiate mean-spirited legislation, directed against targets whom they deem too politically weak to fight back – lesbian, gay, bisexual, and transgender women and men; women who value reproductive options and choices; poor people; the sick and elderly; the environment; African–Americans and, as we are witnessing right now, new immigrants, especially Mexicans.

The Christian Right is a political movement with specific social and political agendas. We need to be clear that there are many good and kind Christians who are socially conservative and disagree with us about many things, including homosexuality. These Christians are often motivated not primarily by fear, and never by hatred, but by a love of God that translates into a love of neighbour and a generosity of spirit. These folks are as distressed as we are by the scapegoating and hatred being spawned by the politicized Christian Right and want no part of it. I know this because some of these good Christian folk are neighbours of ours here in the mountains of North Carolina. Some are members of my own family in the Carolinas. Strategically, these Christians who may imagine themselves to be non-political are potential allies of ours in building a prophetic, justice-loving movement among people of diverse spiritual and faith traditions.

Our call

So then, what is our call in this prophetic historical moment? First we need to be aware that, in both Jewish and Christian traditions, 'prophets' have an empowering and poignant role – prophets speak what they believe to be God's word to their own people, among whom they themselves live. Prophets are always speaking to themselves as well as others. In other words, a prophet doesn't stand above people and speak down to them as if somehow he or she is closer to God or better than others. No, prophetic voices are always right in the midst of the rubble. That means that our own lives and values are always on the line, not just the lives and values of others. Of course we have to speak out against injustice, wherever we find it, but it's not enough to blame others as ignorant, frightened, and hateful. We have to look at ourselves as well to see how our lives are being shaped by the same forces of ignorance, fear, and hatred. What we need always to be seeking is right relation, which involves finding points of connection with others, so that the truths of our lives, including our sexualities, can emerge among us. Martin Buber, Jewish philosopher and social existentialist, wrote 'In the beginning is the relation' (1970 [1948], p. 69). We need to remember this – because this simple and profound truth is the basis of all creative spirituality, all effective community organizing, and any political achievement that has staying power.

Strategically, those of us who are lesbian, gay, bisexual, or trans-gender and our allies need to do several things if we hope to build an effective movement:

1 *We need to make our voices heard!* Wherever possible, we need to come out, and whether we ourselves are able to come out as LGBT, we need to speak out as allies. Lots of straight folks can,

and should, speak out, on behalf of LGBT justice. That's the work of allies, and every movement needs allies. It is time for LGBT folks and our allies to use the media in sharp, strategic ways. Write out. Speak out.

2 *We need to take the initiative, be pro-active, not primarily re-active.* We can 'announce' wonderful celebrations, not only 'denounce' injustice. We should send press releases whenever we hold conferences or events like this one, or cultural events, such as a gay festival, featuring cultural creations – music, art, literature, food, inventions – by LGBT people. We could solicit or write human interest stories about LGBT folk who are out, living and working among us, making many contributions to our common well-being in Hendersonville, Brevard, Asheville, and elsewhere in western North Carolina.

3 *We need to take care of ourselves and one another.* We ought not to be careless or foolhardy in these times too often characterized by hate crimes against LGBT people. This means thinking together about how to be both 'out' and as safe as possible – vocal and visible. Not using home addresses. Working publicly for LGBT justice in groups, rather than alone. Most importantly, seeking genuine allies among law enforcement and other community leaders, including religious leaders who will stand with us, speak out, and make it clear that violence against lesbians, gay men, bisexual, and transgender people, our lives and our loved ones, will not be tolerated.

4 *We need to work together and make connections not only among other LGBT people but also with other justice activists,* understanding that all justice issues are interconnected. There is no good *moral* excuse for victims of one oppression to participate in the oppression of others – for example, for LGBT people to be sexist, racist, or classist in our actions or attitudes; or for African-Americans, Native-Americans, or Hispanics to be homophobic and heterosexist in their actions or attitudes. Of course, the powers that be have much to gain by setting minority groups against each other, African–Americans against

143

Hispanics in the current immigration controversy; poor white folks against people of colour in every social and economic crisis; black Christian churches against LGBT movements for marriage and civil unions . . .

There are important historical reasons why, for example, black Americans may often be especially strong advocates of 'traditional family values', the very values they were not allowed to embrace as slaves, values still elusive for many African–Americans, because the structures of racism and classism to separate continue to break and batter black families. So, of course, gay folk are easy scapegoats in such situations, much the way feminists have been portrayed over the years – as destructive to marriage and family, as damaging to children and hostile to men.

Our call, as LGBT people and our allies, is to understand these historical social dynamics, learn from them and work with them. We can, and must, take the initiative in our communities in not allowing the dynamics of racism, sexism, hetero-sexism, and classism separate us from others who are struggling for justice. We need to find allies and advocates among black, Hispanic, and other communities of colour. They are there and they are many. The best way to find allies is to be allies ourselves in struggles for racial and economic justice.

Biblical authority

Now I want to talk about the Christian Bible. Here I speak specifically as a Christian priest and theologian myself. I trust that my Jewish sisters and brothers, my Unitarian Universalist friends, and folks from other spiritual traditions who may be here, can make some connections between what I have to say about the use and misuse of Christian Scripture and ways in which your own traditions use and misuse texts. Moreover, I hope that what I have to say here about the Bible might help you, regardless of your religious/spiritual tradition, hear something new about how

Christians or any people of faith can (and I believe, must) struggle with questions of religious authority.

This question of religious authority sets us in tension with those many people in the United States who are not religious at all and who worry that 'religious people' are going to turn this nation into a theocracy.

This is the social and political context in which Christians must, in the many names of God, speak a resounding 'NO'. We must not allow the Bible to be used as a bludgeon by Christians against people of other spiritual traditions, cultures, tribes, and nations; people of colour; poor people; women; gay, lesbian, bisexual, and transgender people; people who are older, younger, disabled, or sick; other creatures; and the earth itself.

Christians must reinterpret the Bible. With the help of biblical scholars and God's Spirit, we must reject the authority of those passages and interpretations that hurt human beings, other beings, and the Great Source of all being.

I am suggesting that justice-loving Christians must follow Jesus in rejecting entirely the authority of oppressive tradition, including the oppressive use of scripture. This means that no reading of the Bible should ever be used to demean, violate, or terrorize any brother or sister. This question about how we hold and use Biblical authority is an urgent matter which we share with people of other faith traditions. For example, it is the question of Islamic feminist Irshad Manji as she reflects on the fundamentalist interpretation of the Koran by Mohamed Atta (one of the September 11, 2001, hijackers): 'What if [he] had been raised on soul searching questions instead of simple certitudes? . . . Maybe he would have stepped back. Maybe. The possibility begs for attention' (2003, p. 47).

In the 1960s and 1970s, progressive Christians in North America were introduced to Latin American liberation theology's 'hermeneutic of suspicion', which requires reading the Bible through a critical lens that seeks to understand who is oppressing whom, and who has the power to define whose lives. Christians were urged by such liberation theologians as Gustavo Gutierrez and Juan Luis Segundo to be suspicious of what has come down to us as 'orthodoxy' – traditional theological interpretations that usually serve to hold in place the present social, economic, and political status quo. With a hermeneutic of suspicion, we are better able to see, and critique, Christian anti-Judaism in the Christian Bible and Jewish anti-Palestinianism in the Hebrew Bible. Gustavo Gutierrez spoke of the double task of liberation as 'denunciation' and 'annunciation' (1973, pp. 265–72), denouncing and rejecting oppressive readings of the Bible, and then announcing new interpretations.

Today we Christians are, I believe, being urged by the Spirit beyond the boundaries set by liberation theology. Our work as theologians – and all of us are theologians, not just the professionals among us – is to denounce oppression, including oppressive biblical texts, announce liberating interpretations wherever we can. Our work is to disrupt biblical authority in order to shatter its hold over us. Can we who are Christian read the Bible *despite* its least liberating motifs and patriarchal moorings as a resource for liberation and healing, allowing it to fall into place in our lives as a resource for justice–love? What *authority* can justice–loving women and men give the Bible in their lives as Christians?

First and foremost, we need to re-imagine 'authority' itself – any kind of authority, including biblical authority – not as 'power over', not as that which demands obedience or conformity. *Authority is a relational resource that grows with us, in the Spirit of mutuality, which is the Spirit of God.*

Several years ago, I read Jewish theologian of liberation Marc Ellis' *Unholy Alliance: Religion and Atrocity in Our Time* (1997). In this book, Ellis joins a number of theologians of liberation, Christian as well as Jewish, in naming, as sacred, our power in mutual relation as the only creative spiritual response to the 'God of atrocity', which Ellis understands to be the patriarchal justification for holding power over one's own people and perpetrating violence against one's enemies. Marc Ellis understands that the only way God can be experienced and understood as a source and resource of love, justice, and compassion, rather than as a god of atrocity – is *as a path wide open to the future*. He sees that such a God cannot be known primarily, much less only, through dogma, creeds, or the Bible. Moreover, Ellis insists that God cannot be known 'in advance', or primarily through memorials or religious language. Most importantly, Ellis suggests that God cannot be known or experienced through 'a pretence to innocence', by which Ellis means a self-congratulatory effort to remain pure and spotless, untouched by the sin and evil of the world, spiritually a cut above others (1997, pp. 158–67).

With Marc Ellis, I believe that we humans – together with other creatures – share the sacred work of 'creating the possibility of more truth' (Rich 1979, p. 194), 'the task of making God exist' (Casanas 1983, pp. 138, 141), 'the possibility of swim[ming] with a new stream whose source is still hidden' (Buber 1952, p. 9). As Ellis writes, much in the spirit of the Islamic feminist Irshad Manji, 'Being fully present [in life] has less to do with answers to be dispensed than with a readiness to move within and beyond what is already known' (Ellis 1997, p. 155).

Being fully present in life means a readiness to take a path wide open to God – a path wide open, which is an experience of One whom we can meet in our life together on earth as the dimly lit, sometimes altogether hidden, path itself. Along the way, we encounter forces, we are met by surprises, and we are shaken by events that *disrupt* our lives, shatter our assumptions, and transform, perhaps obliterate, our experiences and understandings of not only the content of Holy Scripture, but also its authority.

No longer are we Christians put *under authority*. No longer are we *under obedience* to Jesus, God, Church, or Bible. We have become friends, justice-loving friends, to Jesus, God, Church, and Bible. Together *with* them we can grow, empowered together through the Sacred Spirit of mutuality that is none other than the

Holy Spirit, the Christic Spirit. From now on, *let us focus on what the Bible calls forth in us rather than in what it tells us.* Often, it is both, yet more radically one than the other: more 'spirit' than 'letter'; more 'inspiration' than 'doctrine'; more mystery than explanation; more what Dorothee Soelle called *'Phantasie'* (a spirited combination of freedom, intuition, and imagination) than obedience to authority (Soelle 1982, pp. 49–53).

We need a multiplicity of interpretations if we genuinely are committed to the struggles for justice, compassion, and non-violence. Trying to make the Bible fit our spiritual yearnings for connection and compassion is seldom the most creative or faithful spiritual effort. Instead, we should be honest with the Bible, much as we should be with any good friend.

So then, in this spirit of mutuality and friendship, let's turn to one of the Biblical texts cited most frequently by Christians who do not wish gay, lesbian, bisexual, or transgender people to be able to marry, form civil unions, or be ordained as religious leaders:

> Their women exchanged natural intercourse for unnatural, and in the same way also the men, giving up natural intercourse with women, were consumed with passion for one another. Men committed shameless acts with men and received in their own persons the due penalty for their error.   Romans 1.26b–7

With many of you, I'm sure, my patience gets worn thin by our Bible-thumping Christian brothers and sisters, who assume that queer folks are damned to hell unless we repent and whose little fear-based slogans serve only one purpose: to stir fear by misleading. But my patience has been pressed also by other liberal and progressive Christians, who often want to use the Bible – a fundamentally patriarchal, hetero/sexist, resource – to find justification for same-sex love. Yes, there are many spiritual resources queer folks can enjoy to make our case for justice for all, including gay, lesbian, bisexual, and transgender people. The Bible can be indeed such a resource for justice-making, advocacy for the oppressed, and love of neighbour. But the Bible cannot be read honestly as either neutral or mute on the subject of homosexuality, any more than it can be read as either neutral or mute on the subject of the full participation and leadership of women in world and Church.

The only way to accept the Bible as in any meaningful sense authoritative in relation to what the Church should teach about homosexuality is to read the Bible *against* itself – to read the Bible, for example, as testimony to a God of justice, mercy, and compassion struggling for right relation and liberation, rather than as a rule book written on behalf of a God who is a sexually proscriptive overseer of patriarchal logic. As bogus as 'proof-texting' is, people on all sides of controversial issues do a lot of it. We lift verses and passages out of context to try to make our points. As intellectually lightweight as this is, it is often spiritually honest. In fact, most Christians 'discuss' the Bible by reading or citing favourite verses. Queer folks can play this game as well, and as validly as those who proof-text to support their homophobia.

If, however, we intend to draw upon our friendship with the Bible in our struggles for sexual justice, we can combat biblical homophobia by reading the Bible *against* itself. For example, we can read Micah 6.8, 'What does the Lord require of you, but to do justice, and to love kindness, and to walk humbly with your God?' *against* Leviticus' condemnations of 'abominable' relations between men (Leviticus 18.22). Or, we can read Mark 12.30–1, 'You shall love the Lord your God with all your heart, and with all your soul, and with all your mind, and with all your strength [and] you shall love your neighbour as yourself. There is no other commandment greater than these' *against* Paul's exhortation against same-sex love in Romans 1.26–7. In fact, we can read Paul against Paul! We can read Romans 8.38–9 and 1 Corinthians 13 – in which Paul is a poet of love – against Romans 1.26–7, in which he sounds more like a homophobic vigilante. We can invite the Bible, as an old friend, to reject its own authority over us and, instead, to join us in our wrestling to live responsible, faithful lives in the Spirit of God.

As a lesbian feminist Christian, my gut level response to the hetero/sexism of the Bible has long been, 'So what?' Regardless of the Bible's messages about lesbians and other women, I intend to lift up and honour my sisters and mothers, my nieces and spiritual daughters, my lovers and friends. It has only been in the last few years, however, that I have been able, along with sisters and brothers throughout the world, to claim the authority to say both 'so what?' to the Bible's hetero/sexism and 'we're going to argue about this, because you – our friend, the Bible – are wrong about it. When you say what you do about what is natural and un-natural in our sexual relationships, you don't make any more sense than you do when you rave on about the patriarchs and their many wives and concubines. God is, after all, the One who loves strong women-loving women, and She is opening the path before us.'

Finally, a little postlude about marriage . . . I have been involved in the 'gay marriage' debate that has been in the news over the past several years. As a priest, I was delighted to officiate at the marriage of several lesbian and gay couples in Massachusetts two years ago! Until then, my position for 30 years had been that, since gay and lesbian people cannot legally marry, I would not offici-ate at any marriage. This is still my position in every state except Massachusetts. I will bless holy unions of gay couples and straight couples, but when I bless the marriage of a heterosexual couple, that couple must have a justice of the peace or another minister 'solemnize' their marriage on behalf of the state. I simply will not do for heterosexual couples what the states will not allow me to do for gay couples. Joe Hoffman and Howard Hanger are two min-isters in Asheville who have made a similar decision. *We ministers who have taken this position will legally solemnize marriages only in those states that allow gays and lesbians to marry.* That seems to me only fair and just – for everyone, heterosexual as well as homosexual partners. Straight folks who are lesbian and gay allies and who wish to marry not only understand this, they are happy enough to go a little out of their way to get someone else to legally sign their papers, thereby making a small gesture of solidarity with gay men and lesbians. This seems to be the least we can do; it may be at this time also the most.

22

Remembering Who We Are:
People of Soul

This sermon was preached on 29 July 2007 at Myers Park Baptist Church in Charlotte, North Carolina. I have often been a guest preacher at Myers Park; in fact, this congregation, renowned for its justice commitments, was one of the first churches in the United States to welcome me as a preacher after I had come out as a lesbian in 1979. Other churches and organizations withdrew their invitations at that time. My understanding of 'soul' is adapted, respectfully, from the black Church tradition in the United States. 'Soul' reflects not an individual's possession but rather a quality of the Sacred that we share, the spiritual foundation of community-building.

Thirty-three years ago today, at almost this very hour, eleven women were ordained to the priesthood of the Episcopal Church in what become known as 'the Philadelphia Ordination'. This ordination of women took place before the organization, the official Episcopal Church, was ready for it. We let go of old habits, old customs, when we are pressed toward something new. That's how change happens, especially hard changes in the society and in our common life in churches, cities, states, nations, families. Seldom do we simply say, 'Oh great, let's change how we've been doing things for 2000 years, or 200 years, or 20 years!' And yet, today there are thousands of women priests throughout this nation, and many Anglican and Episcopal women priests throughout the world, joining the large numbers of women ministers, pastors, priests, and bishops in other churches. Just last year, the Episcopal Church in the United States elected as its Presiding Bishop, its chief priest and pastor, a woman: the Reverend Katharine Jefferts Schori.

Today I want us to think together about who we are and why, so often, we resist change, why we want to stay forever in the same place – with the same ideas and opinions, the same faces and language, food and friends.

Like countless children of all ages, from about 9 to 95, I'm moving along, page by page, through the seventh and final volume of Harry Potter (*Harry Potter and the Deathly Hallows,* 2007). And don't worry, I'm not going to tell you what has happened so far – and I don't want you telling me after the service! I do want to say something about how I experience the spirituality of the Harry Potter epic, the whole saga, from its beginning with the wee wizard orphaned by the murder of his parents at the hand of the evil Lord Voldemort until the end, which as yet I haven't reached with Harry, his friends and adversaries. Regardless of how it ends, however, the imaginative author J. K. Rowling has chosen to draw the story to a close. She has given us a story about soul, about the strengthening of the soul of not only one English boy wizard and his buddies, but also the soul of each of us who has taken the journey with them.

According to the Psalms, the young David exclaims, 'On the day I called, you answered me, you increased my strength of soul' (138.3). In Hebrew anthropology, this understanding of 'soul' and its increase means that the person becomes more fully alive when his soul is 'increased'. The totality of his spiritual grounding – his *'nephesh'* . . . 'soul' . . . 'living being' – is quickened with the breath of God breathing through us. To be soulful, to be in right relation with God, is to breathe with divine breath. Now the people of Israel understood that being in right relation with God was never simply the shape of an individual's 'spirituality', that it was not a private matter. Soul is a collective journey, a shared path, and it is a sacred one *only because it is shared.* If it is not shared, if it does not move us beyond ourselves, narrowly understood: my-self, my family, my nation, and my God, it is not sacred. For the breath of God, the life of God, that which infuses us with soul, is never simply mine. Nor simply yours. Nor simply ours or the spiritual blessings bestowed on those like us. The breath of God moves us along a path we make together by sharing with those who walk-with us and those we meet along the way. For many millennia and certainly today, many Jews have believed that the sharing of sacred ground must always extend beyond Israel itself, as a nation, as a religion, and as a land – to include others as well, most notably the Palestinians. As elusive and confounding as such inclusivity is, it is not merely a matter of political necessity; it is the only way for Israel to live as a genuinely moral and holy people, and many Israelis know this well and passionately.

The most moral and loving characters in Harry Potter are the adults and kids who know, and demonstrate, that what is most important, always most important, is *to love others as we do ourselves*. These are the characters with souls being strengthened rather than weakened by the trials and tribulations that befall them. The gentle giant Hadgrid loves most dearly his many magical creatures. They are as dear to him as any human, and indeed for J. K. Rowling that seems to be just fine, as it is for many environmentalists and animal rights activists. Harry's deceased parents loved their infant son enough to sacrifice their lives in order to save his. 'No greater love', we are told. The wise and kindly headmaster Dumbledore loves his students and the world they share more than anything, including himself. This last volume has many themes and plots and subplots and wonderful adventures and terrifying moments, but the greatest theme in the book is that Harry and his good friends Ron and Hermione, all of them seventeen years old, are learning that, without love for each other and for all that is kind and respectful, life is not worth the bother. Without love for the oppressed and downtrodden, without love for the stranger, those being kept out by the majority, life is not worth living.

Indeed what sets Harry Potter apart from his chief ad-versary, the once handsome and clever young wizard who has de-volved into the evil Lord Voldemort, is that Voldemort does not care about anybody but himself nor about anything that does not secure his power over others. And to make it all a bit more complex, and frightening for Harry and all of us, Harry has to struggle with the knowledge that he is in many ways just like Voldemort, being lured toward the same power over his own and others' lives.

Harry Potter is learning, because the author J. K. Rowling seems to know, that there is not much difference between people who do good and people who do evil. Both the good and the evil ones may be bright and charming, good and evil folks may be rich or poor, we may be religious or non-religious, we may be wizards, witches, or 'muggles' (people who aren't magical). As he matures, Harry is learning that evil is done by those who love only themselves and those who are like them, those who support them, those who admire them, those who give them what they want. Harry Potter realizes, as he grows up, that it's not enough to love and be kind to those whom we like, our own kids and communities, our own nations and cultures and people like us. Harry Potter's 'god' is way larger than any spirit who would prefer the people of one race, one nation, one religion, one way of acting or thinking or being.

My beautiful, soulful sister Ann, a member of this church, is fond of saying to her kids, 'Remember who you are.' I don't know exactly when and how Ann began saying this, but I hear it as a spiritual wake-up call to remember that we are family – that spiritually, we are family. Some of us are family biologically, and many of us here are family culturally. But all of us are family politically and socially and spiritually. We are relatives – sisters and brothers in Spirit, bound to each other as children of God, people on a sacred journey. No one is an island, in the spirit of the words of the seventeenth-century poet John Donne. This is what we are called to remember, when we remember who we are. When we remember this, we become more fully alive, sisters and brothers en-souled by the *nephesh*, the breath, of God. It is who we are.

In his book *I and Thou*, published more than 50 years ago, Martin Buber wrote, 'In the beginning is relation' (1970 [1948], p.

18). This Jewish philosopher and friend of both Israel and Palestine understood that, when we regard each other as 'thou' instead of 'it', we see the depth at which our lives are connected. The soul in me touches the soul in you. People whose souls are being strengthened by the Spirit see that there is no one on this planet, and nothing, that is totally alien to the rest of us. Not Osama bin Laden and his Islamic extremists nor others who do great evil because they have been mis-educated spiritually to believe that they can love only people like themselves. We may be, and surely are, fearful of this 'terrorism', but this does not mean that we are not called by God to figure out how to love these terrifying people who are, at this moment in history, our enemy. For there is nothing totally alien to the daughters and sons of God who are infused with divine breath.

Certainly not our Mexican neighbours and workers and friends and companions. These people are our sisters and brothers, as spiritually and morally complex as we all are, and as worthy of love and respect. Immigration politics have turned ugly, racist, contemptuous of those who do not always speak like or look like or act like the majority of people with power in the United States. There are never easy answers to confounded matters of public policy, but when soulful people err, it tends to be on the side of inclusivity and the building of mutual respect.

People of soul are folks whose sense of connectedness with all living beings gives them strong conscience, a deep intuitive knowledge of right and wrong, of what makes or breaks our love for one another. The great nineteenth-century English pastor and teacher Frederick Denison Maurice is perhaps my favourite theologian because he was not only smart, he was a genuinely good human being who took risks, and sometimes lost, on behalf of women, the poor, and others marginalized by the economic and political forces in England at the peak of the Industrial Revolution. Maurice wrote something that has stayed with me. He wrote that we cannot teach children both conscience and an ethic of obedience to authority (1868). Children, like adults, need to be taught right from wrong by being taught respect and kindness toward all living beings. Whatever is 'wrong' is whatever denies or thwarts this respect and kindness. As children and adults come of age spiritually, as our souls are strengthened, our souls guide us in knowing right from wrong. Our souls are our guidance counsellors, and this guidance work of the soul is our 'conscience'. Conscience is a spiritual strength that cannot be passed on by those who believe that people should simply fall in line and obey those in authority.

In the Harry Potter saga, this distrust of absolute authority is something that the wise old wizard Dumbledore, Harry's mentor, knows and is passing on to Harry. Lord Voldemort doesn't have a clue. Like the police officer Javert in *Les Miserables*, like the Scribes and Pharisees in Jesus' life, like our own President Bush and Vice President Cheney in these challenging times, Lord Voldemort demands total allegiance and absolute obedience to his authority, regardless. No questions asked. No accountability required.

So we are here today, gathered together in this church, seeking to know how we might better love God and our neighbours as ourselves. When I asked my mother Mary Ann several weeks ago what I might preach on today, her response was immediate: 'Uncertainty', she said. And that response of Mama's led me to where we are in this sermon. We don't know much. We don't know how long our lives will be. We don't know for sure what we'll find when we get home today. We don't know what big or small challenges may lie ahead for any of us. We have no idea how we'll cope with all the deaths and losses and disappointments that come with being alive in the world. We don't know what is going to happen in this great nation of ours, or in this world that needs courageous and moral leadership from the United States rather than arrogant aims of global domination and obedience to our authority, an arrogance fastened not in courage but rather in our terrible fear. In every arena, we can do our best – trying one day at a time to live loving lives, our souls sparked by God, our consciences strong and active. But we just don't know what is going to happen, do we?

What we *do* know is who we are, and that is all we need to know.

Jesus said to his disciples (that includes you and me), 'Do not worry about your life, what you will eat, or about your body, what you will wear. For life is more than food, and the body more than clothing. . . . Can any of you by worrying add a single hour to your span of life? If then you are not able to do so small a thing as that, why do you worry about the rest? Consider the lilies, how they grow: they neither toil nor spin; yet I tell you, even Solomon in all his glory was not clothed like one of these.' Luke 12.22–3, 25–7

One way of experiencing the entire Gospel, the whole story of Jesus as our brother and Christ, is as a window into what matters. Through this window, we see ourselves and we remember who we are – sisters, brothers, all of us children of a Mother–Father God, who does not demand obedience but rather teaches us, invites us, implores us, to love one another as we do ourselves and whose abiding promise is to be with us always, breathing through us in our lives and, when we die, carrying us on in the breath of Her Spirit. It is a great spiritual journey! And if we truly remember that we are on it together, every day, one day at a time, our worries will fall away and our fears will evaporate like the morning dew.

23

But How Do We Love?

This essay and the one that follows (Chapter 24) were written as meditations for The Christian Century, *a journal for theologically open-minded Protestant Christians in the United States. I was asked to reflect on particular passages from the Gospel of Matthew and Paul's First Letter to the Thessalonians. These two pieces were an attempt to speak theologically to mainstream church people. This first piece appeared in the 26 October 2008 issue, a little over a week prior to the Presidential Election in the United States.*

You shall love the Lord your God with all your heart, and with all your soul, and with all your mind. This is the greatest and first commandment. And a second is like it: You shall love your neighbour as yourself. On these two commandments hang all the law and the prophets.   Matthew 22.37–40

We were gentle among you, like a nurse tenderly caring for her own children. So deeply do we care for you that we are determined to share with you not only the gospel of God but also our own selves, because you have become very dear to us.
                                                    1 Thessalonians 2.7b–8

Jesus is clear that the greatest commandment is to love God and that a second commandment is like it: to love our neighbours as ourselves, and that all other religious laws should be rooted in these two. The commandment to love is the basis of all the world's major religions. Indeed, few Christians would argue that anything is more important to God than that we love one another. But our agreement often stops here, because love means many different things to many different groups of Christians. For some Christians, loving God requires that we follow religious law as it

159

has been passed down and interpreted over the years for what Christian and cultural leaders have deemed the good order of the community: male headship of family and church, for example; marriage as possible only between men and women; unquestioning obedience to parents, even when parents are abusive or wrong. These are some of the religious laws that many Christians, past and present, have believed to be steeped in the commandment to love God and neighbour.

The worldwide gathering of Anglican bishops at the Lambeth Conference in England this past summer testifies to the fact that many Anglican prelates throughout the world still believe that homosexuality is a grave sin against God and neighbour. Many fear that even to tolerate homosexuality within the community is to sin against God and neighbour and to place oneself outside the boundaries of what is generally accepted as Christian community. Making their case for the exclusion of gay people and their advocates from the Christian Church, some African Anglican leaders, encouraged by 'traditionalist' [overwhelmingly, white] bishops in the United States, contend that affirming gay people will hinder their relationship with the most fearful in the Islamic community within their countries. Furthermore, ever since the 2004 consecration in the United States of Gene Robinson as the Bishop of the Episcopal Diocese of New Hampshire, a number of African Muslim leaders have attacked Anglicanism itself as a 'homosexual church', and some African religious leaders, perhaps both Christian and Muslim, have even interpreted the acceptance of homosexuality as part of the Bush unilateralist policies against the rest of the world!

Through the eyes of progressive Christian faith and liberal Democratic politics, this is astonishing. But it illustrates how a shared desire to love God and neighbour can propel people along such radically divergent spiritual and political courses. Indeed, the commitment to love God and neighbour, a pledge common among Christian, Muslim, Jewish, and other brothers and sisters, traditionalist and progressive, in the United States and throughout the world, keeps us worlds apart. All too often the commandment to love seems to become the basis of violence waged against those whom we perceive to be not only our opponents but also the enemies of God and of all that is good.

But can the love of God and neighbour ever be the basis upon which we seek to destroy our sisters and brothers? I believe not. But I understand this to be a spiritually complex, challenging matter for all humans. Case in point: I can hardly bear to realize what the Taliban in Afghanistan is doing to women. I am outraged when I see images of women being shot in the public square and of young Afghan girls burning themselves to death because the Taliban have accused them of *Sharia* violations or because their own families are beating them, hurting them, shaming them, threatening to kill them because they have offended family 'honour'. Am I a cultural imperialist, a Western feminist critic of another's way of life? Some would say so, and perhaps I am. But my rage and critique is steeped in my understanding that the love of God and neighbour is not being extended to Afghanistan's women and girls, and that, in this context, the Taliban is sinning against God – YHWH, Sophia/Christ, Allah – and is doing great evil, albeit in the name of Allah. So then, do I believe that the United States should be making war against the Taliban?

Yes, I believe we must resist the Taliban. I believe that this is a collective moral as well as political responsibility that we must undertake on behalf of Afghanistan's people, especially its women. But wait then! Aren't we using the love of God and neighbour to justify our efforts to destroy these Afghan men, these Taliban leaders? Aren't we, like the Taliban, like Al Quaeda, like Bush and Cheney, like religious, political, and military leaders from time immemorial, simply declaring that God is on our side – and that, therefore, whatever killing we do is justified by our love of God and neighbour? What, if anything, distinguishes us from the Taliban, from Osama bin Laden, from the self-righteousness of any political leader who dares to assume that God is on his, or her, side?

I believe that what distinguishes any who claim to be lovers of God and neighbour is not simply the claim to love God and neighbour – religious talk is cheap – but how, in fact, people practise this love. How, in real life, do we love? How, in the middle of a war, can we love our enemies? How do we illuminate the love of God and neighbour to be not a pious religious platitude but a way of life?

The oft-cited prophetic passage, Micah 6.8, tells us exactly how we love: We struggle for justice. We show mercy, kindness. And we walk humbly with God. Taken together, as they must be taken if we are embodying the love of God, these three dimensions of God's love give us powerful insight into the very essence not only of God but also of ourselves when we are living most faithfully in God's Spirit. Justice-making, undertaken with mercy and in humility, constitutes the 'how' of God's love whether we experience it between intimate lovers and friends or between ourselves and our enemies in contexts of conflict, including war. Moreover, it is God's Wisdom – Sophia – that opens us humans to the possibilities of living in this Spirit and to realizing the possibilities for good and evil in all of us – our enemies, our friends, and our own lives. But can we actually incarnate these spiritual gifts, because that is what they are – gifts from God – in our daily lives, individually and collectively?

Yes, we can, although only partially. We can't love perfectly. That's not within the realm of human possibility. If it were, there would be no wars. But both as individuals and collectively, we can be lovers of God and one another. Certainly we as a nation can do better than we have done recently. We cannot love anyone, however, especially our enemies, as long as we are in the grip of fear and its pathetic spawn, the demonization of enemies as unworthy of God's love or our own. And while fear is a deep and natural emotion, common to all, we can and should expect our spiritual and political leaders to help lead us through and beyond this paralysing fear, rather than exploit it for their own gain, which is what has happened so tragically in the United States since

11 September 2001. The simple recognition of our enemy's humanity, however distorted by violence it may have become, may crack open a door through which we can imagine meeting the enemy as a brother or sister – even if, in real life, such a meeting cannot take place, at least not now and perhaps not in this generation or for generations to come.

Surely the dreadful history of wars holds stories of mercy and humility manifest in abundance among those who recognize the humanity of the enemy. The film director Clint Eastwood told such a story, imagined through the eyes of the Japanese commander, about one of the iconic battles of World War II. In *Letters from Iwo Jima* (2006), Eastwood portrayed both terrible evil and amazing goodness at the hands of Japanese and United States soldiers. He presented images of kindness extended by each side's soldiers to their enemies; as well as images of unspeakable horror, of men showing no mercy and no love, images of the awful absence of God so characteristic of violence and war. The layers of moral complexity portrayed through this film suggest that it was inspired by God's wisdom and love, working through Director Eastwood.

Finally, on the matter of how we love, let's ask ourselves today what kind of Commander-in-Chief we need here in the United States. Who will be best able and willing to lead us down paths of justice, mercy, humility, and wisdom in relationship to both friends and enemies, in the smallest and largest arenas of our relationships at home and around the world? We need to think, and talk with our companions, about what we need to expect of our President and other spiritual and political leaders. Can we expect them to help us, as a nation and communities, embody the love of God and neighbour? Yes, we can, and we must.

24

Humility: Root of Compassion

'Humility' is a Christian virtue I have long attempted to reinterpret. This piece was published in the religious journal The Christian Century *the week of 2 November 2008, which coincided with the Presidential election in the United States. It was written as the second part of the previous essay on 'love' (Chapter 23). Both were written on scripture passages that had been assigned to me. Theologically, the two pieces should be read together. The reflections on the Trinity in the last paragraphs of this essay illustrate my ongoing interest in traditional notions of Christian theology, which I try to approach in a respectful spirit, both critically and constructively.*

We constantly give thanks to God . . . that when you received the word of God . . . you accepted it not as a human word but as what it really is, God's word, which is also at work in you believers. 1 Thessalonians 2.13

Do whatever they [the scribes and Pharisees] teach you and follow it; but do not do as they do, for they do not practise what they teach . . . They do all their deeds to be seen by others. . . . They love to have the place of honour at banquets and the best seats in the synagogues, and to be greeted with respect in the market-places, and to have people call them rabbi. But you are not to be called rabbi, for you have one teacher, and you are all students. And call no one your father on earth, for you have one Father – the one in heaven. Nor are you to be called instructors, for you have one instructor, the Messiah. The greatest among you will be your servant . . . Matthew 23.3–11

Among spiritual qualities, why is humility one of the hardest to practise and yet probably the easiest to imitate? Why do so many politicians and clergy insist that they work not for themselves but for others – 'not for myself, but for my country', not for my own interests but for what's right, not for me, but for God? I believe that humility eludes us to the extent that we are afraid to notice how utterly common all humans are in our needs for love, justice, compassion, health, and dignity. If we are afraid of one another, afraid of finding ourselves in relation to others in the world, all others not just those most like us, then our 'humility' cannot be genuine. Such false humility is a pretence which masks our contempt and takes root in our fear of those who seem alien to us. Just as Jesus takes the scribes and Pharisees to task for their false humility – doing good deeds to be seen by others – so too we need to be wary of political and religious leaders in our own day whose stories of self-sacrifice and love of God and country are often told in order to stir peoples' fear of those who seem most alien.

Genuine humility is a gift from God which has nothing to do with down-cast eyes, misty voices, and noble stories of sacrifice on behalf of God, country, and other people, always 'instead of myself'. Humility is, rather, living courageously in a Spirit of radical connectedness with others, which enables us to see ourselves as God sees us: We are sisters and brothers, each as valuable and worthy of respect as every other. A truly humble man does not deny his self-interest but rather strives to realize how his interests are connected with the well-being of others, all others, not just those most like him. A genuinely humble woman does not seek to play herself down, as if she should be small and insignificant next to others, but rather is able to love herself and struggles to extend this strong love to all others by advocating their dignity and well-being.

As the 2008 political season draws to a close and we move beyond the bombastic rhetoric that has so bruised our sensibilities, we can't know for sure what Jesus would make of the electoral process in the United States, a political and spiritual context very different from his own. On the basis of the Biblical portrayal of the brother from Nazareth, however, we can imagine that Jesus would have little patience with the arrogance and 'spinning' which characterize public life in the United States and elsewhere, especially as people choose leaders. For the New Testament suggests that the greatest difference between Jesus and the religious leaders who opposed him was humility. Jesus had a strong sense of his place in the larger scheme of things in God's world, and his religious adversaries had hardly any sense at all. He knew that he, and they, belonged to God; they knew the religious law. Jesus, not the scribes and Pharisees, had humility – the deep, embodied realization that we all belong to God. Jesus, unlike the religious leaders, knew – in Thich Nhat Hanh's words – his 'own true names' (1999, pp. 72–3), which involved an acceptance of the truth that he was neither more important to God, nor less, than his neighbour. Jesus' humility was a strong, sacred source of his capacity for faith, hope, and love. It is also ours.

Humility is the root of our compassion, our ability to 'suffer with' one another, because we know ourselves as spiritual kin to everyone. No one is beneath us – or above us – in God's world. Let us imagine that humility was God's gift to Paul at his conversion. Let us imagine also that, from that moment on, Paul recognized his own true self, his own place in God's world and, on that spiritual basis, was able to become the first major Christian evangelist – travelling and teaching among communities filled with people whom he recognized as brothers and sisters. Moreover, like Jesus who preceded him, and whose Christ–spirit accompanied him, the convert Paul realized that it is God's presence working through us that enables us to be humble, God's spirit working in us that empowers us to love, God's grace filling our hearts with compassion, and God's wrath stirring our anger not only at injustice and oppression but also at the false humility that drips from the lips of false prophets then and now.

Now for a brief theological lesson. The doctrine of the Trinity is one of the most elusive and, for many of us, to be honest, one of the least helpful, Christian teachings. Yet it has become for me, over the years, one of the most energizing spiritual images. This reflection on humility – as both a gift from God and a quality manifest by some humans like Jesus and the convert Paul – can serve as a springboard into our understanding the Trinity as a living spiritual resource:

When we meet one another in a Spirit of humility, we are meeting God in one another, that which makes us spiritual sisters and brothers; at the same time, others are meeting God in us. God is not only with us in our encounters but is also moving in us and through us. In other words, we and others are embodying God, through our humility, which comes from God; we are making God incarnate, here in the flesh, tangible and visible. This is what happened in and through Jesus in his time and place, and it is what it means now for us to be Christ's Body in the world, to live 'in Christ', or 'in a christic spirit', or 'in God'. So what does this have to do with the Trinity?

First, the Father. The patriarchal framers of early Christian theology named 'the Father' as the source of our humility, and as the source and constant resource of all that is good. Like Jesus, and in his christic spirit, we humans – and other creatures, many of us would insist – help make God incarnate in the world by loving one another as we do ourselves, which only happens when we are genuinely humble.

Second, the Son. Traditionally, the incarnation of God in human form is imaged as 'the Son'. Many Christians, including most liberal and progressive Christians, look beyond Jesus himself to all of humanity, and even all creation, as 'the Body of Christ'. It is not only Jesus' body, dead and risen; it is our shared christic body, belonging to all humans, other creatures, the earth and cosmos. Our humility enables us to realize our place in the larger Body and, as such, is essential to understanding how humans and the earth and its many, varied creatures can be mutually related. It also shows us how we humans of different tribes, cultures, racial, national, religious, and gender-identities can relate mutually to one another.

Third, the Spirit is the God-energy between us, when we love one another, when we show mercy and compassion, when we walk humbly with our God. It is quite that simple. Keep in mind that we don't need to use religious language at all, much less 'believe in the Trinity', in order to love God and neighbour. We don't even need to 'believe in' God. We do need to believe in ourselves and our shared capacities for justice-making, compassion, and humility. I believe we are strengthened immeasurably if we also believe that 'something' – some Mother Father Christic Spirit – connects us and grounds our capacities, as moral subjects, to love one another.

25

God's Fierce Whimsy[1]

This sermon was preached at Myers Park Baptist Church, a progressive, justice – seeking church in my home town of Charlotte, North Carolina, on 27 July 2008. I have been a regular guest preacher in this parish for many years.

Who are our spiritual mentors? People who open us to the Spirit? We all have spiritual mentors. Who are some of yours? This morning I want to tell you something about two: One, an Episcopal bishop, a white economically privileged man of faith; the other, a small writing collective of black, white, and Latina women to which I belonged in the 1980s.

In 1973, while a student at Union Theological Seminary in New York and just days before I was to be ordained a deacon in the Episcopal Church, I had a panic attack – I couldn't get ordained, I had decided, because I could not in good conscience take the 'oath of conformity', which every ordinand in the Episcopal Church has to take prior to his or her ordination. It begins with these words: 'I believe the Old and New Testaments to be the Word of God and to contain all things necessary to salvation. . . .' For me, this oath was a stumbling block, so I called the office of the Bishop of Pennsylvania, Robert DeWitt, because I knew from several of our mutual friends that this man was an intelligent, compassionate man of faith to whom I could turn. He was not my own bishop. Paul Moore, Bishop of New York, was with his critically ill spouse and was not available. Bishop DeWitt said he

---

1 The title was taken from a book written by a small collective of Christian feminists in the mid-1980s: The MudFlower Collective, *God's Fierce Whimsy: Christian Feminism and Theological Education*, Cleveland, OH: Pilgrim, 1985.

would be happy to meet me in New York's Pennsylvania Station for a cup of coffee a couple of days hence. When we met, I explained my problem with the Oath of Conformity and Bishop DeWitt smiled: 'Let me tell you how I've always thought about it: To affirm the Old and New Testaments to be the Word of God is not to say that they are the *only* Word of God; and to acknowledge that they contain all things necessary to salvation is by no means to contend that *everything* they contain is necessary to salvation.' We continued to talk and the upshot of our conversation was my decision to proceed with ordination.

As the story suggests, Bishop DeWitt took the *concept* of God seriously but not too seriously. An intelligent, thoughtful man who took the *experience* of God way more seriously than his dogma. Yet he was, to most observers, a religious man, a churchman, a bishop – for many of us, a very wonderful bishop indeed, a brother in Christ whose serendipitous way of being in church, as in life and friendship, sparked my image of the Holy Spirit as playful, whimsical, and delightful.

As a bishop and friend, Bob DeWitt helped me realize a couple of paradoxical dimensions of God and ourselves in God: on the one hand, we see the *vastness of God* – while understanding that our ideas – especially our ideas about God – are so small, so limited by our senses of ourselves and of what we can imagine. To affirm Jesus as Brother and Friend and Christ, one through whose life we meet God, doesn't mean that Jesus of Nazareth was or is the *only* window into God. God is so far beyond our capacities to 'know' or wrap up neatly in packages of doctrine and dogma. To me, the greatest Christian theologians have always been those whose understandings of God, and of religion at its best, have been to open us more and more to that which we don't yet, and may not ever, know fully. So we simply cannot, in good faith, insist that our way is the *only* way.

In one life, the life of Jesus, we catch a glimpse of the universal Spirit of God. And Jesus' lesson for us – the Good News – is that in our own lives, we can experience and glimpse the Spirit whenever we are rooted and grounded in God. Feminist Christians often affirm, in making our communion, that 'the body of Christ' is our Body. It is who we are called to be in the world. And the blood of Christ is our blood as well, a sacred river of life connecting us all, most holy whenever we offer it for the well-being of others – a mother giving birth to her newborn, a man or woman sacrificing whatever need be, including sometimes life itself, to save or help others.

The life of Jesus helps us see that, paradoxically, in the midst of God's vastness and universality, we are touched by the *smallness and simplicity of God*. Not only is God so much more than we can imagine, God is also tiny, here in the midst of us, in each of our lives, in ways so small we may not notice: The sacredness in this moment, the holiness of the man, woman, child sitting beside you here this morning, the greatness of God in our own yearnings and sadnesses, our own hopes and gratitudes. Whenever two or three of us are gathered together, Jesus is with us, a spiritual brother/sister. Indeed, wherever we are, in our living, dying, playing, winning, losing, holding on, letting go, God is with us. And what is it that God asks of us? That we 'do justice, love kindness and mercy, and walk humbly with God' (Micah 6.8).

And let us imagine that God is not just with us humans. God is dancing throughout creation, the sacred rhythm far beyond our capacities to know or understand. But as we listen we find ourselves tapping out God's beat, moving in concert with strains of praise and play, grief and mourning, justice and kindness. Scotsman Sidney Carter wrote a hymn which became a favourite among Christian young people in the 1960s and has remained a delight to this day – 'The Lord of the Dance' images a dancing deity who leaps and swirls his way along, calling us into being as She goes. Some of you elders like me may remember a little film about Jesus called *Parable* (1964), in which Jesus was a whimsical Clown. And over the years, I dare say, many of you have seen and sung and clapped along with the characters in *Godspell* (1970).

Which brings me back to Bishop DeWitt. He was a simple man.

His moral compass was clear: we are here to do God's work and enjoy God's life on this earth. The *we* is not just *us* and folks like us. It's everybody and all of creation. So it is the moral and political work of Christians to help open up space for everyone. No one is excluded. Robert DeWitt was elected Bishop of Pennsylvania in early 1964 as a compromise candidate between a liberal and a conservative. But then, the unexpected occurred.

Girard College had been chartered decades earlier as an all-white school, and a number of prominent Episcopalians were on its board. At about the time Bob DeWitt was being consecrated as Bishop of Pennsylvania in 1964, an effort was being mounted to integrate Girard College. As Bishop DeWitt himself put it years later, 'I had to decide where to stand, and neutrality was not, it seemed to me, an option.' For the first time in his life, then and there, in his early 50s, Bob DeWitt joined a picket line and, in a way, he never left it. One justice struggle or another became part of the warp and woof of his ministry as a priest and bishop of the Church. Before long he was involved in the peace movement, the context being the Vietnam War, and he continued his work in civil rights.

In the early 1970s he joined women who were seeking ordination, and Bishop DeWitt presided at the 'irregular' ordination of the eleven women priests in 1974, before the Church had authorized women's ordination. He resigned after ten years as Bishop of Pennsylvania, in 1974, because he didn't believe it was healthy for the Church or the bishop for any one person to hold that amount of institutional power for longer than ten years. For the next seven years – from 1974 to 1981 – he edited *The Witness* magazine, a monthly launched earlier in the twentieth century by another Episcopal bishop, who had decided to cast his lots with those whom the Church and society disregarded: labour organizers, pacifists, civil rights leaders, and later feminists, gay folks, and environmentalists.

When asked what motivated him, Bishop DeWitt would cite the Bible, which was for him a powerful spiritual resource – 'the Word of God'. He took its stories and its spirit to heart. He studied it earnestly. He taught it prayerfully. He respected it intellectually and was delighted and challenged, comforted and unsettled, by it personally. No part of the Bible was more descriptive of how Bishop DeWitt reached his values and clarified his priorities than the famous Markan passage we heard this morning: For like Jesus and every prophet in the Hebrew Scripture, Bob DeWitt understood that the Sabbath was made for humankind, not humankind for the Sabbath (Mark 2.23–8). He knew that religion ought not to be a spiritual box of dogma and discipline into which we humans have to squeeze our spirits and bodies in order to be right with God. We are not asked by God to downsize our spirits and constrict our bodies. We are rather invited to come along with Jesus and other brothers and sisters on a journey on God's earth, not grovelling or shrinking before God, but rather moving along in a spirit of mutual respect as we find the rhythms of our lives, one spirited step at a time.

About 25 years ago, I was one of eight women – black, Latina, and white women; married, single, and divorced; lesbian and straight – from several different Christian traditions. We called ourselves the MudFlower Collective (it's hard for flowers to grow in mud!). And we wrote a book together called *God's Fierce Whimsy: Christian Feminism and Theological Education*. For a year, we met together to wrestle with questions of what, from our perspectives as Christian feminists, the churches and seminaries ought to be teaching about God, Christ, and Church; about gender, race, sexuality, and economics; about prayer and social action; about good and evil. The MudFlower Collective had quite a time of it, because we discovered – this was in the mid 1980s – how difficult it was to talk to each other about religion and spirituality across lines of race, class, and sexual identity.

In the current presidential campaign [2008], our nation has an opportunity to wrestle with many of the same questions that baffled the MudFlower Collective in the 1980s: I can imagine, for example, that no woman of colour in our group, then or now, would have found either remarkable or offensive Revd Jeremiah Wright's indictment, over the years, of our society as racist, violent, classist. I also assume that every woman in our small collective would be delighted today by Barack Obama's call to join in a national dialogue on race. For, even back in the 1980s, we believed strongly that the time was coming when folks in our churches and nation would have opportunities to learn together about race, and also about class, sexuality, the economy, the environment, war and the military. We would have opportunities to think together about how these structures of our lives interact in ways that too often tear us apart, here in this nation and throughout the world.

The MudFlower Collective's conversations were heavy, intense, and often peppered with anger. So perhaps the most surprising thing about our work was that, through our frustrating process, we experienced so much whimsy in God. Despite our tensions, despite our shame and frustration as women trying to communicate across the historic lines that divide us, despite the anger and aggravation that made us all want to throw in the towel many times during our process of writing the book together, we kept on keeping on. We didn't throw in the towel – seven of the eight of us didn't. No, the MudFlower Collective plodded on together, sometimes alienated from each other, but refusing to give up. After about a year, meeting every month or two for long weekends, we reached a unanimous conclusion: we realized that in our process of wrestling with each other, we had been touched and changed by the force of God's relentless passion for justice working through us and by God's serendipitous delight in every one of us for keeping on keeping on, with a little bit of faith in each other and quite a bit more faith in God's mysterious ways! In spite of our tensions, we had had such fun together, doing theology and struggling for justice. Somehow, in the midst of it all, our faith had soared.

Like Bishop DeWitt, the MudFlower Collective came to realize that only our faith in God's 'fierce whimsy' will see us through this life together on earth. Our faith in God's relentless passion for justice and her playfulness and joy will heal us as individuals and communities. We saw that God compels us to march and pray and work for a better world by resisting injustice and oppression and that this same God calls us to join together in making music, making gardens, making bread, making love, making wonders of many kinds. We came to experience the Lord of the Dance as our Best Friend, our Mother, Father, Sister, Brother. We realized, with repentant hearts, that She is also the angry judge of our injustice, oppression, and the violence we do to one another and ourselves, that She is judge of our wars and our refusals to learn from our wars. Together, we experienced this God as a merciful and compassionate companion. Together, we came to believe that it is our faith in God's fierce whimsy that will see us through. And it will!

26

Light as a Feather

Almost two decades after the MudFlower Collective worked on God's Fierce Whimsy *(1985; see Chapter 25), I discovered the joy of horses as seren-dipitous friends, powerful spiritual resources, vibrant sources of healing, and embodiments of God's fierce whimsy. The following is adapted from my 2005 book* Flying Changes: Horses as Spiritual Teachers.

In the last quarter of the twentieth century, feminism was coming alive as a force to be reckoned with inside the churches in the United States and elsewhere. Many women were being called by the Spirit to leave the religion that was breaking their spirits and bodies much as men have always broken horses. During this time, I wasn't alone in my dismay that women, in and out of the Church, were being set against themselves, against other women, and against men by the strange teachings and practices of patriarchal spiritualities in a patriarchal society. I count myself fortunate that I was alive at a moment in history in which women were struggling for social and religious change through the 'second wave' of the feminist movement. This followed the 'first wave', which took place in the late nineteenth and early twentieth centuries as mostly white women in England and the United States launched a movement for full human rights for themselves and other women.

I didn't leave the Church earlier in my life, because I believed I could help transform it from within and help call it to work for social change. Indeed, over the past three decades, I've been able to work with many sisters and some feminist brothers in this work of social and religious transformation. Our efforts continue as a work-in-progress. Whether or not they will have been worth it, time will tell.

Of course the feminist movement in western Christianity was no new thing, even in its earlier manifestation. It was kin to all those efforts in history that have challenged the teachings and practices of established religion. We've been taught to brand as 'heresy' any significant departure from the doctrines, or central teachings, of a religious tradition. Most heresies, however, are rooted in intuitions of truth and wisdom that are threatening to transform the organized Church and, for that reason, are perceived as dangerous and must be banned or buried.

Like the Judaism from which it sprang, Christianity has been patriarchal to its bone. This is not to blame Judaism for Christianity's problems with women but rather simply to draw a historical line between these two major patriarchal forces. In fact, most feminists – Christians, Jews, and others – agree that, due to the strength of its Neoplatonic heritage, Christianity is especially oppressive to women. Much of Christianity is culturally more hostile than most of Judaism to sexuality and, in most matters, more contemptuous toward our experiencing God in the midst of embodied pleasures such as singing our hearts out about love, marching our feet off for justice, having great sex, dancing with abandon, giving birth, looking into the face of a newborn, or galloping through a field of goldenrod.

Two decades ago, seven Christian women co-authored a book we named *God's Fierce Whimsy* (see Chapter 25), in which we concluded that Christian theology, in its mainstream and male-stream, has been not only sexist but too ponderous and heavy, not reflective enough of the whimsy of God. We testified to more serendipitous and good-humoured spiritualities, all the while recognizing the oppression and terror that breaks the world, its people and creatures. We bore witness to a God who moves the struggles for justice and peace, One whose ways are not only reproachful toward injustice and violence but also joyful and playful among us. This God, we affirmed, is truly our Sacred Source of liberation and healing.

New birth

I got a jubilant sense of 'God's fierce whimsy' in the summer of 2003, when I saw the Sacred squeezed out into this world again, wet and sticky and tired but, as usual, a source of great joy. She was born right before midnight on 17 June, my quarter horse Red's little filly arriving two weeks later than expected. She pushed her way into this world right before my eyes and those of a dozen family and friends who'd gathered at the barn to witness this birth. Two of us were present at Red's side during the delivery – Jennifer, a college student majoring in animal sciences, who'd been helping midwife Red through her pregnancy, and me. Everyone else stood at a distance, outside the stall, trying to stand back a little since mares, like human moms, appreciate some privacy. Jennifer and I stood back and waited until the baby's front legs, followed by her head, began to emerge. My companion Sue remarked later that the newborn looked like a space ship getting ready to land. In the moment, Sue like the rest of us was simply awestruck. 'Wow, wow,' she whispered, barely audibly, again and again.

I had done everything I could to prepare for this event. But as anyone who's given birth (or even witnessed it close up) knows, there's no way to prepare fully for it. There's something totally magical, miraculous, stunning beyond belief in that moment when new life actually appears and begins to make itself known to those who've been waiting for it to arrive as it begins to take shape and develop its own personality.

Almost from the day Red entered my life, in the summer of 2000, I wanted her to have a foal. I reasoned that since she was fourteen when I acquired her, Red would be well into her twenties as I moved into my sixties, and I probably should be thinking not only of a younger horse, if I hoped to keep riding into my seventies and eighties, but also I should be thinking of a smaller horse. On the advice of one of my trainers, I decided to breed Red to a Connemara pony, a small, sturdy Irish breed with an easy disposition. I took great care in planning the pregnancy, beginning with making certain Red was in good health. Our vet assured me that there was no reason why, even at age seventeen, Red couldn't have a safe delivery. Two of her previous caregivers, whom I'd been able to locate by phone, did not believe Red had ever foaled, but we had no way of knowing for sure. The vet said this probably wouldn't matter if she were in good shape, which he assured me she was. Through the last half of her eleven-month gestation, I was in Massachusetts teaching. Not being able to be present in North Carolina with Red during this period was hard for me, but my helper Jennifer and other friends were wonderfully attentive to her, and periodic vet checks confirmed that Red and the little one were coming along fine.

In late May, once I arrived home from Massachusetts and then from a short, sad trip to Berlin for a memorial service for my friend and sister theologian Dorothee Soelle (see Chapter 33), I spent time every day hanging out with Red in her stall and small paddock. I also tried each day to walk her down the road or around the riding arena, to help relieve her boredom, give her a little exercise, and show some sisterly solidarity.

By the due date in early June, I had selected several possible names – Redwing after the mom; Ariel after the god of wind and air, Angela or Angelo after my beloved friend Sister Angela (see Chapter 31); Wingo, just for fun. But I knew that I wouldn't be able to really name the foal until after the birth. I imagined that, somehow, the baby would name him/herself. I would just know its name. Names are important, for humans and other creatures, conveying something about who we really are and how we are connected to each other. I knew that the foal's name would be the right one, and that I'd know it only after she or he arrived. Like most human parents, I didn't give a whit whether it was a girl (filly) or boy (colt) as long as mom and babe were safe. The late arrival, which turns out to be pretty routine in the equine world, was a bit unnerving, but our vet kept assuring me that all was well and that we had done everything we could to get ready for the imminent birth. All we could do now was wait and wait and wait.

As the expected date passed and days followed days, I found I couldn't sleep well or think about much of anything except Red and this baby. I spent most of my waking hours over at the stable with Red, walking her, grooming her, talking and singing to her, sitting on the floor of her stall – reading, thinking, praying – bending beside her and caressing her very large belly, and occasionally feeling the foal kick or move. Red's appetite, always large, never abated – a good sign, I was told. She may have been feeling good, as our vet assured me, but it was also a hard time for Red. Besides the discomfort of carrying around sixty or seventy extra pounds, Red really dislikes long periods of confinement. Usually when horses have to be kept in stalls for more than a day or two because of an illness or injury, we're able to hand-graze them, lead them into a grassy pasture and hold their leads while they nibble. A pregnant mare, however, must be kept off pasture because of an ingredient in fescue, a common pasture grass, that can cause complications in the delivery.

Though I'd never experienced a pregnancy myself, I felt much empathy for Red as she waddled about in the heat of early summer, unable to play, run, eat grass, cut off from the rest of the herd, carrying a baby who wasn't ready, until 17 June, to deliver its mom from her discomfort.

Feather

The phone rang at 11:40 pm. 'Carter, we've got ourselves a baby coming!' It was Heidi, Jennifer's younger sister. They were staying over at the stables together, waiting for this moment. We had heard that many foals are born between 11 pm and midnight, and so it was.

My companions Sue, Bev, and I live about five minutes from the stables, so we were able to get there in a flash, several minutes before the foal's legs began to exit her mom's body. Red seemed amazingly calm, at ease, as she lay with her head in the fresh straw bedding. She was groaning but her eyes and body conveyed no fear. Whatever pain she was experiencing, I imagined, was being offset by a great embodied sense of relief.

'Imprinting' is a process of introducing a newborn to the strange phenomenon of human life and the odd things humans do like touch horse faces, stick human fingers in horse mouths and ears and other orifices to take horse temperatures, rub human hands all over horse bodies, slap the bottoms of horse feet, and wrap human arms around horse chests and bellies. The idea is to desensitize the horse to human touch so that the horse, by nature a fear-based animal, will not fear human engagement.

We weren't sure whether the baby needed help getting out of the birth sac, so Jennifer and I gently cut the sac open to release the baby's face and legs. We then began rubbing our hands all over the newborn. We massaged its wet little neck, head, and mane as they appeared. The foal appeared to be buckskin, a light tan. As more of its slippery little body emerged, we could see that, like Red, this baby had a dark dorsal stripe running down its spine. Its mane was black and stood on end like the hair of a punk rocker, all slicked and spiked and pointing in all directions. We continued to touch and rub its body.

Next thing I knew, the baby was all the way out, and Jennifer was turning it over, 'We've got us a little filly!' she exclaimed.

'A little filly!' I announced to everyone. 'We've got a little filly!' I could hear the excitement in my own voice. Here she was – a healthy newborn, lying there still attached to her mom. We knew to leave the umbilical cord alone; Red would chew it loose when she got around to it.

One of the most remarkable sights of the evening was watching Red, having broken the cord, get to her feet and figure out how to manoeuvre around the stall without stepping on her baby. Red moved like a dancer, with grace and deliberation. She took great care to bend herself in whatever directions necessary and to lift each leg as slowly as she had to in order to step around or over or beyond the foal. I stepped to the side of the stall to watch and was aware of the tears in my eyes. I really loved and admired Red so much.

From that point, I have some memory of folks 'oohing' and 'aahing' and moving in and out of the stall for the next couple of hours as several friends helped the baby, once on her feet, try to find her mom's nipples, which she seemed to think were up between Red's front legs.

By 3 am, everyone else had left the stables. Red was standing in the middle of the stall, attending calmly to the little one, licking her all over as she lay at her feet. As I prepared to leave, I realized that I didn't know the baby's name. None of the names I'd chosen in the abstract was right. I leaned over the stall door, took another look, thanked God for this incredible gift of an evening, a birth, an experience. I asked that she keep them through the night and then I went home to sleep.

At 4.30 am, I awoke, popped up in bed, suddenly aware that the foal's name was 'Feather'.

What is taking us so long?

Since that night, Feather has introduced me to God in ways that have helped me realize more fully than ever before that God – Holy Spirit, Sophia, she and he of many names and none at all – has *always* been around, through the cosmos and the struggles for justice, through our yearnings and hopes, through our sad times and happiness, through our loves and losses and gains and more losses. She has always been here with us on the earth, as ancient as the Appalachian mountains and as light and fresh as the Feather who was born in these hills, daughter of Red the quarter horse and Hideaway Sebastian the Connemara pony. God has been with us in the earth's soil, with the earth's suffering and struggles for better water and air. God has been shaping and shifting the earth and other planets in and beyond the galaxies as we know them or imagine we do. The Most Holy has been with us in our most intimate relationships, in our shared sensualities and sexualities, in our celibacies and celebrations, our friendships and partnerships, our sacred unions and our connections with children and elders and one another and other creatures too. She has revelled with us playfully, leaping in joy, bucking enthusiastically, kicking up her heels when she is human, and her hooves when she is horse. The Spirit has been walking us through and leading us beyond the bleakest, hardest times in our lives as communities, as individual creatures, and as the earth. She has been and will always be our power in the struggles against oppression, injustice, violence, and fear-based politics. She has been and will always be our power for right, mutual relationship; for justice, compassion, and peace. She will always be whoever she will be, and she will be our rock, our light, our wisdom, our joy, and the root of our repentance for violence, greed, and the fear in which such evil festers.

All the horses have been my priests. All the horses teach me. But in a special way Feather and Red have me by the heart and are prancing. As my Spirit-guides, they are taking me home to our jubilant Mother, wellspring of Wisdom, creative partner of the Father, Lover of all creatures great and small, who surely must be wondering what is taking us so long.

Part 3: Celebrating Our Friends

Introduction

Part 3 was the most evocative for me to gather up and offer for publication, because it is so deeply personal and because the last five pieces are sermons or speeches at memorial services for people who were not only significant religious leaders from around the world, but also beloved friends of mine and each, in a unique and special way, a mentor. I hope that the reader will not only take courage from all nine pieces but will also enjoy meeting some remarkable women, and one man, who touched the world and changed it.

Chapter 27, 'Womanism and Feminism', was part of a panel presentation honouring Delores S. Williams upon her retirement in 2004 as the Paul Tillich Professor of Theology at Union Theological Seminary in New York City. Delores and I had been graduate students together at Union and, over the years, had taught several courses and led workshops together on womanist and feminist theologies. Chapter 28, 'The World According to Bev', was my presentation at a 2007 celebration in Asheville, North Carolina, of Beverly Wildung Harrison's remarkable contributions to theological and ethical scholarship as a feminist social ethicist.

Chapter 29, 'Beyond Liberal Feminism', is my panel response, at the 2007 meeting of the American Academy of Religion, to Rosemary Radford Ruether's *America, Amerikkka: Elect Nation and Imperial Violence*. Rosemary Ruether has long been one of the most intelligent and consistently radical Christian feminist theologians in the world, and I was delighted to be able to publicly acknowledge her contributions. Nine years earlier, in 1998, on a panel at the American Academy of Religion, I responded to feminist philosopher Mary Daly's 1998 book, *Quintessence: Realizing the Archaic Future – A Radical Elemental Feminist Manifesto*. Chapter 30, 'Biophilic Courage and Be-Dazzling Creativity', is my response. It was a memorable moment for me because Mary Daly and I had not been easy colleagues over the years. For many years, however, I had learned from Mary and admired her 'biophilic courage' and 'be-dazzling creativity'.

The remaining chapters are sermons or speeches at memorial services. In 31, 'An Almost Unbearable Lightness of Being' (2002), I remember Sister Angela from the Community of Saint Clare and my beloved spiritual companion in North Carolina and Massachusetts for the last two years of her life. Chapter 32, 'What Will We Do Without Sue?' (2002), is my sermon at the celebration of the life of Sue Hiatt, my remarkable colleague and best friend at the Episcopal Divinity School, and our leader in the movement for the ordination of women in the Episcopal Church. In Chapter 33, 'Making Us Homeless' (2003), I speak as a representative of people throughout the United States in paying tribute to Dorothee Soelle at an ecumenical service in Berlin. I had known Dorothee as a cherished friend, as a teacher at Union Theological Seminary, a sister sojourner in Nicaragua on a Witness for Peace delegation in 1990, and a colleague in teaching and leading workshops on liberation theologies in the United States, Latin America, and Europe.

Chapter 34, 'Keep Your Courage' (2004), was my sermon at the memorial service for Bishop Robert L. DeWitt in Cambridge, Massachusetts. Along with Sue Hiatt, Bob DeWitt had engineered the 'irregular' ordination of women priests and, along with Sue, had become a pastor, counsellor, and friend to each of the women he ordained. As I note elsewhere in this book, Bishop DeWitt was a 'spiritual dad' to me. Finally, in 35, 'Like a Little Child' (2009), I give thanks for the profoundly loving life of my mother, Mary Ann Carter Heyward.

27

Womanism and Feminism: Honouring Delores S. Williams

This statement was part of a 2004 panel presentation honouring womanist theologian Delores S. Williams upon her retirement as Paul Tillich Professor of Theology at Union Theological Seminary in New York City. Originally published in The Union Seminary Quarterly Review, *Festschrift for Delores S. Williams, Vol. 58, 2004, Numbers 3–4, pp. 180–2, it has been slightly adapted and is reprinted here with permission.*

Let me say that I treasure the opportunity to be part of this celebration of Delores Williams' groundbreaking womanist work. Over the now going-on four decades that she and I have worked together, beginning here at Union as graduate students, Delores has been truly a friend, a comrade in the struggle for justice, and a spiritual sister to me as we, along with many others, have attempted to navigate and re-configure theological channels marked previously by generations of largely white Euro-American men.

One aspect concerning feminism that I learned about early in my experience at Union, often through the insights of Delores, was about the dreadful, devastating dimensions of white women's unexamined and unacknowledged racism. Indeed, for white people, including white feminists, racism is like the air we breathe, an apt image of apartheid offered by white South African feminist theologian and activist Denise Ackermann. In the late twentieth/early twenty-first centuries, a professional and personal relationship between a black and a white woman, one less forged in struggle against injustice, could not, I believe, have survived.

In 2000, Delores and I co-led, with Episcopal Bishop Barbara Harris, a conference in North Carolina on how the 'daughters' of slaves and slave owners might together, in Katie Cannon's words, 'unmask, disentangle, and debunk' the slave master's religion. Of course those who invited us to lead this conference, a good and challenging educational opportunity – but basically one for white Southern Christian women – insisted that we name the conference something that would be less threatening to white (and perhaps black) women. There could be no mention in the title of the 'slave master's religion', so difficult is it for white Christians in the United States to look honestly and critically at our own social and spiritual history.

This leads me to one of the major challenges facing womanists and feminists today across the historical social borders into the public spaces which we share either by choice or necessity. It is a challenge, in two parts, to be ever-more adamant in speaking truth to power:

First, how can we more effectively encourage one another to speak truthfully *among ourselves,* not muting our message: womanist to womanist, feminist to feminist, womanist and feminist to one another? How can we encourage each other to speak truthfully about the ongoingness of the slave master's Christianity and its effects? To speak truthfully requires that we learn together how to recognize and name truths about classism and empire as racist and about the hetero/sexist underpinnings of right wing Christianity's stranglehold on the United States of America in 2004. I am aware that one of the boldest womanist spokeswomen on matters of class and colonialism, and their effects on black women's lives, is Joan Martin, my esteemed colleague at the Episcopal Divinity School.

How do we speak truthfully together about the ongoing effects of the 'bloody Jesus' tradition – Delores Williams' reference to the effects of the blood-sacrifice atonement tradition – on the bodies of women of all colours and cultures? Not only do we have here Delores Williams' gutsy, intelligent, and infamous contribution to the Re-Imagining Conference in Minneapolis in 1993, but also the womanist Christological visions of such sisters as Jacquelyn Grant, Kelly Brown Douglas, and Joanne Terrell.

How do we encourage one another to speak our truths, womanist and feminist, about our lesbian, bisexual, heterosexual, transgender, and omnigender lives being lived in black Churches as well as in white churches and other churches throughout this and other lands? Here I want to lift up the bold womanist voice of Kelly Brown Douglas on the subject of 'sexuality and the black Church'. I also want to lift up the courageous voice of our black lesbian feminist colleague Irene Monroe, whose work as a public theologian has been a beacon of hope for black queer folk as the issue of 'gay marriage' has become a strong divisive wedge in black communities, especially in Massachusetts this spring.

How, in these times of social crisis which are far worse, I believe, than we tend to imagine, can we empower one another, womanists and feminists, to speak boldly and truthfully, even among ourselves – perhaps, at times, even to ourselves?

Second, how do we steadfastly, cunningly and effectively, counter the efforts of leadership, in Church and academy, to ignore womanist wisdom and anti-racist feminism whether through co-optation, trivialization, or rejection?

At no time have our churches and our theological and religious education centres been in greater need of womanism's theological wisdom and spiritual colourfulness! Yet because we are in a nation and world that is feeding on '9/11', never have our religious institutions been more fearful of speaking truth to power. How can we keep ourselves from being silenced and overcome by this fear draped like a pall over most of our public space? How can we build a creative political resistance to what Dorothee Soelle named in 1981 (early in Reagan's first term) as the 'christofascism' she detected on the horizon in the United States? Today, 25 years into christofascism's spread among us, how can we feminists and womanists resist the efforts of our churches to smooth over the rough edges of our passionate voices in order to render us bland

and tame? How do we help spark and sustain a serious, sustainable movement of justice, transformation, and hope in this nation that is teetering on the brink of total social and moral collapse?

28

The World According to Bev: Honouring Beverly Wildung Harrison

On 23 March 2007, Holy Ground, a feminist spirituality resource centre in Asheville, North Carolina (Chapter 11), held a celebration of the contributions of Christian feminist social ethicist Beverly Wildung Harrison, who had retired in 1999 from more than 30 years on the faculty of Union Theological Seminary in New York City. Bev has been a significant person in my life, since I entered Union Seminary as a student in 1967. She has been a mentor and teacher to me, as she has been to hundreds of feminist and womanist theologians and ethicists throughout the world. After I graduated from Union Seminary in 1980, Bev and I became lovers and partners for over a decade. Bev continues as a beloved friend, one of my life-companions, family. I was invited to make this presentation at the celebration honouring her work as an advocacy-scholar of Christian ethics.

This is undoubtedly one of the greatest honours, and challenges, which has come my way as a feminist theologian – to try to set in theological and ethical context the contributions of Beverly Wildung Harrison, and to do so in about 30 minutes! Those of you familiar with Bev's work know that, in response to any serious ethical question from a student or reader, Bev herself may easily take 30 minutes. Bev says it's because she's from a German stock and the weird theological complexity of that culture. Most of us think it's because she's so smart! I mean it often takes Bev 20 to 30 minutes just to get started in a serious moral discourse, given the complexities, nuances, and sheer elegance of her mind and the way she approaches ethics. I mean by this the way Bev, as a Christian feminist ethicist and teacher, thinks about all ethical issues in view of women's lives; the way she thinks about procreative freedom; the way she thinks about the ongoing struggle against white racism, or white supremacy; the way she thinks about the nefarious character of advanced global capitalism (ever more apparent during the presidency of the man dubbed by Molly Ivins as 'Shrub'), the way Bev thinks about the ambiguities and challenges in the struggles for gender and sexual justice and, especially, during the last couple of decades, the fight for LGBT justice; the way she thinks about the rise and (perhaps, now) the imminent decline of the 'Religious Right'; and, of course, the way – as a teacher and an intellectual – Beverly Harrison thinks about teaching and thinks about thinking!

Tomorrow, thanks to the presence here of a number of Bev's most celebrated students, who are themselves now teachers of ethics, we'll have a chance to hear in some detail, and discuss the implications of, Bev's own thinking and teaching in such areas as teaching itself, or in pedagogy, economic justice, sexual/gender/racial justice, and the global character of these and other matters facing us today. Tonight, in the next few minutes, I'll be trying to help set the stage for these discussions by telling you a little about my experiences of Beverly Harrison over a 40 – year period – what I have learned from her, and about her, and why I believe Bev is celebrated throughout the world as the 'mother of Christian feminist ethics'.

My earliest experience of Bev was in my first semester as a student at Union Theological Seminary in New York City in the fall of 1967. Right out of a southern woman's college and white, middle-class southern women's culture, I was emotionally un-prepared for either New York City or the radical anti-war and sexual politics of my seminary classmates. As it happened, Bev Harrison was not only a junior professor of Christian Ethics on Union's Faculty, she was also the Associate Dean for Women – so that many women like me, who were coming unglued by the pace and passions of graduate school life in 1967, had an advocate. So my first experience of Bev was as my advocate in a situation that otherwise would have overwhelmed me. Several years later, in the context of a women's consciousness raising group at Union Seminary, I would hear every other woman student bear similar witness to Bev's powerful role in their lives, like mine, as an advocate. She believed in us before we believed in ourselves. In that way, Bev – a Presbyterian laywoman and scholar – was pastor and counsellor to women students from diverse cultures and denominations in ways that few of us had ever experienced. Bev asked me to say here that some of her interests were methodological: She developed various theological and moral 'hermeneutical circles' to show how Christian ethics could be simultaneously advocative (normative toward justice) and objective or fair in its descriptive work.

I had a similar experience of Bev three years later, in the first course I took from her. It was in the fall of 1970 (I had returned to pick up my studies at Union after a two-year leave of absence). The course was 'The Sociology of Knowledge'. For me, it was like taking a foreign language, so alien were such concepts as 'epistemology' (how we know what we know) and 'hermeneutics' (how we interpret the material before us). I had to struggle to catch up with my classmates, who were themselves having to struggle to keep up with Bev. As it happened, the class worked like magic for one primary reason: Bev believed in our capacities to catch up, keep up, and understand what was going on. She did not talk down to us. She did not patronize us. She did not allow us to undercut our capacities for scholarship by failing to believe in ourselves as first-rate students, thinkers, scholars, and teachers. It didn't matter whether we were women or men, gay or straight, black or white, Australian, German, Korean, or from the United States South or Midwest. We were all way more capable than almost any of us had believed we were. Here, as in her work as Dean of Students, Bev believed in us, before we believed in ourselves, and because she did, many of us began to grow and blossom with Beverly Harrison as our mentor.

Years later, I listened as Bev reflected on these years. She spoke of how it was in those days at Union, the 1960s and early 1970s, when women were beginning to come to seminary in large numbers, but often with very little self-confidence. She said that very often her male colleagues looked down on these women students, refusing to take us seriously. In fact, she said that it took her some time – and the emergence of the women's movement in the early 1970s – to realize that she had allowed herself to become 'the exceptional woman', the one (and too often the only) woman respected by her male colleagues. In her own successful professional journey, Bev had become 'one of the boys' in the eyes of some male colleagues. Later Bev would say that it was only with the help of women students that she began really to see how trivialized women were by some male theologians and teachers. At Union some senior scholars gave her top grades but resented her as 'too political'. She had become lonely as a woman treated by men as smarter and more competent than other women.

Looking back, Bev was able to recognize this particular dynamic – the trivialization of women and being set apart from other women if you happened to be especially smart and articulate – as her springboard into feminism. This would become the foundation of the rest of her professional and personal life.

Beverly Wildung Harrison's roots are in the small town of Luverne in southwestern Minnesota. She was born in 1932, the fourth of five kids – with two older brothers (one of them Richard Wildung, a star player for the Green Bay Packers), an older sister, and a younger brother, Hal, her only surviving sibling and a great music teacher and choral conductor in Minneapolis. Bev's father died when she was a little girl and she was raised by her mother Dale, who ran a women's clothing store and raised her five children at the same time – a matter of economic necessity and not simply the love of fashion. Bev describes her family of origin as made up largely of Republicans and Presbyterians who were, and still are, more conventional than conservative. Her older sister Ginny, younger brother Hal, and Bev herself, along with a number of the younger generation of Wildungs, have left the Republican Party and, for some, the Presbyterian Church behind.

One of Bev's own mentors, who helped shepherd her in more liberal intellectual and radical spiritual and political directions, was the great liberation theologian, Robert McAfee Brown, a faculty member at Macalester College in St Paul, Minnesota, when Bev was a student there in the early 1950s. The social and political climate at the time was a rabid anti-Communism, and Bev found herself being mentored by men like Robert McAfee Brown and Macalester's President, Charles Turk, who were themselves being 'baited' by their Wisconsin neighbour, Senator Joseph McCarthy. She became a Democrat while working for Congressman Eugene McCarthy, who led opposition to the Vietnam War.

My hunch is that Bev's early and ongoing ethical interest in matters of political economy, Marxism, capitalism, and economic justice has roots in a combination of her family origins in Luverne, a widowed mother who ran a successful local dress shop, together with the raging anti-labour message that resounded throughout the anti-Communism craze of the early 1950s. In the 1980s, while most twenty-year-old white, middle-strata women were settling into marriage, motherhood, and family, allowing their husbands be the breadwinners, Beverly Wildung began to develop critical insights on our national political and economic life. Her studies at Macalester in social ethics later, and later at Union throughout the 1960s, would give her an opportunity, as well as professional platform, to pull together her interests in social justice, Christian ethics, philosophical ethics and moral theory.

In the early 1970s, Bev's ethical interests began to focus on social theory and political economy. These she would weave through feminism into an analysis of the fabric of women's lives. As the 1970s gave way to the Reign of Ronald Reagan in 1980, and into the 1990s, Bev's converging interests in economic and gender justice would be deeply impacted by her commitments to exposing white racism.

The 1970s and 1980s had witnessed the emergence here in the United States of Latin American, African, and Asian Liberation Theologies, and Bev's ethical interests increasingly assumed global proportions, which meant that her travels and her professional colleagues and collaborators increasingly introduced her to many parts of the world. I think of Reinhild Traitler from Switzerland, the Sophia Center and Angela Moloney in Australia, Susan Adams in New Zealand, Denise Ackermann in South Africa, Mercy Amba Oduyoye in Kenya, Grace Jantzen and Mary Grey in Great Britain, Chung Hyun Kyun and Yung Ja Kim from Korea, Gustavo Gutierrez from Peru and Ivone Gebara from Brazil, Dorothee Soelle and Luise Schottroff from West Germany, and Brigitte Kahl from East Germany. These friendships and collaborations served to sharpen and clarify for Bev what she had been learning for several decades from women at the World Council of Churches and, certainly, from many students at Union who had come from many parts of the world.

These names represent only a fraction of the theologians, ethicists, Biblical scholars, and other religious activists around the world who, over the past 20 to 30 years, have proudly referred to Bev as not only their esteemed colleague in ethics but, even more importantly for most of them, as their good friend, Bev Harrison, whose apartment in New York was always open to them as a second home and whose table was always set as a welcoming table for friends and sojourners in the struggles for justice-love.

Here's a poem written by Dorothee Soelle for Beverly Harrison and published in Dorothee Soelle's autobiography *Against the Wind* (1995):

Seven Paradoxes for Beverly
You are younger than I
but when someone came on to me recently
in a particularly mean way
I said you just wait I'll get my big sister

You have no children
But your apartment declares merrily
children wanted come one come all

Once I saw you crying
with rage about an injustice
but you were stronger than the strong

You think about abortion
but I have never seen a teacher
who drives away so little of life

Sometimes you are so buried in work
that I cannot see your face
but I have learned something
it is like the moon it returns again

Once I saw you crying
with happiness there is no paradox for that
once I saw you crying
and was happy

Sometimes I am sad
because I sense a thin wall between us
but it has doors
(Soelle 2005, pp. 65–6)

Even as Bev Harrison's ethical and theological interests were becoming more and more multi-cultural throughout the 1980s and 1990s and up to the present, so too was her special interest in the lives of women and of all people – men and women – who suffer sexual or gender injustice, which means of course all lesbian, gay, bisexual, and transgender women and men, as well as all victims of sexual, gender, and 'domestic' or 'intimate' violence. Some of Bev's most compelling work as a teacher, writer, and speaker over the last three decades has been in relation to the struggles for gender and sexual justice and their connections to struggles for racial and economic justice. Her first book, *Our Right to Choose: Toward a New Ethic of Abortion* (1983), has become a classic among religious advocates to keep abortion and pro-creative options safe and legal for all women in the United States and elsewhere, especially poor women and women of colour. (The book was published last year in Mexico, where several hundred people, largely women and their daughters or women and their mothers, showed up in Mexico City to meet and raise a glass to toast Beverly Harrison.)

One of her most widely read essays, 'The Power of Anger in the Work of Love', by now published in several dozen languages, debunks the assumption, widespread among white Christians, that 'anger' is a 'sin' and suggests, to the contrary, that anger is indispensable to the work of making justice–love in history; and that one of the problems with anger, in heterosexist patriarchy, is that it is confused with violence. In her essay, 'Misogyny and Homophobia', Bev makes clear the connection between the hatred of women in patriarchy and the fear of homosexuality. In this essay, Bev Harrison insists that we cannot understand the struggle for the liberation of women (women of colour and poor women as well as white privileged women) apart from working for justice for lesbian, gay, bisexual, and transgender people, whether Anglicans in Nigeria or Roman Catholics in the United States.

Like many other feminists, Bev has incorporated into her work, more and more over the last decade, a deep concern for what her colleague at Union Larry Rasmussen has named 'earth ethics'. Alongside other feminists and liberation theologians, Bev recog-nizes that humans are doing terrible violence to the earth, water, air, and creatures – and that humankind must undergo a con-version to an ethic of sustainability if we are to survive as a species. Making such connections, persistently and ever-more deeply, is her intellectual and political trademark. It is why it often takes her twenty minutes to begin to answer a question! Her former graduate students and colleagues, several with us tonight, will attest to how glad they are that they learned, over the years, to wait with Bev as, together, they learned to weave intelligent responses to difficult questions about how theology and ethics inform significant life-issues like sex and money and violence and environmental racism.

Needless to say, throughout these many years, the Christian Right has had no use for Beverly Harrison, nor she for them. Bev does not suffer fools gladly – and she can be strident or harsh with people she does not experience as truthful or as open to learning anything they don't already know. But those who know her (and thank her for who we have been able to become, professionally and personally) are deeply aware of how seriously Bev takes anyone, from right, left, or centre, who is struggling to speak truthfully or to figure out how better to participate in the struggles for justice–love.

Finally, a personal word. Bev and I have been life-companions in one form or another for some 27 years. Prior to that, for about 13 years, we were becoming friends (as teacher and student and, after a while, as teacher and teaching assistant). It is hard to find a language intelligible to us, much less to others, for who we are to each other today. But we know each other well, and love each other, and I can speak to you with authority about Bev's ongoing passion for justice and her rage against injustice. And I can speak to you about her loving, sweet adoration of her animal-companions, her brother and nieces and nephews, and my family as well. Moreover, I believe that the breadth and depth of Bev's mind – her sheer intellectual power – is also the source of some real loneliness and mental anguish for Bev in these years approaching 'seniorhood'. She is fond of saying, 'Ageing is not for the faint-hearted'. What she means, I believe, is not only that our bodies become increasingly unreliable and can require almost full-time maintenance, but also that what we have learned, by the time we are 75 or 80, if we share Beverly Harrison's passion for justice, is almost more than we can bear in the context of the present world and this nation's place in it.

And so, life for Bev, and for the rest of us, her sisters and brothers, becomes increasingly a challenge in a number of ways, does it not? But she would be quick to insist that, on the journey, today and tomorrow, our most valuable resource will always be one another's companionship and our commitment to the struggles for justice–love, a commitment that is sacred because it is shared.

Hanging on the wall of Bev's guest room today is a magnificent quilt of 50 or 60 patches held together by a bright purple border. Each patch was made or contributed by one of Bev Harrison's graduate students or former students, or friends – and most say something like 'Blessed are the Bold!' or 'Mother of us all' or simply 'Thank you, Bev'. This conference, tonight and tomorrow, is a small way of saying, again, 'Thank you, Bev'.

Those who have had a meal at Bev's table any time during the last 20 or so years have heard her say the grace that is attributed to two old friends who wished to dine together – one an Episcopal Bishop who wouldn't dine without saying grace and the other a Communist activist who wouldn't say grace. As a way of launching our celebration of Bev Harrison, I invite those of you who know the blessing to join now: 'Some have bread. Some have none. God bless the Revolution!'

29

Beyond Liberal Feminism: Responding to Rosemary Ruether

This paper was presented as a panel response to Rosemary Radford Ruether's book, America, Amerikkka *at the 2007 meeting of the American Academy of Religion in San Diego, California, 7 November 2007.*

What Rosemary Radford Ruether has done for half a century, and continues to do in *America, Amerikkka* (2007), is to help Christians and doubtlessly others think about ourselves collectively, as historical people, shaped by forces for good and for evil. As for the evil, the problems that violate and break us, Ruether has helped us realize that, while these immense problems – such as sexism, racism, and empire – are beyond our personal fault, they are not beyond our personal and collective responsibility for solving. Indeed, for Rosemary Ruether, as historian, theologian, and activist, the revolution is never won, and Christians are never off the hook as persons with revolutionary vocations and responsibilities.

Anyone alert to the ugly dynamics being unleashed today, as in the past, against Hillary Clinton, will notice the depth of sexism permeating our society, which counterrevolutionary sisters and brothers insist upon describing as 'post-feminist'. Today, as over the last half century, no Christian theologian has been more responsive to the depth and pervasiveness of sexism in church and society, this nation and around the world, than Rosemary Ruether. Moreover, no Christian theologian has become more emblematic of feminism as a strong, liberative response to sexism, misogyny, homophobia, racism, militarism, classism, economic exploitation, environmental assault, and other structures of systemic violence.

Even as early as the 1970s, Rosemary Ruether had emerged as a leading Christian feminist theologian, and I was permitted to take one of my doctoral field exams in 1978 on her work. I noted at that time that, while liberal Christian churches in North America were just beginning, in timid ways, to make space for some feminism in language and liturgies, Rosemary Ruether was moving Christian feminism way beyond the soft-mushy-brain notion that feminists are interested primarily, if at all, in gaining equal rights with men in static patriarchal institutions. Ruether was clear that feminism always involves justice-making and as such is inherently a struggle *against* patriarchy, a movement to *transform* patriarchal institutions, not simply for equality within them. That was why Ruether emphasized the struggles by and for women of all cultures, religions, and classes, and not only women, but by and for all who are oppressed. For Rosemary Ruether, feminism has always required, in Beverly Wildung Harrison's language, 'making the connections' between and among the structures of systemic violence that shape our lives. Like Harrison, Ruether was never a 'soft' feminist, never simply a white middle-class Christian woman's advocate for equality in an unjust social order. She has always been a liberation theologian, even before she/we were able to articulate clearly the language of 'liberation theology', which began to catch fire among white theologians, feminists, and others in the mid-1970s. Rosemary Ruether understood and wrote about economic exploitation and the problems of rich v. poor nations and cultures at least a decade before Latin American Liberation Theologies began to appear in the North. She also addressed racism as a systemic problem, well before most white progressive Christians had begun to read black theologies or ponder the ongoing challenges of white racism and the white privilege that had all along been shaping our theological assumptions.

As I was reading *America, Amerikkka,* three characteristics of Rosemary's theological work in this book stood out:

1 *As an historian, Rosemary Ruether uses historical precedents and analogies to help us better understand where we are today and where we are not.* We are likely to feel less alone, less crazy, more empowered, and better informed as historical actors ourselves the better acquainted we become with those who have gone before us. What can we learn for our contemporary struggles by studying the trials and tribulations of such characters in United States history as Anne Hutchinson, Eugene Debs, Jane Addams? Ruether helps us realize how connected our lives and struggles are, historically, with those who have gone before. Indeed, their most revolutionary contributions continue to find and take shape among us in the twenty-first century.

2 *Rosemary Ruether has always been a 'utopian' theologian.* She asks us to look ahead of where we are – to where we are 'not yet' – while insisting that we be grounded in the realities of the present time and place. For Ruether, it is not okay to pretend that, in some spiritual realm, everything is okay. It is not okay to pretend that all is right with God and God's world because it most assuredly is not. People and other creatures are dying violently everywhere in the world. Women and children are suffering unspeakable abuses in every nation. Ethnic cleansings are mounting from continent to continent. Racism, sexism, and fascism are marching along together. Imperialist aims, especially those of the United States, arrogantly threaten to gobble up planet earth, its people, creatures, water, land, and air. All is not right with God's world – in the midst of this grave situation, you and I are beckoned by God's Spirit to join in the historical struggles to make Jubilee a reality, to bring into being, in ways great and small, a world in which everyone is cherished and respected.

3 *Acknowledging the tension between the utopic vision and the real praxis of our lives, Rosemary Ruether's theology has always manifested a 'dialectical' sensibility.* She is a dialectical theologian more in line with the aims of liberation theologian Ignacio Ellacuría than the neo-orthodoxy of Karl Barth. Unlike

Barth, she does not 'read the Bible in one hand and the newspaper in the other'. Ruether interprets both scripture and the daily news with a critical consciousness seeking ways to strengthen the justice motifs and possibilities in both. Her critical consciousness positions her in the tensions between past and present, then and now, here and there, us and them. Wrestling intellectually and politically in these tensions, Ruether expects to uncover much value and truth in the relation between 'them' and 'us', between our perspectives and traditions and those of others. Her understanding of Christian Antisemitism as 'the left hand of Christology', and her critique of Israel's reprehensible treatment of the Palestinians reflect her dialectical understanding of both historical and theological truths, which cannot be contained within any one religious tradition – Christian, Jewish, Muslim – nor any single national or cultural identity, be it (United States of) 'American' Israeli, or Palestinian. Again and again, for Ruether, the revolution is never won.

Finally, let me say a word about how wonderfully accessible Rosemary's work is to non-scholarly lay folks. A vital quality of a good theology is that it be intelligible to people other than academic theologians, as is much of Rosemary's work, including *America, Amerikkka*. Beverly Harrison and I belong to a small mission church in the mountains of Western North Carolina, which will be reading and discussing *Amerikkka* as our educational focus in this coming Epiphany season. The members of this small church are progressive Christians looking for ways to make a difference in the world. We need help in thinking about our roles in this historical moment of empire-building in which evil seems to have an upper hand. Who better to turn to than Rosemary Ruether? And so we do, again.

30

Biophilic Courage and Be-Dazzling Creativity: Responding to Mary Daly

This presentation was made at the 1998 meeting in Orlando, Florida, of the American Academy of Religion. I was on a panel of feminist theologians celebrating Mary Daly upon publication of her seventh book, Quintessence: Realizing the Archaic Future – A Radical Elemental Feminist Manifesto (1998). Quintessence *is an imaginative account of life among women and girls in another place and time, on Lost and Found Continent in 2048. Readers unfamiliar with Mary Daly's startling word-plays are likely to be mystified by my response, in which I attempted to meet this creative philosopher fifty years in the future on Lost and Found Continent.*

Drawn by the Magnetic Presence of these pages over the last few days, I shouldn't have been surprised to discover that my cat Rubyfruit has conjured me this morning and spirited me off with Her through time and space to Lost and Found Continent. I had thought Rubyfruit was biding her time in the Southern Comfort Pet Resort near my home in western North Carolina, waiting for my return later today, just as I had thought that I was biding my time in this set of plastic boxes [reference is to the hotel in which we were meeting].

But no, we have arrived Here and Now, my familiar and I, in a semitropical paradise of ferns and mango trees, in the year 2048 B. E. (for the 'Biophilic – love of life – Era', which has followed the demise of much patriarchy on planet earth). Here on this redis-covered continent, there are no men – only women and girls in the company of other animals and trees, plants and rocks, water and air, mostly clean and fresh. My heart is leaping, my mind sparking with Elemental Feminist Gynergy, as my eyes scan the Landscape for some sign of Mary Daly, whom Rubyfruit has assured me is Here and Now. And sure enough, as quick as I can think it, I see Mary, 'more Present to me than she [perhaps] consciously realizes' (p. 228), and to you, too, if you realize that you are Here and Now, in the Presence of Wild Women who are becoming 'more rooted [together] in the State of Natural Grace' (p. 228).

Back in the twentieth century, fifty years ago, Mary wrote, 'Biggest lies were as Big as Lies can get' (p. 192). During those death-dealing days in the Deadzone, we women – even Radical feminists – were weighed down by many 'ingrained bad habits' (Mary's words), including the difficulties we all had sustaining right, mutual relation (my words) with so many other Desperately Revolting Sisters. In those times – the energizing 1970s, ominous 1980s, dreadful 1990s – as we struggled to stay alive and alert as Radical Elemental Women, Mary and I often missed each other. We did not often recognize the depth and strength of our connection as Wicked Women, Grieving and Raging, and yes also Hoping and Dancing always in the Lively, Living Interfaces of Future, Present, and Past.

Clearly, one of the Big Reasons Rubyfruit brought me here into this meeting with Mary Daly and the rest of you, if you are with us, is to give us a chance to look backward through a window into the Future which is ours, in Mary's language, to 'concreate'. It is an Archaic Future that we once have known and can rediscover with the 'Wildness of Creative Courage' (p. 20). And I have come here, into this Future, to say Thank You, Mary Daly, for some particular Gifts you gave me and women like me in the twentieth century. I am thinking of other Christian feminists, Postchristian women, Lesbian women, and other Radical Elemental Feminist women voyaging in the Fifth Direction which you named as the Centre.

First was the Gift of your A-mazing, Be-Dazzling Creativity. You were a poet whose Elemental Feminist Genius spun Magical Fabrics, which women could put on, and wear, and dare to flaunt before the Deadheads of our time, knowing that these Fabricated

Magical Powers would protect us. You wrote that 'We were all philosophers when we were five.' And we were. You, as much as any woman on the planet in the last century, helped call forth the imaginative, daring girlchild in us all who was, and still is, yearning to create and dance and fly! Thank you, Mary, for the Gift of your Crafty Creativity.

Second was the Gift of your own Biophilic Courage, which you called the 'quintessential ingredient in Elemental Feminist Genius'. In *Quintessence,* speaking through the character Kate, of Life even among women Here and Now on Lost and Found Continent, you said, 'We need once again to discover Fire!' Well, Mary, your work was Fire among us in the twentieth century. It caught on. It burned. It bothered us and made us hot, and fierce, and dangerous. Most of all, it en-couraged us. There were Christian priests, pastors, and ministers like myself who, because of you, Mary, knew very early in our professional sojournings that God the Father was a necrophilic overseer of nothing but Lies. And a number of us Harrowing Harpies spent much of our lives speaking this Truth in a thousand different ways to our Sisters who, for a thousand different reasons – some good, some not so good, but all real, reasons – were in the Church. Being a Radical Feminist Christian seemed as much like an oxymoron to many of us as it did to you, I suspect. Year after year, I stayed, we stayed, those of us who *did* stay in the churches, to help those who needed to leave find their way out – often through your books – and to help those who needed to stay find the courage to stay on their own Elemental Feminist terms, making no peace with their own or others' oppression. Thank you for your Creative Courage, Mary, which not only made many of our lives easier – in or out of the Church – but also, I am sure, in some cases possible. Your work was literally a life-line.

Third, thank you for the cunning, cut-dead-throat clarity with which you named the evils in both Church and academy – or, as you described it, 'the academonic invasion of women's psyches'. I personally delighted in your 'Sado-Ritual Syndrome' analysis of post-modern feminism – an expression which, I agree with you in some ways, is an oxymoron. In other ways, I think it is redundant. And as for the Church, well, Mary, your indictment of Christianity was far and away the clearest and most uncompromising of any public Feminist voice in our time or any time. I also appreciated your Scathing Scepticism of Sisters' spiritual escapes in the 1980s and 1990s into the sometimes softer patriarchal logic of some Eastern religious traditions. You warned us, 'All patriarchal religions sap female energy.' You were clear, and you were right about this. Thank you for your Dis-illusioning Clarity.

Now you were not always right, of course! Who is? I suppose that one of the necrophilic reversals inherent always as a possibility in such Cutting Clarity as yours, Mary, is what you yourself named as the first component of the Sado-Ritual Syndrome – 'an obsession with purity'. You identified this as a problem with post-modern feminism. I found your work at least as much as that of our post-modern colleagues, ironically, to be overly committed to an intellectual, spiritual, and political Purity. You seemed to me in the twentieth century to have little Elemental Space or Time for the ambiguities, messes, divided loyalties, confused commitments and contradictions which I see as inherent in the Fifth Direction – the Expanding Here.

I think your Lust for Purity pulled against your making strong connections between patriarchy, capitalism, and class privilege (including your own, and mine); between patriarchy, racism, and white privilege (including yours and mine); or between patriarchy, sexism, and anything except the necrophilial anti-nature of patriarchy, a connection you made passionately. It was, for the most part, as if you believed that the evils of patriarchy and sexism could be best comprehended in pure form, undiluted by other historical systems of death-dealing oppressions like white racism and the Euro-American colonization of the earth's resources.

Looking back, I'd say that Wild Women need not have been so Pure to have been Clear, Strong, and Effective; and that we might have given ourselves and other Sisters more Time and Space to be messy and full of contradictions, even wrong, again and again.

Moving on now, I want to Thank You, Mary, for the fourth Gift you gave us in the last century – your Vision, your Trans-spatial, Trans-temporal Vision of the Expanding Here and Now. Because you were such a Revolting Hag, it was not always easy for Christian women to recognize in you the same mystical – you named it 'Magical' – Gynergy that sparked among women like Hildegard. You wrote that 'those who can pull us ahead may be our Foresisters of the Future'. As early as 1968, Mary, you were such a Foresister, writing to us simultaneously from the twentieth century, and beyond, and before. It is hardly surprising that, in your public work, you so often conjured Sojourner Truth, Matilda Joslyn Gage, Virginia Woolf and other Foresisters. I have no doubt that they played, and play still, no small part in concreating your work. Thank you for your Magical Vision.

Fifth and finally, thank you, Mary, for the Gift of your Grief and Rage in the context of Nectech, the technology of death, genetic manipulation, Human Genome Project, etc. In naming this stinking, rotten 'doodoo of the Daddies of the Deadzone', you poured out some of your Most Passionate writings, as of 1998, on behalf of our Sister the Earth and Her many varied Creatures who were being viciously tortured and torn apart in those terrible times. Nowhere was your Fire hotter than in the connections you dared to make between Nectech Future as the End of Nature and Nectech Future as the End of Women. Thank your for making these connections, and for your Grief and Rage. The twenty-first century has borne Witness to the Truths you spoke in 1998, and 1988, and 1978, and 1968. 'Our Grief is not passive', you wrote. 'We do not consume our time in depression. Our Grief combines with Rage. Our Wailing is our Railing.' You bet it is.

And now. I return to 1998 so that I can release myself from this strange Disney tomb and get on back to North Carolina, where my cat Rubyfruit is waiting to be released from the kennel. As I leave, I hope it is clear to you, Mary Daly, how immensely grateful I am for the last 30 years of your work in the twentieth century, in which you laid many of the most durable foundations for feminist theologies and philosophies that would be concreated in decades and centuries to come. Without your work, no feminist theologian of any tradition would have been where she was in 1998 – or would be where she is today, 50 years later.

As for the fact that you and I so often missed each other in the last century, it seems that just when I was rolling my eyes that you were out to lunch, you were shaking your head that I was out to church!

31

An Almost Unbearable Lightness of Being: Remembering Sister Angela

At the time of her death, in January of 2002, Sister Angela Solling of the Community of Saint Clare, in England and Australia, had been living in our small intentional community in the mountains of North Carolina for three years. Angela and I had met in January 1991 at the Clare Monastery in Stroud, New South Wales, where Australian friends had taken me to meet her and to lead a conversation on feminist theology. From the moment of our meeting, Angela and I become spiritual companions at a depth which transformed us both. Over the next decade, our relationship stirred my mystical sensibilities and sparked Angela's passion for justice. She died on 20 January 2002, following a massive stroke several days earlier. On 9 February 2002, Angela's friends in Brevard, North Carolina, held a memorial service at St Phillip's Episcopal Church and scattered her ashes at the farm where she and I had worked with our horses and with Free Rein Center for Therapeutic Riding. On 5 March 2002, Angela's friends and colleagues in Massachusetts held another memorial service for her at the Church of the Good Shepherd in Watertown, Massachusetts. I preached this sermon at both services. Later, some of Angela's ashes were taken by her Australian friends and scattered at the Monastery in Stroud, which she had founded almost three decades earlier.

What did you most treasure about Angela? Was it her way of greeting every living soul, 'Hello daahling'? Was it her use of words like 'dancey' and 'gorgeous' to describe every glorious waking moment with every person and creature she ever met? Was it her energy, enthusiasm, and excitement about being alive in the Light which she believed to the core of her being was the essence of God and of all that matters in this and every world? Or was it the plain and simple fact that, when you were with her, you felt so loved, affirmed, and good about yourself?

I met Angela in January 1991, eleven years ago, when I was a guest at the Monastery in Stroud, New South Wales, several hours northwest of Sydney. As many of you know, Angela and several other nuns and helpers had built the monastery at Stroud with their own hands. The sisters and their friends had done this with mud bricks, which they themselves made out of Australian clay. 'Sister Angela', as she was known in England and Australia, oversaw this construction project some twenty-five years ago, immediately after she had been diagnosed with colon cancer and given two months to live, or two years at the outside. 'No daahling,' she told her doctor, 'it's not my time. I have a monastery to build.' And so she did.

Some of you may not realize that Wendy Hope Solling (later, Sister Angela) was one of Australia's premier young sculptors in the late 1940s and 1950s, working in wire and metal on themes related to the Australian outback. Later, when she entered the Anglican Community of Saint Clare at Freeland in England, she began working in wood, stone, and metal to make religious sculptures, which today are treasures in various churches, mon-asteries, and cathedrals in England and Australia. Just last month, a member of one of the Franciscan communities told me that she recently had had the 'privilege' of cleaning several of Sister Angela's sculptures in England – and that a startling light comes through, or emanates from, each of these pieces in a mysterious way, giving each sculpture a special sense of lightness and grace.

The thing about Angela, which I was – and am – most touched and transformed by, was – and is – the lightness of her being, a quality of body and soul, of intuition and insight, of artistic genius and athletic grace, which had – and has – nothing to do with size and everything to do with a quality of relational presence which we often call 'love'.

As you can tell, it is difficult to speak of Angela in the past tense, not because I am in denial about her death, but because Angela herself would be the first to insist that far from being gone from us, those who have died have simply moved on into another dimension of life in the Spirit – and are, in some ways, even more present to us now than when they were living persons here on earth. So, please bear with me, as I fumble around among verb tenses for a few minutes this evening in reflecting on the spiritual legacy of Wendy Hope Solling, whom we knew as Sister Angela or simply as Angela.

The passage from Wisdom reminds those of us steeped in patriarchal Christianity that Wisdom, or Sophia, is an eternal image of Sacred Power. Indeed, just as Jesus is for Christians the Word of God and the Christ of God, so too is Jesus the Sophia or Wisdom of God. She was with God in the beginning. All that came to be had life in Her, and that life was the Light of humankind and creature-kind, a Light that shines in the darkness, a light that darkness cannot overcome. The passage from Wisdom (Wisdom 7 and 8) was read here to remind us that Sister Angela was a feminist Christian, a woman who refused to forget her sisters or to ignore their struggles for justice, struggles which over time she recognized as her own.

It is imperative that we today not bury our female saints, priests, and prophets without recognizing how trivialized or dismissed most of them were, and are, to this day. Angela's femaleness was not an insignificant dimension of who she was. It mattered to her. It mattered to her because it gave her particular perspectives, as both artist and religious leader, in a world and church dominated by men. Again and again, like many women religious and women priests, the Reverend Sister Angela's mystical spirituality was dismissed by the powers that be as 'flaky', less than serious. All the while, her genius – as a world-class sculptor – was much admired throughout her life and sometimes sought after by those church leaders who winked and smiled at her spirituality. It never seemed to dawn on those custodians of the faith that the light which shines through her sculpture is the same God who shone through her embodied person here on this earth!

But being a woman mattered most to Sister Angela, because her womanness was a place of relational connectedness with women of all ages and conditions, who frequented the monastery and sought her out for counsel. Later in her life, Angela's spirituality and wisdom, seasoned through her experience as the leader of the Clare Community in Australia, provided a path to Aboriginal women whose own leaders teamed up with Angela to share sources of spiritual strength, hope, and experience.

Before meeting Angela, I had seen a film called *The Fully Ordained Meat Pie*, a reference to a quip made by a priest in the Anglican Church of Australia that ordaining a woman would be like ordaining a meat pie. In case you don't get it – and many sane and intelligent people don't! – many guardians of patriarchal religion have argued over time that it is impossible for God to ordain women, because we lack something that God needs his priests to have. Your guess is as good as mine as to what it is we may lack! Be that as it may, the great film on the meat pie showed Sister Angela consoling a group of Australian women in the aftermath of yet another defeat for the ordination of women in 1987. She spoke with such passion to the grieving and angry women gathered in the monastery, 'Now daahlings, you must not let them get you down. You must laugh in the face of the tiger! That's what you must do – *laugh*, daahlings, in the face of the tiger!'

I'll never forget watching that film in Massachusetts and asking my colleagues, 'Who *is* that woman, that wonderful nun?' For Angela was – is – like Jesus. And that was, and is, the point.

For those of us who would at times find ourselves befuddled and frustrated by the possibility that Angela never had a linear thought in her life, try to imagine what it must have been like hanging out with Jesus of Nazareth in his more mystical moments! Angela knew that she wasn't always the easiest person to work with, but this was of little bother to her, unless she felt that either she or others were lacking compassion or generosity of spirit. She didn't often get angry, but when she did, watch out! Usually in response to an experience or report of some cruelty or injustice, she would let it rip! This was no sugar-coated sister.

The Gospel of John was Angela's favourite book in the Bible, and of course, because the author of John believes that God is not only with us; God lives through us! Indeed, for John and Angela, the good news is not merely that God is our Father or Mother or that Jesus is our Saviour. This is good news, but the best news is that we ourselves are God-bearers! That's what it means to be 'the Body of Christ', that was the heart of Angela's faith and it is, I believe, what drew us to her – and her to us.

For Angela, like the author of John, life was not primarily religious worship, nor was it about waiting to be more fully in the light of God some day. For Angela, like the author of the Gospel of John, each day was a participation in the living God of Light and Love. Her whole reason for being was to let God's light shine through her – which brings me to her 'angelic' lightness of being. Was it not because the Light of God shone through her right into our lives that we felt so affirmed and good when she was with us?

Is this not what all angels do? Illuminate our lives, shine sacred light upon us, help us see ourselves as we are meant to be. My mother has a poem and colourful graphic on her wall, which reads, 'Most people don't know that there are angels whose only job is to make sure you don't get too comfortable and fall asleep and miss your life' (Andreas, StoryPeople).

'Come on, Carter, you don't believe in angels, do you?' some of you are probably whispering to yourselves! Well yes, actually, I do. Not the Hallmark Card variety, but something much more like our Angela. Not only human angels and not simply individuals, but divine beings beyond our capacities to imagine – mighty spiritual forces that come to us through people and water and rocks and birds and beasts and the power of collective memories and stories, forces with the power and energy of God, connecting us generation to generation, moving our struggles, touching our hearts, opening our minds, transforming our lives, and seasoning our capacities to bear the Sacred Spirit with and for one another so that we do not miss our lives.

Dear sisters and brothers, Wendy Hope Solling, our friend Angela, was and is an angel. But lest we give her too much spiritual authority, and ourselves too little, let's look a little deeper still at what is going on here. A number of interesting things have happened in my waking and sleeping life since Angela's death on 20 January, each of them shaking me up so that I will not miss my life. And with the passing of each day, the force of this beloved sister's Love has become clearer and ever more compelling, and her Word to me, and to you, is this:

'Dear heart, the point is not that *I* am in the Light. Of course I am. But the point is that *you* are in the Light! We are all here together in the Light of God – but isn't it just *glorious!*'

It's what she was all about, and what she still is all about – to help us see that it's what *we're* all here to do: to live fully in the Light of God, to let the light shine through us, to share a way of being that is so light and so loving and so good humoured and, yes, sometimes so angry at cruelty and injustice as to be almost unbearable.

It is a vocation we share – to be God-bearers, to share sacred power, to take flight with Angela through all eternity, beginning here and now wherever we are. We are called through Angela's spirit, wherever we are, to live with eyes open to the world and God and to let ourselves – our minds and spirits – expand. We are invited by Angela, whoever we are, to grow spiritually larger, a day at a time – and as we grow, not to give much of a whit about others' opinions of us. The vocation we share with our beloved sister is to foster loving, mutual relationships and to do whatever we can to help build a just and compassionate world in which all humans and creatures are respected.

Angels, of course, see through the eyes of God. As we learn to see more clearly through the eyes of God, we will be learning how better to love ourselves, the world, and God. Like Angela, and like Jesus, we too will care less about rules than about love, justice, and compassion; and we will care much less about strange human fixations like overly-zealous patriotism and overly-structured religion than about doing whatever we can on behalf of the well-being of the entire created order – across lines of race, culture, religion, class, nation, gender, sexual identity, and even species. But let's not think that it's all seriousness and struggle. Angels have fun and great senses of humour! In Angela's spirit, we are free to play and laugh and enjoy these lives of ours. She, for example, would have loved the Superbowl last Sunday, especially – sitting up there in Boston – its patriotic outcome! She was so looking forward to going to Red Sox games (she called them 'Red Stockings') as well as working on perfecting her canter with Red, the quarter horse, whom she and I shared.

I will always remember one of the last moments she and I spent together, the day before her stroke. We were in the car, headed down Becky Mountain Road for church. I had on a clerical collar, which was too tight, and I was feeling generally stressed. But Angela and I had our own little way of handling stress, when things got to us. So, mimicking Red the horse – who is a 'cribber', which means she chews on wood for the purpose of windsucking – I glanced over at Angela and went [Carter imitated Red cribbing]. Angela instantly went [Angela imitated Red cribbing) right back at me – 'Daahling!' We burst out laughing, and the tension floated out of the car as lightly as a summer breeze.

Two days later, which was the day after her stroke, I left the hospital and drove home from Asheville to take a bath and do a few errands. On the way home, I stopped by the stables to visit for a few minutes with our friends there, human and horses. After visiting briefly with Carolyn our friend and stable manager, I spent about ten minutes in the pasture with Red the horse. As I cried into her fur, I said some words like these to her, 'I don't know what to say to you, sweet Red, but if you were human, I'd ask you to pray with us.' Then I stroked her neck for a few moments, gave her some carrots, and left.

Later that day, Carolyn told me that after I left, she noticed that Red was down on the ground with her front legs folded up under her as if she were a foal, which is apparently not a common position for an adult horse. Red's nose was touching the ground, and her eyes were glazed over, as if she were in a trance.

Who knows? I know that Angela and Red had – and have – a special bond, and I believe that animals and other forms of life 'know' more than we humans can begin to imagine. Angela, who was a Franciscan to her bones, believed this, too.

When we leave St Phillip's today, we'll be going out to the Stables at Las Praderas, where Angela helped initiate Free Rein Center for Therapeutic Riding and Education. There, led by Patience, the other horse most special to Angela (since Red has gone to Massachusetts with me for the spring), we will scatter her ashes and lift our voices in blessing and gratitude for this remarkable woman and friend. But before we go, we will celebrate communion, as Angela would wish, giving thanks to God for this astonishing teacher of love, this priest of God, and her almost unbearable lightness of being.

In St John Chrysostom's words, 'She whom we love and lose is no longer where she was before. She is now wherever we are.' Hallelujah, daahlings! Amen.

32

What Will We Do Without Sue? Remembering Sue Hiatt

The Reverend Dr Suzanne R. Hiatt, known to her friends and colleagues simply as 'Sue', was the prime mover behind the ordination of women priests in the Episcopal Church. Educated to be a social worker and community organizer, as well as a priest, Sue's combined training and talents served us well, we who were seeking to become priests at a moment in which the institutional Church was fiercely and – thanks largely to Sue Hiatt, futilely – fighting to hold back the tide of women's ordination. Following our 'irregular' ordination in July of 1974, Sue and I joined the faculty of the Episcopal Divinity School, where she taught pastoral theology until her retirement in 1998. To her great sadness, and mine, and that of all who loved her, Sue was diagnosed in February 2001 with an anaplastic thyroid tumour, a fast-acting terminal cancer. Still, Sue managed to outlive her four-month prognosis by more than a year. She died on 30 May 2002 at Chilton House, a hospice facility, in Cambridge, Massachusetts. The following sermon was given at her memorial service in St John's Memorial Chapel at the Episcopal Divinity School in Cambridge on 17 June 2002.

There is no question that nothing will separate us from the love of God in Christ Jesus, but what will we do without Sue? How are we to go forward without Sue Hiatt's wit and wisdom, her love and leadership, in the midst of world crisis such as ours today? How do we Christians and we others cope with this 'war against terrorism' being staged by an Administration in which she, like many of us, had less than zero confidence? And what are we to make of the mess in the Roman Catholic Church, which (though greater in drama and degree than its kindred messes in other religious communities) nonetheless has been shaped and seasoned by the same patriarchal Christianity which Sue spent her entire life not simply lamenting personally nor resisting professionally but building and leading a movement against?

It's a question of strategy, as Sue would say. Not whether we will go on, because by the grace and power of God, we will go on, but the question is 'how will we build our movement?' How will we choose our battles? How will we resist injustice? How will we keep on keepin' on in a church, nation, and world that urge us to hush our mouths and take off our marchin' shoes and retire not simply from our professional jobs but from the struggle which, as Sue believed, is life itself? This is why, following her retirement from the Episcopal Divinity School in 1998, she revved up to continue building the movement. This she was doing through blessing lesbian and gay unions in Episcopal parishes, preaching a Gospel of radical economic justice-making to affluent Episcopalians, and plodding on, steadfastly, in her work as 'bishop to the women'. She was especially concerned for those lay women, deacons, priests, bishops, and other ministers who struggle daily to live with integrity in the confusion of a patriarchal church that remains to this day profoundly ambivalent toward strong, woman-affirming women. Sue was a constant advocate for those called to resist patriarchal power-relations throughout the Church's structures, liturgies, theologies, and pastoral relationships.

Sisters and brothers, it was more than her job, more than her profession, more even than her vocation as a priest. It was Sue Hiatt's life, the very core of her Christian identity, the basis of how she understood not simply her ordination but moreover her baptismal vows – to struggle irrepressibly and without distraction for justice for all women of all cultures, races, classes, nations, religions, ages, abilities, and sexual identities.

Like all great leaders, she was misunderstood by some and no doubt mistaken in some of her judgments. She was, for example, misunderstood by those who thought that her work was more on behalf of white middle-class women than women of other races, classes, and cultures. The fact is, Sue Hiatt was an organizer and historian by trade and training who saw white middle-

and upper-class women – indeed the Episcopal Church itself – as a strategic location of social, economic, and political power that needed to be organized and put to work on behalf of social justice. Women's ordination and the Church itself were not, for Sue, ends in themselves but steps along the way toward the Promised Land. This larger view of hers is what Bishop DeWitt, David Gracey, Barbara Harris, Paul Washington, Ann Smith and other colleagues in Philadelphia saw in Sue and affirmed in her, as she sought to be ordained a deacon and to work in mobilizing white suburban Episcopalians to cast their lots with the poor and with sisters and brothers of colour in the city of Philadelphia and elsewhere.

She lived on the basis of a tenacious faith in the capacities of her brothers and sisters, including white affluent folks like most of us here today, to help make 'justice roll down like waters and righteousness like an ever-flowing stream' (Amos 5.24), and she had faith in our willingness to step forward and offer ourselves as labourers in God's harvest. In this way, Sue Hiatt was an heir of the same hope and enthusiasm that have historically shaped the great Christian movements for social justice and the irrepressible passion for justice among such great Anglican divines as F. D. Maurice, William Temple, John Hines, Verna Dozier, William Stringfellow, and Desmond Tutu. Among those who've gone on before, and with countless saints of God still here on this earth, our beloved sister stands tall today, a great Episcopalian, a great Christian feminist leader of the twentieth century, a great Christian pastor and prophet and priest.

And it wasn't that she always got it exactly 'right', though often she did. Some of us affectionately called her 'Eeyore' after the donkey in *Winnie the Pooh* who believed that 'it's all the same at the bottom of the river'. Sometimes it seemed as if Sue's belief in our capacities to help God create this world would fall victim to a pessimism, even at times a cynicism and anger, that bordered on despair. In those gloomy moments, this wise and good-humoured sister would withdraw and seek primarily her own counsel and that of her animal companions like Job and Annie and Sissy and Ginger. In such moments, she invariably would be shocked and amazed if something good happened! It took me a long time to begin to understand and fully appreciate Sue's courage: I came to realize that her pessimism was not simply the flip-side of her passion for justice. It was a visceral, embodied response to what she saw when she prayed, a vision of a world in crisis and a Church too seldom up to the task. The sort of vision that drives prophets mad – as Eeyore would say, 'You see, it *is* all the same at the bottom of the river.' It was, I believe, against this grim, depressing picture that Sue struggled courageously throughout her life to build and lead a movement for justice for all, never failing to believe that, against the odds, folks like you and I could rise to the task. This, I figured, is what Bishop Bob DeWitt meant when he wrote to Sue and to all of us ordinands, and still to this day writes us: 'Keep your courage.' Despite her vision of a chaotic world and an often feckless church, Sue Hiatt kept her courage.

Exactly one week before her death, Archbishop Desmond Tutu, who was at the Episcopal Divinity School last semester as a Visiting Professor, paid a visit to Sue in her room at Chilton House, a hospice residence here in Cambridge. Sue had met the Archbishop several months earlier, when she had been able to attend one of his lectures and, several days before his visit, she had called out for him there in Chilton House. When he arrived, Sue was still able, barely, to communicate verbally – and she spoke to him very slowly and clearly: 'Meeting you has been the thrill of my life. You help me see that the truth will go on.'

But how will the truth go on? How will we keep our courage? What will we do without Sue? Here is what, I believe, Sue would say and – through the power of the Spirit in which she is so fully involved – what she is saying to us right now:

We must never retire from the struggle. We must always, as Ed Rodman reminds us, refuse to participate in our own oppression or that of others, *and yet* we must never get too busy to take time out, to rest by the lake, to walk the dogs, plant the irises, eat truffles with buddies, pray quietly in the morning and in the evening, 'pleasure ourselves', as Sue would cajole us.

We have to organize! Justice doesn't just 'happen'. We can't do it alone, not as heroes', not as Lone Rangers or Superwomen or Spidermen. We must do it together, *and yet* we need to learn not only to tolerate the personal loneliness which, to some degree, inheres in the prophetic life. We need to accept it gratefully and patiently and learn to live in it without regret or pity.

We need to put action over talk, the common good over our personal fortunes however great or small, substance over style, and ethics over etiquette, which is why our sister had so little use for most politicians and prelates. *And yet* we need always to be cultivating a gentleness of spirit and a sense of humour, which will help us speak the truth in love, like when Sue told EDS's faculty in 1975 that they needed to hire not one, but two, women priests, so that these women priests 'could walk back-to-back together down the hall'.

If we live this Spirit, which is Holy, which is God, and which is today Sue with and in God, she will never be far from us. This is how the truth will go on. It is how we will keep our courage. It is what we will do without Sue, *and yet* it is what we will do with her in our midst. Because she whom we loved and lost is no longer where she was before. She is now wherever we are. Alleluia! And let the people say, Amen!

33

Making Us Homeless: Remembering Dorothee Soelle

In the spring of 2003, the sad news reached me at a faculty retreat outside Boston. Dorothee Soelle, my friend, mentor, and sister theologian, had died suddenly of a heart attack, while she and her husband Fulbert Steffensky were leading a retreat in Germany. Our mutual friend Reinhild Traitler of the Boldern Institute outside Zurich asked if I would deliver a statement on behalf of Dorothee's friends and colleagues in the United States at a memorial service in May. This is the statement I made at the service for Dorothee Soelle, which took place at the Kirchentag celebration in Berlin on 29 May 2003.

Dear sisters and brothers, how grateful I am to have been invited to join you here to celebrate the love and work of our beloved friend and theological mentor Dorothee Soelle. When Reinhild Traitler phoned me, she asked if I would be able to come to this Kirchentag event and say a little about Dorothee's theological impact on those of us in the United States, who have shared her passion for justice as the passion of God. I am honoured to do so, and I bring greetings to you today from men and women throughout the United States, who, upon learning that I would be attending this service, asked me to please let people know how deeply grieved they are by Dorothee's death and how their lives have been transformed spiritually and radicalized politically by Dorothee's work.

For example, my colleague at the Episcopal Divinity School in Cambridge, theologian and teacher Kwok Pui-lan, asked me to tell you how much her students, during this past semester, loved Dorothee's 'politically subversive mysticism'.

A student of mine named Mark Kozielec wrote, 'I think it's clear in my [term] paper how much of an impact Dorothee Soelle's *Creative Disobedience* has had on me. I'm planning on buying several copies of it to send to people.' Another student, Frank Clarkson, wrote, 'I'm just discovering Dorothee Soelle. But I am touched by her willingness and her ability to get to the heart of the matter, to tell the truth that sensing God's presence is bliss.'

But as Dorothee Soelle says in *The Silent Cry,* life in the spirit also 'makes one homeless' (2001, pp. 195–9). Soelle is describing something I have experienced but that I haven't been able to articulate.

Have we in the United States ever been more in need than we are right now, in these times, of politically subversive spiritualities? Have we ever been in greater need for theologies to call us 'beyond mere obedience'? Has the need ever been more urgent for the building of networks and communities of mysticism and resistance that make us simultaneously 'blissful and homeless'?

It is truly, as Dorothee declared, 'blissful' to share the marvellous companionship of friends old and new, comrades in struggle and hope – people like you, gathered here at this Kirchentag, and throughout the world wherever even two or three are gathered together in the Spirit of the brother from Nazareth who stood with the poor, the marginalized, the outcast. And yet, as Dorothee herself deeply knew, it also makes us 'homeless' – following Jesus. Dorothee helped us realize, we Christians in the United States, that we are called to the margins of our homeland and that we may wind up being imprisoned or exiled by it. Also that we are called to the margins of our institutions – our churches, academies, other places of professional involvement – and that there, too, we may wind up being rejected.

Dorothee Soelle may well have been the most influential Christian theologian among progressive Christians in the United States in the last quarter of the twentieth century. Among Roman Catholics and Protestants, among men and women, among people of different ages, among people still involved with the organized churches and those who had left religious institutions out of boredom or disgust, Dorothee Soelle represented a resurgence of faith, hope, and radical love. In the United States, she is often cited along with contemporaries Thich Nhat Hahn and the Dali Lama as a shining beacon for peace – but not just any peace. Peace with justice. There's a song in the United States labour and socialist tradition called 'Bread and Roses', which is about how fighting for bread (food, survival) isn't enough. We must also have roses (beauty and sweetness). Dorothee understood that the two go together – peace and justice, roses and bread, mysticism and resistance. We can't have one, not for long, unless we also have the other. This is what her last book, *The Silent Cry*, is all about and it is, of course, what her love and work was all about.

One of my life companions, Beverly Harrison, a renowned Christian feminist social ethicist in the United States, was also a very dear friend of Dorothee's. Beverly asked me to bring you her love and add her voice to the throng of sisters and brothers celebrating Dorothee today. And Beverly Harrison also asked me to say something about how important it was to her, as an ethicist and as a citizen of the United States, that Dorothee insisted that 'collective shame' is a moral requirement for people with a history like Germany's or like ours today in the United States. Dorothee Soelle realized the creative, revolutionary character of collective shame wherever gross injustice and moral evil has been either embraced or ignored by groups of people bound by nation, patriotism, race, tribe, religion or gender.

I want to echo my sisters Beverly Harrison and Dorothee Soelle on this point. Christian theology is not about being nice, being popular, staying safe, or avoiding conflict. About 15 years ago, back in the United States, in response to a university president, who had asked Dorothee and me not to embarrass the school by being too outspoken in our opposition to an antisemitic sermon we had heard in the university chapel, Dorothee and I had a batch of t-shirts made that said, 'Ethics, Not Etiquette' – and we and many others wore these t-shirts to the Commencement ceremony of the university.

Personally, as a younger scholar/activist many years ago, I was touched and transformed along the way of my vocational path by Dorothee Soelle's theological intelligence, moral courage, and spiritual vision. She was, in a very real way, my chief theological mentor, spiritually and politically my 'big sister', a source and resource not only of wisdom but of good humour, strong opinions, and delight in music and food and play and prayer. I speak here today, however, not only for myself, but for countless women and men in the United States, many of whom never had the privilege of actually meeting Dorothee, for whom nonetheless she was also *their* 'chief theological mentor', *their* spiritual and theological guide.

What then will we do without Dorothee? We will miss her terribly. With Fulbert and her children and grandchildren, we do and will grieve for her. Yet, like Jesus' friends after his death, we too will realize more and more that we are surrounded by Dorothee's presence. We will realize, a day at a time, that we are infused with Dorothee's spirit which, as she herself well knew, was becoming more and more fully a dimension of God's own Sacred Power. More and more, we will know, by the power of Jesus, which is now also the power of Dorothee, that she is with us, to guide and strengthen us, as we continue doing what we can to build the realm of God, which is the realm of justice–love, the realm of justice and peace on earth, the realm of well-being for every human being and all creatures and creation.

Nancy Hawkins, a sister feminist theologian in the United States, wrote me about Dorothee the other day, 'Dorothee taught me that what we stand for theologically can make a real difference in our world. I believe her final book on Mysticism is the jewel in her crown', Nancy Hawkins wrote, and she continued, 'Dorothee came to understand, I believe, that after all is said and done, and one's life is lived, that we simply stand in naked contemplation of the God we love. Now that God is returning the favour.'

Surely God is today celebrating the presence of Dorothee Soelle among the heavenly host. And surely Dorothee is already at work here, sparking among us, drawing us toward homelessness and promising us the bliss of her eternal companionship!

Thanks be to the Sacred Spirit for the gift of this most amazing sister and friend, our beloved Dorothee. And thanks be to you, my friends in Germany, for asking me to join you here as a representative of Dorothee's many friends and comrades in the United States.

34

Keep Your Courage: Remembering Bishop DeWitt

Several months after retiring as Bishop of Pennsylvania, Robert L. DeWitt joined the Reverend Sue Hiatt in organizing the first ordination of women priests in the Episcopal Church, in July 1974, prior to the Church's authorization of women's ordination. Bishop DeWitt's advocacy of women priests was one among many such justice commitments he pursued during his tenure as Bishop of Pennsylvania (1964–74) and then as editor of The Witness magazine (1974–1981). When he died in November, 2003, his family asked me to help organize and speak at his memorial service. This is the sermon from the service held at the Episcopal Divinity School in Cambridge Massachusetts on 15 May 2004.

He was to me a spiritual dad, a personal confidante, a singing buddy, a political consultant, a good and sometimes best friend, a remarkably pensive person, often witty, usually good-humoured and almost always self-deprecating. I would call him up to talk about things, and I *still* call him up to talk about things, decisions to be made, struggles to be engaged, controversies to be weathered, within and beyond the Church.

From time to time, Bob was a quiet, melancholy man, who would sing the blues. I figured that some of this sadness – as also with his beloved friend and mine Sue Hiatt – was simply a response to the real world and, too often, the real Church. In any case, I learned from this man we are here to remember that the world and Church are contexts for justice making and struggle and humour and revolutionary patience and that these are ingredients of all love and work, without which our lives fall flat.

I know from his strong and feisty family – you lovely, loving folks here with us today, Becky, Larry, Kathy, Kirsten, kids, grand-kids, great grand-kids, aunts and uncles, in-laws, cousins, others – and I know also from his most cherished, intelligent, outspoken wife Bobbie before her sad, strange journey into Alzheimer's so long ago, that we should not, indeed we can not, idealize Bob DeWitt if we are actually to remember him.

I suspect, for example, that he could be too busy to be fully present to those he loved most. I sometimes wondered how on earth he could do all he did, and I figured he actually couldn't do it all without failing, sometimes, to be where he most wanted to be or do what he most needed to. This must be a liability of being one to whom so many turn for wisdom, counsel, friendship, time. Like most men of his generation, Bob could be too reticent to share much about himself. As a younger woman – more or less the age of his own children – I imagined that they, like I, would find themselves frustrated that he sometimes seemed better able to give advice than to receive it! I am sure he was at times impatient, out of sorts, stubborn, wrong. We are not here to remember him as 'more' or 'larger' than he was, but rather to celebrate the life and wisdom and music and leadership of a man whose courage changed the world and Church around him and whose integrity touched and changed each of us in ways we realize and, perhaps, in ways we don't.

There are so many stories we have already begun sharing, which is fitting, because Bob DeWitt loved stories! But I'm most haunted today, as I have been for a year (since I last visited with him), by something Bob said to me quietly, almost as an aside, as we walked to my car outside his retirement community in Saratoga Springs last May. 'You know, I don't think we've ever been in the serious trouble we're in right now as a nation, it troubles me.' Then, in characteristic DeWitt mode, he looked down and became quiet. When he looked back up at me, he looked so sad I thought he would cry. I imagine that, had his health been better, we would have gotten quite a few more sad and angry songs from this singing, sad bishop to help us cope spiritually, as well as politically, with this awful period in the United States.

I have a couple of stories to tell you about Bob DeWitt, which will convey something about how we ourselves can keep our courage, as he would have it, in these challenging times:

Last spring, Bob told my companion Sue and me a story in response to my asking him whether he had ever had any particular religious or spiritual – mystical – experience. He said that, when he was a boy, maybe about 16, or maybe even as young as 12, he and his family were vacationing in Canada, and he was in a little boat out on a lake. All of a sudden he sensed something. He didn't hear any words or see any vision. Rather, he just knew that he was surrounded by – 'for lack of words', he said – 'a presence'. He said that, if it had used words, which it didn't, it would have said something like, 'I see you. I know you're there. I'm glad you're there.' 'Even now,' Bob said, 'it's as clear to me as if it were yesterday.'

Now, I believe that Bishop DeWitt's courage was rooted in this experience of being surrounded by a God who was glad he was here, doing what he was doing: rowing a boat, going to seminary, having a family, helping desegregate an all-white boys' school, organizing Episcopalians for justice, ordaining women, editing *The Witness*, lobster fishing on Isle au Haut, sitting with Bobbie over breakfast, playing the accordion for his great granddaughter.

In June of 1973, about a week before I was to be ordained a deacon in New York City, I panicked. I can't be ordained, I said to myself, because I can't, in good faith, take that damn 'Oath of Conformity', which goes something like this: 'I believe the Old and New Testaments to be the Word of God and to contain all things necessary to salvation and I promise to conform to the doctrine, discipline, and worship of the Episcopal Church.' My own good bishop, Paul Moore, was unavailable to talk with me about this, because his wife Ginny was dying of cancer at the time. So I phoned Bishop DeWitt of Pennsylvania, whom I had met and begun to know through the movement for the ordination of women. I told him over the phone what my problem was. 'I tell you what,' he said. 'Let's meet tomorrow in Penn Station (New York City) and have coffee.'

What I recall is my own hyped-up anxiety about the situation being met by Bishop DeWitt's *laughter* – not at me, of course, but at the situation. What he said to me was hugely important to me then and has been ever since: first, he said, to affirm the Bible as the Word of God doesn't mean that it's the only Word of God; second, to say that it contains all things necessary to salvation doesn't mean that everything it contains is necessary to salvation; and third, to promise to conform to the doctrine, discipline, and worship of the Church means only that, as with any vow, you'll do your best, ask God to help you, and use your common sense.

As important as these words were to me, there was something even more important about that meeting with Bishop DeWitt: I think I was a bit like he himself had been in that boat so many years before. In this meeting in New York's Penn Station, I sensed myself surrounded by God, by a Spirit much larger than us both and much larger than the Episcopal Church, and much larger than the Anglican Communion, and much larger than Christianity. Bishop DeWitt's ministry to me on this occasion was to laugh! In this Spirit, he helped me see that basic to the ministry I was being ordained into was a deep, soulful recognition that, in the larger scheme of things in God's world, the Oath of Conformity in the Episcopal Church does not rank very high! On the subway, headed back up to the seminary from Penn Station, I remember thinking, 'He's talking about keeping things in perspective!'

The third story is not so much a story as a lamentation Bob De-Witt shared with me, as I imagine and hope he did many of you in these last years. About ten years ago I asked him what regrets he had about his life. He looked down pensively for a few moments, then responded, 'I wish I had gone to live on the Island earlier.' This, of course, was about his wishing he had had more time to spend with Bobbie before her illness and also I'm sure with his sons John and Rob and their families and the fisher-folk and community on Isle au Haut which was, as he sang, 'the place I want to be'. I thought a lot about this several years later, as I began to move away from full-time teaching here at this seminary toward settling into life with my loved ones in the hills of Western North Carolina. It was a move that, much as Bob loved the Episcopal Divinity School, he encouraged me to make.

So over the years I came to realize that these are some of the spiritual gifts Bishop DeWitt wished for us, when he charged us, as he did us women priests so often, to 'keep our courage':

• The gift of knowing deep in our bones that we are surrounded by God in all times and all places for ever and ever;
• The gift of realizing that in God's life – especially God's on-going, relentless struggle for justice and peace – the rules and regulations and protocols of our organizations, including the Church, much as we may love and respect it, are not all that big a deal;
• The gift of recognizing the time when it comes – a time so easy to miss in our overly-busy lives – when we need to step down or away from our professions or routines in order to follow our hearts to the places we want to be.

Last night Bob's daughter Kathy showed me something a friend of hers wrote about Bob: 'Life is not a journey to the grave with the intention of arriving safely in a pretty, well-preserved body, but rather to skid in broadside, thoroughly used up, totally worn out, and loudly proclaiming, "Wow! What a ride!"'

Shortly after the Philadelphia ordination, Bob wrote me a note about what he imagined might follow. He ended his note with these words – a Godly admonition which I believe he is – in God's Spirit – making to all of us today, in the midst of the struggle:

'Stay in the saddle and enjoy the ride! Love, Bob.'

35

Like a Little Child:
Remembering My Mother

On 18 October 2009 my ninety-four-year-old mother, surrounded by loved ones, slipped away gently into death. What follows is what I shared in the Memorial Service for Mary Ann Carter Heyward at St Martin's Episcopal Church, in Charlotte, North Carolina, on 21 November 2009.

David Conolly, one of my most cherished friends and formerly a priest in this parish, wrote me several weeks ago from his native Australia, where he lives in retirement:

> Oh Carter, how my heart takes flight to reach you! The long and lovely journey of Mary Ann's grace-filled life has come to its full and rich home-coming. Her strength, her sparkle, her down-right goodness, though, will never die. She distributed these, and much, much more like she was scattering candy to eager children.

'Children . . .' as we heard a few minutes ago, Jesus said, 'whoever does not receive the Kingdom of God as a little child will never enter it' (Luke 18.17). What might this mean for us, gathered here to celebrate our mother, grandmother, sister, aunt, neighbour, and friend Mary Ann Heyward? Let's assume, as we can in faith, that the 'Kingdom', or Realm, of God is wherever God is, and that 'God' is wherever Love is; and more even than that, God is the power, the energy, the force, which passes Love on, causing it to grow, surprising us with the joy and peace that is rooted and grounded in God.

A friend wrote the other day,

I offer you and your family my deep sympathy on the death of your beloved mother. I think that I met her only once, yet Mary Ann left a very strong impression, as did the wonderful stories you have told us about her. One night, a small, snappily-dressed, elderly lady took me by the hand and led me away to a private place and told me that I am beautiful. She is one of two people that I can remember telling me that I am beautiful.

The thing about it is – Mama meant it! She saw the beauty in us, the beauty in every one of us – not just her own children and grandchildren – but every single one of us. And how blessed were those with ears to hear and eyes to see that, through my mother, they were meeting God. Through Mary Ann's life, God was speaking directly to us.

She was, in the way I believe Jesus meant it, 'like a little child', alive and at play in the Kingdom of God. Her grandson Rob said that she was 'more present to the moment than anyone he ever met'. That, dear friends, is descriptive both of childhood and of life with and in God – being present to the moment. Think about what we've just heard – stories about Mama being thrilled as a boat she was in got caught up in nets and had to be hauled in, delighting in a McDonald's Happy Meal as the best hamburger she'd ever tasted and the ice cream on a stick at the Quick Stop as the best ice cream in the world.

Another friend wrote us, 'Your mother always made me feel so special. She obviously made everyone feel that way! She was so small, and yet so big and strong. She truly had a heart filled with love.' Along with love and being present to the moment, a quality often associated with little children is their openness to the new and different – new and different ideas, places, people, cultures, customs. It's not that my mother wasn't afraid. In fact, she was afraid that she or others would get hurt, would fall, would find ourselves in harm's way. But she was not afraid of people who didn't look like her, or think like her, or speak of God in the way she did.

Robbie, Ann, and I have often said that one of the greatest spiritual gifts we received from both of our parents was their openness to the new and different, which meant that their life together, and with us, was an adventure: not necessarily fun, although it often was, but an engagement with the world that was sometimes hard and sometimes controversial. Still, for Mary Ann, it was always an adventure, filled with wonder and beauty.

In 1993, when she was seventy-eight, my mother joined my brother, sister, and several of my close friends at a gay pride march in Washington. The night before she caught the train to D.C., she phoned me to tell me that, although she was coming, she really didn't want to march 'beside a man in a feather boa'. Having been to a number of marches myself, I told mama that we can't often decide who we march beside. That's not quite how it works! So, the day came and there we were, milling around on the mall, waiting for the march to begin, when lo and behold, over the hill came a striking 'queen', tall, buxom, long blond hair – draped in a turquoise feather boa! Well, Mama took one look at this person and squealed with delight, 'Look at that marvellous woman! She looks just like Auntie Mame!' 'Mama,' I said, 'I don't think that's a woman. I think that's a man!' 'I don't care whether she's a woman or a man,' my mother exclaimed, 'she's beautiful!' And with that, Mama took out across the mall, camera in hand, chasing after the queen!

Another friend wrote us: 'Mary Ann was an amazing person: smart, funny, totally devoted to her children and grandchildren, and a gutsy justice-lover who managed to keep the twinkle in her eye.' To experience life like a little child, with a twinkle in the eye, learning more and more to see the world, its people and other creatures through the eyes of God. Seeing the beauty and the best in everyone and everything, from the drag queen in Washington to the ice cream at the Quick Stop. Life in the Kingdom of God. As her nephew Bill Fenner wrote her years ago, 'You seem to like everyone better than I like anyone.' And so, what we celebrate about Mary Ann Carter Heyward was the bigness, indeed the greatness, of her spirit, which offered us a window into God. Through our mother, we were met by the very opposite of whatever is cynical or judgmental, unkind or harsh, close-minded or indifferent. She loved us and, through her, God loved us.

In the last years of her life, our mother, and we her kids, were much blessed by the presence of an angel, who loved our mother and took care of her with us and for us. Her name was Ofa Tonga, and she is here today with us, as a sister and a friend – Mary Ann, an elderly angel, and Ofa, a younger one, both like little children, playing together, but also working very, very hard in the Kingdom of God, especially the younger taking such tender care of the elder.

Maya Angelou wrote, 'A great soul serves everyone all the time. A great soul never dies. She brings us together again and again' (Angelou in Whitaker 1986, p. 178). Another friend wrote us, 'What a truly great soul, Mary Ann! I will miss her presence in the world.' And so will we all, especially her children, Robbie, Ann, and I, and her grandchildren Rob, Isabel, Kate, Ramsey, and her brother Luther, and her nieces Amy and Marsha, and all the various spouses and in-laws. And yet, in the words of St John Chrysostom, 'She whom we love and lose is no longer where she was before. She is now wherever we are.'

Bibliography

Denise Ackermann, 1999, 'Becoming fully human: an ethic of relationship in difference and otherness', Episcopal Divinity School Occasional Paper, Cambridge.

Nafeez Mosaddeq Ahmed, 2005, *The War on Truth: 9/11, Disinformation, and the Anatomy of Terrorism*, Northampton, MA: Olive Branch.

Marcella Althaus-Reid, 2000, *Indecent Theology: Theological Perversions in Sex, Gender and Politics*, London: Routledge.

Nancy T. Ammerman, 1994, 'Accounting for Christian Fundamentalisms', in Martin E. Marty and R. Scott Appleby (eds), *Accounting for Fundamentalisms: The Dynamic Character of Movements*, Chicago: University of Chicago.

James Baldwin, 1989, *Conversations with James Baldwin*, Fred R. Standley and Louis H. Pratt (eds), Jackson, MS: University Press of Mississippi.

W.O. Beeman, 'Follow the oil trail–mess in Afghanistan partly our government's fault', *Jinn* (online magazine), San Francisco: Pacific News Service, 24 August (1998), website: www.pacificnews.org/jinn

The Book of Common Prayer According to the use of The Episcopal Church (1979), New York: The Church Hymnal Corporation.

Martin Buber, 1970 (1948), *I and Thou*, Trans. and notes Walter Kaufmann, New York: Charles Scribner's Sons.

Martin Buber, 1952, *The Eclipse of God: Studies in the Relation Between Religion and Philosophy*, New York: Harper and Row.

Joel Carmichael, 1993, *The Satanizing of the Jews: Origins and Development of a Mystical Anti-Semitism*, New York: Fromm.

Rachel Carson, 1962, *Silent Spring*, Greenwich, CT: Fawcett.

Joan Casanas, 'The Task of Making God Exist', in Pablo Richard (ed.), trans. Barbara Campbell and Bonnie Shepherd, *The Idols of Death and the God of Life: A Theology*, 1983, Maryknoll, NY: Orbis.

Steven Charleston, *The Middle Way: A Congregational Resource for Discussing the Lambeth Commission Report*, available on the website of the Episcopal Divinity School, www.eds.edu

The Christian Century, 104 S. Michigan Ave, Suite 700, Chicago, IL 60603, www.christiancentury.org

Citizen-Times, Asheville, N.C., Wednesday, 11 January, 2005.

The Crisis: Official Magazine of the NAACP, Baltimore, MD, Nov/Dec 2005.

Peggy Barrow Culbertson, 2005, *Southern Sampler: Women of Courage*, Cornelius, NC: Warren Publishing Co.

Mary Daly, 1998, *Quintessence: Realizing the Archaic Future – A Radical Elemental Feminist Manifesto*, Boston: Beacon.

Kelly Brown Douglas, 2000, *Sexuality and the Black Church: A Womanist Perspective*, Maryknoll, NY: Orbis.

Christopher Duraisingh, 2001, 'Toward a postcolonial re-visioning of the church's faith, witness, and communion', in Ian Douglas and Kwok Pui-lan (eds), *Beyond Colonial Anglicanism: The Anglican Communion in the Twenty-First Century*, New York: Church Publishing Inc., pp. 337–67.

Michael Dyson, 2000, *I May Not Get There With You: The True Martin Luther King, Jr*, New York: Free Press.

Barbara Ehrenreich, 2009, *This Land is Their Land: Reports from a Divided Nation*, New York: Holt McDougal.

Marc H. Ellis, 1997, *Unholy Alliance: Religion and Atrocity in Our Time*, Minneapolis, MN: Fortress.

Marvin M. Ellison and Sylvia Thorson-Smith (eds), 2003, *Body and Soul: Re-thinking Sexuality as Justice–Love*, Cleveland, OH: Pilgrim.

Feminist Theology, Vol. 17 (2), January 2009, Issue on Rosemary R. Ruether's *America Amerikkka* (2007), Editorial by Lisa Isherwood, London: Sage.

Michelle Fine, Lois Weis, Linda C. Powell, L. Mun Wong, 1997, *Off White: Readings on Race, Power, and Society*, New York/London: Routledge.

Rolf Forsberg, 1964, *Parable*.

Ivone Gebara, 1999, *Longing for Running Water: Ecofeminism and Liberation*, Minneapolis, MN: Fortress.

Robin Hawley Gorsline, 1999, *Bearing Witness to the Dark: Resources for Anti-White-Supremacist, Pro-Same-Sex(es), Pro-Feminist Theologizing in Queer Modes*, unpublished doctoral dissertation, Union Theological Seminary, New York City.

Gustavo Gutierrez, 1973, *A Theology of Liberation: History, Politics, and Salvation*, Trans. and ed. Sister Caridad Inda and John Eagleson, Maryknoll, NY: Orbis (orig. published *Teologia de la liberacion, Perspectivas*, 1971).

Beverly Wildung Harrison, 2004, *Justice in the Making: Feminist Social Ethics*, E. M. Bounds, P. K. Brubaker, J. E. Hicks, M. J. Legge, R. T. Peters, T. C. West (eds), Louisville, KY/London: Westminster John Knox.

Beverly Wildung Harrison, 1983, *Our Right to Choose: Toward a New Ethic of Abortion*, Boston: Beacon.

BIBLIOGRAPHY

Beverly Wildung Harrison, 1985, 'The Power of Anger in the Work of Love', in Carol S. Robb (ed.), *Making the Connections: Essays in Feminist Social Ethics*, Boston: Beacon.

Jennifer Harvey, Karin A. Case, and Robin Hawley Gorsline (eds), 2004, *Disrupting White Supremacy from Within: White People on What We Need to Do*, Cleveland, OH: Pilgrim.

Carter Heyward, 'But how do we love', *The Christian Century*, 26 October 2008.

Carter Heyward, 2005, *Flying Changes: Horses as Spiritual Teachers*, Cleveland, OH: Pilgrim.

Carter Heyward, 'Forgiveness', *The Witness*, 16 February 2004.

Carter Heyward, 2002, *God in the Balance: Christian Spirituality in Times of Terror*, Cleveland, OH: Pilgrim.

Carter Heyward, 'Humility: root of compassion', *The Christian Century*, 2 November 2008.

Carter Heyward, 2010 (1982), *The Redemption of God: A Theology of Mutual Relation*, Eugene, OR: Wipf and Stock.

Carter Heyward, 1999, *Saving Jesus from Those Who Are Right: Rethinking What it Means to be Christian*, Minneapolis, MN: Fortress.

Carter Heyward, 'Womanism and Feminism', *Union Seminary Quarterly Review*, 58 (2004), pp. 180–2.

Mary Elizabeth Hobgood, 2000, *Dismantling Privilege: An Ethics of Accountability*, Cleveland, OH: Pilgrim.

Lisa Isherwood, 1999, *Liberating Christ: Exploring the Christologies of Contemporary Liberation Movements*, Cleveland, OH: Pilgrim.

Molly Ivins and Lou Dubose, 2000, *Shrub: The Short But Happy Political Life of George W. Bush*, New York: Random House.

'Keeping body and soul together: sexuality, spirituality, and social justice', *A Report of a General Assembly Task Force on Human Sexuality, Presbyterian Church (U.S.A.)*, 1991.

Catherine Keller, 2008, *On the Mystery: Discerning God in Process*, Minneapolis, MN: Fortress.

Martin Luther King, Jr, 1963, 'Letter from Birmingham City Jail', in James M. Washington (ed.), *A Testament of Hope: The Essential Writings of Martin Luther King, Jr.*, San Francisco: Harper, 1986, pp. 289–302.

Martin Luther King, Jr, 1964, *Why We Can't Wait*, James M. Washington (ed.), *A Testament of Hope: The Essential Writings of Martin Luther King, Jr*, San Francisco: Harper, 1986.

Martin Luther King Jr, 1967, *Where Do We Go From Here: Chaos or Community*, New York: Harper.

Paul Krugman, 2009, *The Return of Depression: The Economy and the Crisis of 2008*, New York: W. W. Norton.

Kwok Pui-lan, 2001, 'The Legacy of Cultural Hegemony in the Anglican Church', in Ian T. Douglas and Kwok Pui-lan (eds), *Beyond Colonial Anglicanism: The Anglican Communion in the Twenty-First Century*, New York: Church Publishing Inc., pp. 47–70.

Kwok Pui-lan, 2005, *Postcolonial Imagination and Feminist Theology*, Louisville, KY: Westminster John Knox.

Andrew Linzey and Richard Kirker (eds), 2005, *Gays and the Future of Anglicanism: Responses to the Windsor Report*, London: O Press.

Sallie McFague, 1997, *Super, Natural Christians: How We Should Love Nature*, Minneapolis, MN: Fortress.

Sally Noland MacNichol, 2004, 'We Make the Road by Walking', in Jennifer Harvey, Karin A. Case, and Robin Hawley Gorsline (eds), *Disrupting White Supremacy from Within: White People on What We Need to Do*, Cleveland, OH: Pilgrim, pp. 188–215.

Irshad Manji, 2003, *The Trouble with Islam: A Muslim's Call for Reform in Her Faith*, New York: St Martin's.

Frederick Denison Maurice, 1872 (1868), *The Conscience: Lectures on Casuistry*, 2nd Ed., London: Macmillan and Sons.

Frederick Denison Maurice, 1905 (1853), 'Concluding Essay: Eternal Life and Eternal Death', *Theological Essays*, London: Macmillan and Sons.

Nelle Morton, 1985, *The Journey is Home*, Boston: Beacon.

The Nation, 33 Irving Place, New York, NY 10003, www.thenation.com

William Nicholls, 1995, *Christian Antisemitism: A History of Hate*, Lanham, MD: Jason Aronson, Inc.

Darlene O'Dell, 2001, *Sites of Southern Memory: The Autobiographies of Katharine Du Pre Lumpkin, Lillian Smith, and Pauli Murray*, Charlottesville: University Press of Virginia.

James W. Perkinson, 2004, *White Theology: Outing Supremacy in Modernity*, New York: Palgrave Macmillan.

James Piscatori, 1994, 'Accounting for Islamic Fundamentalisms', in Martin E. Marty and R. Scott Appleby (eds), *Accounting for Fundamentalisms: The Dynamic Character of Movements*, Chicago: University of Chicago.

Larry L. Rasmussen, 1996, *Earth Community Earth Ethics*, Maryknoll, NY: Orbis.

Robert Reich, 2007, *Supercapitalism: The Transformation of Business, Democracy, and Everyday*, New York: Vintage/Random House.

Adrienne Rich, 1978, *The Dream of a Common Language*, New York: W. W. Norton.

Adrienne Rich, 1979, *On Lies, Secrets, and Silence: Selected Prose, 1966–1978*, New York: W. W. Norton.

J. K. Rowling, 1997, *Harry Potter and the Sorcerer's Stone*, New York: Arthur A. Levine Books, an Imprint of Scholastic Inc.

BIBLIOGRAPHY

J. K. Rowling, 1998, *Harry Potter and the Chamber of Secrets*, New York: Arthur A. Levine Books, an Imprint of Scholastic Inc.

J. K. Rowling, 1999, *Harry Potter and the Prisoner of Azkaban*, New York: Arthur A. Levine Books, an Imprint of Scholastic Inc.

J. K. Rowling, 2000, *Harry Potter and the Goblet of Fire*, New York: Arthur A. Levine Books, an Imprint of Scholastic Inc.

J. K. Rowling, 2003, *Harry Potter and the Order of the Phoenix*, New York: Arthur A. Levine Books, an Imprint of Scholastic Inc.

J. K. Rowling, 2005, *Harry Potter and the Half-Blood Prince*, New York: Arthur A. Levine Books, an Imprint of Scholastic Inc.

J. K. Rowling, 2007, *Harry Potter and the Deathly Hallows*, New York: Arthur A. Levine Books, an Imprint of Scholastic Inc.

Rosemary Radford Ruether, 2007, *America, Amerikkka: Elect Nation and Imperial Violence*, London: Equinox.

Rosemary Radford Ruether, 1996 (1971), *Faith and Fratricide: The Theological Roots of Anti-Semitism*, Eugene: OR, Wipf and Stock.

Stephen Schwartz and John Michael Tebelak, 1970, *Godspell.*

Lillian Smith, 1949, *Killers of the Dream*, New York: W. W. Norton.

Dorothee Soelle, 1974, *Revolutionary Patience*, Trans. Robert and Rita Kimber, Maryknoll, NY: Orbis (orig. published *Die revolutionäre Geduld*, 1974).

Dorothee Soelle, 1982, *Beyond Mere Obedience*, Trans. Lawrence W. Denef, New York: Pilgrim (orig. published *Phantasie und Gehorsam*, 1968).

Dorothee Soelle, 1999, *Against the Wind: Memoir of a Radical Christian*, Trans. Barbara and Martin Rumscheidt, Minneapolis, MN: Fortress (orig. published *Gegenwind: Erinnerungen*, 1995).

Dorothee Soelle, 2001, *The Silent Cry: Mysticism and Resistance*, Trans. Barbara and Martin Rumscheidt, Minneapolis, MN: Fortress.

Thich Nhat Hanh, 1999, *Call Me by My True Names: The Collected Poems of Thich Nhat Hanh*, Berkeley, CA: Parallax Press, pp. 72–3.

James M. Washington, ed., 1986, *A Testament of Hope: The Essential Writings of Martin Luther King, Jr.*, San Francisco: Harper.

Traci C. West, 2006, *Disruptive Christian Ethics: When Racism and Women's Lives Matter*, Louisville, KY: Westminster John Knox.

Charles Whitaker, 'W. E. B. Du Bois: a Final Resting Place for an Afro-American Giant', *Ebony*, November (1986), p. 178.

Delores S. Williams, 1993, *Sisters in the Wilderness: The Challenge of Womanist God-Talk*, Maryknoll, NY: Orbis.

David Sloan Wilson, 2002, *Darwin's Cathedral: Evolution, Religion, and the Nature of Society*, Chicago: University of Chicago.

JoAnn Wypyewski, 'State of Emergency', *Mother Jones*, January/February (2007).